CHIPS

FROM

A GERMAN WORKSHOP

BY

F. MAX MULLER M. A.

FOREIGN MEMBER OF THE FRENCH INSTITUTE, ETC.

VOLUME V.

MISCELLANEOUS LATER ESSAYS

NEW YORK
CHARLES SCRIBNER'S SONS
1881

[*Published by arrangement with the Author*]

RIVERSIDE, CAMBRIDGE:
STEREOTYPED AND PRINTED BY
H. O. HOUGHTON AND COMPANY.

CONTENTS OF FIFTH VOLUME.

I.

ON FREEDOM.

PRESIDENTIAL ADDRESS DELIVERED BEFORE THE BIRMINGHAM MIDLAND INSTITUTE, OCTOBER 20, 1879.

NOT more than twenty years have passed since John Stuart Mill sent forth his plea for Liberty.[1]

If there is one among the leaders of thought in England who, by the elevation of his character and the calm composure of his mind, deserved the so often misplaced title of Serene Highness, it was, I think, John Stuart Mill.

But in his Essay "On Liberty," Mill for once becomes passionate. In presenting his Bill of Rights, in stepping forward as the champion of individual

1 Mill tells us that his Essay *On Liberty* was planned and written down in 1854. It was in mounting the steps of the Capitol in January, 1855, that the thought first arose of converting it into a volume, and it was not published till 1859. The author, who in his Autobiography speaks with exquisite modesty of all his literary performances, allows himself one single exception when speaking of his Essay *On Liberty*. "None of my writings," he says, "have been either so carefully composed or so sedulously corrected as this." Its final revision was to have been the work of the winter of 1858 to 1859, which he and his wife had arranged to pass in the South of Europe, a hope which was frustrated by his wife's death. "The *Liberty*," he writes, "is likely to survive longer than anything else that I have written (with the possible exception of the *Logic*), because the conjunction of her mind with mine has rendered it a kind of philosophic text-book of a single truth, which the changes progressively taking place in modern society tend to bring out into strong relief: the importance to man and society, of a large variety of character, and of giving full freedom to human nature to expand itself in innumerable and conflicting directions."

liberty, he seems to be possessed by a new spirit. He speaks like a martyr, or the defender of martyrs. The individual human soul, with its unfathomable endowments, and its capacity of growing to something undreamt of in our philosophy, becomes in his eyes a sacred thing, and every encroachment on its world-wide domain is treated as sacrilege. Society, the arch-enemy of the rights of individuality, is represented like an evil spirit, whom it behooves every true man to resist with might and main, and whose demands, as they cannot be altogether ignored, must be reduced at all hazards to the lowest level.

I doubt whether any of the principles for which Mill pleaded so warmly and strenuously in his Essay "On Liberty" would at the present day be challenged or resisted, even by the most illiberal of philosophers, or the most conservative of politicians. Mill's demands sound very humble to *our* ears. They amount to no more than this, "that the individual is not accountable to society for his actions so far as they concern the interests of no person but himself, and that he may be subjected to social or legal punishments for such actions only as are prejudicial to the interests of others."

Is there any one here present who doubts the justice of that principle, or who would wish to reduce the freedom of the individual to a smaller measure? Whatever social tyranny may have existed twenty years ago, when it wrung that fiery protest from the lips of John Stuart Mill, can we imagine a state of society, not totally Utopian, in which the individual man need be less ashamed of his social fetters, in which he could more freely utter all his honest convictions, more boldly propound all his theories, more fearlessly agitate for their speedy realization; in which, in fact, each man can be so entirely himself as the society of England, such as it now is, such as generations of hard-thinking and hard-working Englishmen have made it, and left it as the most sacred inheritance to their sons and daughters?

Look through the whole of history, not excepting the brightest days of republican freedom at Athens and Rome, and you will not find one single period in which the measure of liberty accorded to each individual was larger than it is at present, at least in England. And if you wish to realize the full blessings of the time in which we live, compare Mill's plea for Liberty with another written not much more than two hundred years ago, and by a thinker not inferior either in power or boldness to Mill himself. According to Hobbes, the only freedom which an individual in his ideal state has a right to claim is what he calls "freedom of thought," and that freedom of thought consists in our being able to think what we like — so long as we keep it to ourselves. Surely, such freedom of thought existed even in the days of the Inquisition, and we should never call thought free, if it had to be kept a prisoner in solitary and silent confinement. By freedom of thought we mean freedom of speech, freedom of the press, freedom of action, whether individual or associated, and of that freedom the present generation, as compared with all former generations, the English nation, as compared with all other nations, enjoys, there can be no doubt, a good measure, pressed down, and shaken together, and sometimes running over.

It may be said that some dogmas still remain in politics, in religion, and in morality; but those who defend them claim no longer any infallibility, and those who attack them, however small their minority, need fear no violence, nay, may reckon on an impartial and even sympathetic hearing, as soon as people discover in their pleadings the true ring of honest conviction and the warmth inspired by an unselfish love of truth.

It has seemed strange, therefore, to many readers of Mill, particularly on the Continent, that this plea for liberty, this demand for freedom for every individual to be what he is, and to develop all the germs of his nature, should have come from what is known as the freest of all countries, England. We might well understand such a cry of indignation if it had reached us from Russia; but why should English philosophers, of all others, have to protest against the tyranny of society? It is true, nevertheless, that in countries governed despotically, the individual, unless he is obnoxious to the Government, enjoys far greater freedom, or rather license, than in a country like England, which governs itself. Russian society, for instance, is extremely indulgent. It tolerates in its rulers and statesmen a haughty defiance of the simplest rules of social propriety, and it seems amused rather than astonished or indignant at the vagaries, the frenzies, and outrages of those who in brilliant drawing-rooms or lecture-rooms preach the doctrines of what is called Nihilism or Individualism,[1] — viz., "that society must be regenerated by a struggle for existence and the survival of the strongest, processes which Nature has sanctioned, and which have proved

[1] Herzen defined Nihilism as "the most perfect freedom from all settled concepts, from all inherited restraints and impediments which hamper the progress of the Occidental intellect with the historical drag tied to its foot."

successful among wild animals." If there is danger in these doctrines the Government is expected to see to it. It may place watchmen at the doors of every house and at the corner of every street, but it must not count on the better classes coming forward to enrol themselves as special constables, or even on the coöperation of public opinion which in England would annihilate that kind of Nihilism with one glance of scorn and pity.

In a self-governed country like England, the resistance which society, if it likes, can oppose to the individual in the assertion of his rights, is far more compact and powerful than in Russia, or even in Germany. Even where it does not employ the arm of the law, society knows how to use that quieter, but more crushing pressure, that calm, Gorgon-like look which only the bravest and stoutest hearts know how to resist.

It is against that indirect repression which a well-organized society exercises, both through its male and female representatives, that Mill's demand for liberty seems directed. He does not stand up for unlimited individualism; on the contrary, he would have been the most strenuous defender of that balance of power between the weak and the strong on which all social life depends. But he resents those smaller penalties which society will always inflict on those who disturb its dignified peace and comfort: — avoidance, exclusion, a cold look, a stinging remark. Had Mill any right to complain of these social penalties? Would it not rather amount to an interference with individual liberty to deprive any individual or any number of individuals of those weapons of self-defence? Those who themselves think and speak freely, have hardly a right to complain, if others claim the same privilege. Mill himself called the Conservative party the stupid party *par excellence*, and he took great pains to explain that it was so not by accident, but by necessity. Need he wonder if those whom he whipped and scourged used their own whips and scourges against so merciless a critic?

Freethinkers — and I use that name as a title of honor for all who, like Mill, claim for every individual the fullest freedom in thought, word, or deed, compatible with the freedom of others — are apt to make one mistake. Conscious of their own honest intentions, they cannot bear to be misjudged or slighted. They expect society to submit to their often very painful operations as a patient submits to the knife of the surgeon. This is not in human nature. The enemy of abuses is always abused by his enemies. Society will never yield one inch without resistance, and few reformers live long enough to receive the thanks of those whom they have reformed. Mill's unsolicited election to Parliament was a triumph not often shared by social reformers; it was as exceptional as Bright's admission to a seat in the Cabinet, or Stanley's appointment as Dean of Westminster. Such anomalies will happen in a country fortunately so full of anomalies as England; but, as a rule, a political reformer must not be angry if he passes through life without the title of Right Honorable; nor should a man, if he will always speak the truth, the whole truth, and nothing but the truth, be disappointed if he dies a martyr rather than a Bishop.

But even granting that in Mill's time there existed some traces of social tyranny, where are they now? Look at the newspapers and the journals. Is there any theory too wild, any reform too violent, to be openly defended? Look at the drawing-rooms or the meetings of learned societies. Are not the most eccentric talkers the spoiled children of the fashionable world? When young lords begin to discuss the propriety of limiting the rights of inheritance, and young tutors are not afraid to propose curtailing the long vacation, surely we need not complain of the intolerance of English society.

Whenever I state these facts to my German and French and Italian friends, who from reading Mill's Essay "On Liberty" have derived the impression that, however large an amount of political liberty England may enjoy, it enjoys but little of intellectual freedom, they are generally willing to be converted so far as London, or other great cities are concerned. But look at your Universities, they say, the nurseries of English thought! Compare their mediæval spirit, their monastic institutions, their scholastic philosophy, with the freshness and freedom of the Continental Universities! Strong as these prejudices about Oxford and Cambridge have long been, they have become still more intense since Professor Helmholtz, in an inaugural address which he delivered at his installation as Rector of the University of Berlin, lent to them the authority of his great name. "The tutors," he says,[1] "in the English Universities cannot deviate by a hair's-breadth from the dogmatic system of the English Church, without exposing themselves to the censure of their Archbish-

[1] *Ueber die Akademische Freiheit der Deutschen Universitäten*, Rede beim Antritt des Rectorats an der Friedrich-Wilhelms-Universität in Berlin, am October 15, 1877, gehalten von Dr. H. Helmholtz.

ops and losing their pupils." In German Universities, on the contrary, we are told that the extreme conclusions of materialistic metaphysics, the boldest speculations within the sphere of Darwin's theory of evolution, may be propounded without let or hindrance, quite as much as the highest apotheosis of Papal infallibility.

Here the facts on which Professor Helmholtz relies are entirely wrong, and the writings of some of our most eminent tutors supply a more than sufficient refutation of his statements. Archbishops have no official position whatsoever in English Universities, and their censure of an Oxford tutor would be resented as impertinent by the whole University. Nor does the University, as such, exercise any very strict control over the tutors, even when they lecture not to their own College only. Each Master of Arts at Oxford claims now the right to lecture (*venia docendi*), and I doubt whether they would submit to those restrictions which, in Germany, the Faculty imposes on every *Privat-docent*. *Privat-docents* in German Universities have been rejected by the Faculty for incompetence, and silenced for insubordination. I know of no such cases at Oxford during my residence of more than thirty years, nor can I think it likely that they should ever occur.

As to the extreme conclusions of materialistic metaphysics, there are Oxford tutors who have grappled with the systems of such giants as Hobbes, Locke, or Hume, and who are not likely to be frightened by Büchner and Vogt.

I know comparisons are odious, and I should be the last man to draw comparisons between English and German Universities unfavorable to the latter.

But with regard to freedom of thought, of speech, and action, Professor Helmholtz, if he would spend but a few weeks at Oxford, would find that we enjoy it in fuller measure here than the Professors and *Privat-docents* in any Continental University. The publications of some of our professors and tutors ought at least to have convinced him that if there is less of brave words and turbulent talk in their writings, they display throughout a determination to speak the truth, which may be matched, but could not easily be excelled, by the leaders of thought in France, Germany, or Italy.

The real difference between English and Continental Universities is that the former govern themselves, the latter are governed. Self-government entails responsibilities, sometimes restraints and reticences. I may here be allowed to quote the words of another eminent Professor of the University of Berlin, Du Bois Reymond, who, in addressing his colleagues, ventured to tell them,[1] "We have still to learn from the English how the greatest independence of the individual is compatible with willing submission to salutary, though irksome, statutes." That is particularly true when the statutes are self-imposed. In Germany, as Professor Helmholtz tells us himself, the last decision in almost all the more important affairs of the Universities rests with the Government, and he does not deny that in times of political and ecclesiastical tension, a most ill-advised use has been made of that power. There are, be-

1 *Ueber eine Akademie der Deutschen Sprache*, p. 34. Another keen observer of English life, Dr. K. Hillebrand, in an article in the October number of the *Nineteenth Century*, remarks: "Nowhere is there greater individual liberty than in England, and nowhere do people renounce it more readily of their own accord."

sides, the less important matters, such as raising of salaries, leave of absence, scientific missions, even titles and decorations, all of which enable a clever Minister of Instruction to assert his personal influence among the less independent members of the University. In Oxford the University does not know the Ministry, nor the Ministry the University. The acts of the Government, be it Liberal or Conservative, are freely discussed, and often powerfully resisted by the academic constituencies, and the personal dislike of a Minister or Ministerial Councillor could as little injure a professor or tutor as his favor could add one penny to his salary.

But these are minor matters. What gives their own peculiar character to the English Universities is a sense of power and responsibility: power, because they are the most respected among the numerous corporations in the country; responsibility, because the higher education of the whole country has been committed to their charge. Their only master is public opinion as represented in Parliament, their only incentive their own sense of duty. There is no country in Europe where Universities hold so exalted a position, and where those who have the honor to belong to them may say with greater truth *Noblesse oblige.*

I know the dangers of self-government, particularly where higher and more ideal interests are concerned, and there are probably few who wish for a real reform in schools and Universities who have not occasionally yielded to the desire for a Dictator, of a Bismarck or a Falk. But such a desire springs only from a momentary weakness and despondency; and no one who knows the difference between being governed and governing one's self, would ever wish to descend from that higher though dangerous position to a lower one, however safe and comfortable it might seem. No one who has tasted the old wine of freedom would ever really wish to exchange it for the new wine of external rule. Public opinion is sometimes a hard master, and majorities can be great tyrants to those who want to be honest to their own convictions. But in the struggle of all against all, each individual feels that he has his rightful place, and that he may exercise his rightful influence. If he is beaten, he is beaten in fair fight; if he conquers, he has no one else to thank. No doubt, despotic Governments have often exercised the most beneficial patronage in encouraging and rewarding poets, artists, and men of science. But men of genius who have conquered the love and admiration of a whole nation are greater than those who have gained the favor of the most brilliant Courts; and we know how some of the fairest reputations have been wrecked on the patronage which they had to accept at the hands of powerful Ministers or ambitious Sovereigns.

But to return to Mill and his plea for Liberty. Though I can hardly believe that, were he still among us, he would claim a larger measure of freedom for the individual than is now accorded to every one of us in the society in which we move, yet the chief cause on which he founded his plea for Liberty, the chief evil which he thought could be remedied only if society would allow more elbow-room to individual genius, exists in the same degree as in his time — aye, even in a higher degree. The principle of individuality has suffered more at present than perhaps at any former period of history. The world is becoming more and more gregarious, and what the French call our *nature moutonnière*, our tendency to leap where the sheep in front of us has leapt, becomes more and more prevalent in politics, in religion, in art, and even in science. M. de Tocqueville expressed his surprise how much more Frenchmen of the present day resemble one another than did those of the last generation. The same remark, adds John Stuart Mill, might be made of England in a greater degree. "The modern *régime* of public opinion," he writes, "is in an unorganized form what the Chinese educational and political systems are in an organized; and unless individuality shall be able successfully to assert itself against this yoke, Europe, notwithstanding its noble antecedents and its professed Christianity, will tend to become another China."

I fully agree with Mill in recognizing the dangers of uniformity, but I doubt whether what he calls the *régime* of public opinion is alone, or even chiefly, answerable for it. No doubt there are some people in whose eyes uniformity seems an advantage rather than a disadvantage. If all were equally strong, equally educated, equally honest, equally rich, equally tall, or equally small, society would seem to them to have reached the highest ideal. The same people admire an old French garden, with its clipped yew-trees, forming artificial walls and towers and pyramids, far more than the giant yews which, like large serpents, clasp the soil with their coiling roots, and overshadow with their dark green branches the white chalk cliffs of the Thames. But those French gardens, unless they are constantly clipped and prevented from growing, soon fall into decay. As in nature, so in society, uniformity means but too often stagnation, while variety is the surest sign of health and vigor. The deepest secret of nature is its love of continued novelty. Its tendency, if unrestrained, is towards constantly creating new varieties, which, if they fulfil their purpose, become fixed for a time, or, it may be, forever; while others, after they have fulfilled their purpose, vanish to make room for new and stronger types.

The same is the secret of human society. It consists and lives in individuals, each meant to be different from all the others, and to contribute his own peculiar share to the common wealth. As no tree is like any other tree, and no leaf on the same tree like any other leaf, no human being is, or is meant to be, exactly like any other human being. It is in this endless, and to us inconceivable, variety of human souls that the deepest purpose of human life is to be realized; and the more society fulfils that purpose, the more its allows free scope for the development of every individual germ, the richer will be the harvest in no distant future. Such is the mystery of individuality that I do not wonder if even those philosophers who, like Mill, confine the use of the word *sacred* within the very smallest compass, see in each individual soul something sacred, something to be revered, even where we cannot understand it, something to be protected against all vulgar violence.

Where I differ from Mill and his school is on the question as to the quarter from whence the epidemic of uniformity springs which threatens the free development of modern society. Mill points to the society in which we move; to those who are in front of us, to our contemporaries. I feel convinced that our real enemies are at our back, and that the heaviest chains which are fastened on us are those made, not by the present, but by past generations — by our ancestors, not by our contemporaries.

It is on this point, on the trammels of individual freedom with which we may almost be said to be born into the world, and on the means by which we may shake off these old chains, or at all events learn to carry them more lightly and gracefully, that I wish to speak to you this evening.

You need not be afraid that I am going to enter upon the much discussed subject of heredity, whether in its physiological or psychological aspects. It is a favorite subject just now, and the most curious facts have been brought together of late to illustrate the working of what is called heredity. But the more we know of these facts, the less we seem able to comprehend the underlying principle. Inheritance is one of those numerous words which by their very simplicity and clearness are so apt to darken our counsel. If a father has blue eyes and the son has blue eyes, what can be clearer than that he inherited them? If the father stammers and the son stammers, who can doubt but that it came by inheritance? If the father is a musician and the son a musician, we say very glibly that the talent was inherited. But what does *inherited* mean? In no case does it mean what *inherited* usually means — something external, like money, collected by a father, and, after his death, secured by law to his son. Whatever else inherited may mean, it does not mean that. But unfortunately the word is there, it seems almost pedantic to challenge its meaning, and people are always grateful if an easy word saves them the trouble of hard thought.

Another apparent advantage of the theory of heredity is that it never fails. If the son has blue, and the father black, eyes, all is right again, for either the mother, or the grandmother, or some historic or prehistoric ancestor, may have had blue eyes, and atavism, we know, will assert itself after hundreds and thousands of years.

Do not suppose that I deny the broad facts of what is called by the name of heredity. What I deny is that the name of heredity offers any scientific solution of a most difficult problem. It is a name, a metaphor, quite as bad as the old metaphor of *innate ideas;* for there is hardly a single point of similarity between the process by which a son may share the black eyes, the stammering, or the musical talent of his father, and that by which, after his father's death, the law secures to the son the possession of the pounds, shillings, and pence which his father held in the Funds.

But whatever the true meaning of heredity may be, certain it is that every individual comes into the world heavy-laden. Nowhere has the consciousness of the burden which rests on each generation as it enters on its journey through life found stronger expression than among the Buddhists. What other people call by various names, "fate or providence," "tradition or inheritance," "circumstances or environment," they call *Karman*, deed — what has been done, whether by ourselves or by others, the accumulated work of all who have come before us, the consequences of which we have to bear, both for good and for evil. Originally this *Karman* seems to have been conceived as personal, as the work which we ourselves have done in our former existences. But, as personally we are not conscious of having done such work in former ages, that kind of *Karman*, too, might be said to be impersonal. To the question how *Karman* began, what was the nucleus of that accumulation which forms the condition of present existence, Buddhism has no answer to give, any more than any other system of religion or philosophy. The Buddhists say it began with *avidyâ*, and *avidyâ* means ignorance.[1] They are much more deeply interested in the question how *Karman* may be annihilated, how each man may free himself from the influence of *Karman*, and Nirvâ*n*a, the highest object of all their dreams, is often defined by Buddhist philosophers as "freedom from *Karman*." [2]

What the Buddhists call by the general name of *Karman*, comprehends all influences which the past exercises on the present, whether physical or mental.[3] It is not my object to examine or even to name all these influences, though I confess nothing is more interesting than to look upon the surface of our modern life as we look on a geological map, and to see the most ancient formations cropping out everywhere under our feet. Difficult as it is to color a geological map of England, it would be still more difficult to find a sufficient variety of colors to mark the different ingredients of the intellectual condition of her people.

That all of us, whether we speak English or German, or French or Russian, are really speaking an

1 Spencer Hardy, *Manual of Buddhism*, p. 391.

2 Spencer Hardy, *Manual of Buddhism*, p. 39.

3 "As one generation dies and gives way to another, the heir of the consequences of all its virtues and all its vices, the exact result of preëxistent causes, so each individual, in the long chain of life, inherits all, of good or evil, which all its predecessors have done or been, and takes up the struggle towards enlightenment precisely where they left it." Rhys Davids, *Buddhism*, p. 104.

ancient Oriental tongue, incredible as it would have sounded a hundred years ago, is now recognized by everybody. Though the various dialects now spoken in Europe have been separated many thousands of years from the Sanskrit, the ancient classical language of India, yet so close is the bond that holds the West and East together, that in many cases an intelligent Englishman might still guess the meaning of a Sanskrit word. How little difference is there between Sanskrit sûnu and English *son*, between Sanskrit duhitar and English *daughter*, between Sanskrit vid, to know, and English *to wit*, between Sanskrit vaksh, to grow, and English *to wax!* Think how we value a Saxon urn, or a Roman coin, or a Keltic weapon! how we dig for them, clean them, label them, and carefully deposit them in our museums! Yet what is their antiquity compared with the antiquity of such words as *son* or *daughter*, *father* and *mother?* There are no monuments older than those collected in the handy volumes which we call Dictionaries, and those who know how to interpret those English antiquities — as you may see them interpreted, for instance, in Grimm's Dictionary of the German, in Littré's Dictionary of the French, or in Professor Skeats' Etymological Dictionary of the English Language — will learn more of the real growth of the human mind than by studying many volumes on logic and psychology.

And as by our language we belong to the Aryan stratum, we belong through our letters to the Hamitic. We still write English in hieroglyphics; and in spite of all the vicissitudes through which the ancient hieroglyphics have passed in their journey from Egypt to Phœnicia, from Phœnicia to Greece, from Greece to Italy, and from Italy to England, when we write a capital F 𝓕, when we draw the top line and the smaller line through the middle of the letter, we really draw the two horns of the cerastes, the horned serpent, which the ancient Egyptians used for representing the sound of f. They write the name of the king whom the Greeks called *Cheops*, and they themselves *Chu-fu*, like this: [1]—

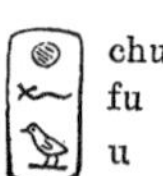

Here the first sign, the sieve, is to be pronounced *chu;* the second, the horned serpent, *fu*, and the little bird, again, *u*. In the more cursive or Hieratic writing the horned serpent appears as ϟ; in the later Demotic as Y and ч. The Phœnicians, who borrowed their letters from the Hieratic Egyptian, wrote 𐤅 and 𐤅. The Greeks, who took their letters from the Phœnicians, wrote ꟻ. When the Greeks, instead of writing, like the Phœnicians, from right to left, began to write from left to right, they turned each letter, and as ꓘ became K, our k, so ꟻ, vau, became F, the Greek so-called Digamma, F, the Latin F.

The first letter in *Chu-fu*, too, still exists in our alphabet, and in the transverse line of our H we may recognize the last remnant of the lines which divide the sieve. The sieve appears in Hieratic as ⊘, in Phœnician as 𐤇, in ancient Greek as ⊟, which occurs on an inscription found at Mycenæ and elsewhere as the sign of the spiritus asper, while in Latin it is known to us as the letter H.[2] In the same manner

Bunsen, *Egypt*, ii. pp. 77, 150.

[2] *Mémoire sur l'Origine Egyptienne de l'Alphabet Phénicien*, par E. de Rougé, Paris, 1874.

the undulating line of our capital 𝓛 still recalls very strikingly the bent back of the crouching lion, 𓃭, which in the later hieroglyphic inscriptions represents the sound of L.

If thus in our language we are Aryan, in our letters Egyptian, we have only to look at our watches to see that we are Babylonian. Why is our hour divided into sixty minutes, our minute into sixty seconds? Would not a division of the hour into ten, or fifty, or a hundred minutes have been more natural? We have sixty divisions on the dials of our watches simply because the Greek astronomer Hipparchus, who lived in the second century B. C., accepted the Babylonian system of reckoning time, that system being sexagesimal. The Babylonians knew the decimal system, but for practical purposes they counted by *sossi* and *sari*, the *sossos* representing 60, the *saros* 60×60, or 3,600. From Hipparchus that system found its way into the works of Ptolemy, about 150 A. D., and thence it was carried down the stream of civilization, finding its last resting-place on the dial-plates of our clocks.

And why are there twenty shillings to our sovereign? Again the real reason lies in Babylon. The Greeks learnt from the Babylonians the art of dividing gold and silver for the purpose of trade. It has been proved that the current gold piece of Western Asia was exactly the sixtieth part of a Babylonian *mnâ*, or *mina*. It was nearly equal to our sovereign. The difficult problem of the relative value of gold and silver in a bi-metallic currency had been solved to a certain extent in the ancient Mesopotamian kingdom, the proportion between gold and silver being fixed at 1 to 13⅓. The silver shekel current in

Babylon was heavier than the gold shekel in the proportion of 13⅓ to 10, and had therefore the value of one tenth of a gold shekel; and the half silver shekel, called by the Greeks a drachma, was worth one twentieth of a gold shekel. The drachma, or half silver shekel, may therefore be looked upon as the most ancient type of our own silver shilling in its relation of one twentieth of our gold sovereign.[1]

I shall mention only one more of the most essential tools of our mental life — namely, our *figures*, which we call Arabic, because we received them from the Arabs, but which the Arabs called Indian, because they received them from the Indians — in order to show you how this nineteenth century of ours is under the sway of centuries long past and forgotten; how we are what we are, not by ourselves, but by those who came before us, and how the intellectual ground on which we stand is made up of the detritus of thoughts which were first thought, not on these isles nor in Europe, but on the shores of the Oxus, the Nile, the Euphrates, and the Indus.

Now you may well ask, *Quorsum hæc omnia?* What has all this to do with freedom and with the free development of individuality? Because a man is born the heir of all the ages, can it be said that he is not free to grow and to expand, and to develop all the faculties of his mind? Are those who came before him, and who left him this goodly inheritance, to be called his enemies? Is that chain of tradition which connects him with the past really a galling fetter, and not rather the leading-strings without which he would never learn to walk straight?

Let us look at the matter more closely. No one

[1] See Brandis, *Das Münzwesen.*

would venture to say that every individual should begin life as a young savage, and be left to form his own language, and invent his own letters, numerals, and coins. On the contrary, if we comprehend all this and a great deal more, such as religion, morality, and secular knowledge, under the general name of *education*, even the most advanced defenders of individualism would hold that no child should enter society without submitting, or rather without being submitted, to education. Most of us would even go farther, and make it criminal for parents or even for communities to allow children to grow up uneducated. The excuse of worthless parents that they are at liberty to do with their children as they like, has at last been blown to the winds, and among the principal advocates of compulsory education, and of the necessity of curtailing the freedom of savage parents of savage children, have been Mill and his friends, the apostles of liberty and individualism.[1] I remember the time when pseudo-Liberals were not ashamed to say that, whatever other nations, such as the Germans, might do, England would never submit to compulsory education; but that faint-hearted and mischievous cry has at last been silenced. A new era may be said to date in the history of every nation from the day on which "compulsory education" becomes part of its statute-book; and I may congratulate the most Liberal town in England on having proved itself the most inexorable tyrant in carrying it into effect.

But do not let us imagine that compulsory educa-

1 "Is it not almost a self-evident axiom, that the State should require and compel the education, up to a certain standard, of every human being who is born its citizen? Yet who is there that is not afraid to recognize and assert this truth?" *On Liberty*, p. 188.

tion is without its dangers. Like a powerful engine, it must be carefully watched, if it is not to produce, what all compulsion will produce, a slavish receptivity, and, what all machines do produce, monotonous uniformity.

We know that all education must in the beginning be purely dogmatic. Children are taught language, religion, morality, patriotism, and afterwards, at school, history, literature, mathematics, and all the rest, long before they are able to question, to judge, or choose for themselves, and there is hardly anything that a child will not believe, if it comes from those in whom the child believes.

Reading, writing, and arithmetic, no doubt, must be taught dogmatically, and they take up an enormous amount of time, particularly in English schools. English spelling is a national misfortune, and in the keen international race among all the countries of Europe, it handicaps the English child to a degree that seems incredible till we look at statistics. I know the difficulties of a Spelling Reform, I know what people mean when they call it impossible; but I also know that personal and national virtue consists in doing so-called impossible things, and that no nation has done, and has still to do, so many impossible things as the English.

But, granted that reading, writing, and arithmetic occupy nearly the whole school time and absorb the best powers of the pupils, cannot something be done in play-hours? Is there not some work that can be turned into play, and some play that can be turned into work? Cannot the powers of observation be called out in a child while collecting flowers, or stones, or butterflies? Cannot his judgment be strengthened either in gymnastic exercises, or in measuring the area of a field or the height of a tower? Might not all this be done without a view to examinations or payment by results, simply for the sake of filling the little dull minds with one sunbeam of joy, such sunbeams being more likely hereafter to call hidden precious germs into life than the deadening weight of such lessons as, for instance, that *th-ough* is though, *thr-ough* is through, *en-ough* is enough. A child who believes that will hereafter believe anything. Those who wish to see Natural Science introduced into elementary schools frighten school-masters by the very name of Natural Science. But surely every school-master who is worth his salt should be able to teach children a love of Nature, a wondering at Nature, a curiosity to pry into the secrets of Nature, an acquisitiveness for some of the treasures of Nature, and all this acquired in the fresh air of the field and the forest, where, better than in frowzy lecture-rooms, the edge of the senses can be sharpened, the chest widened, and that freedom of thought fostered which made England what it was even before the days of compulsory education.

But in addressing you here to-night, it was my intention to speak of higher rather than of elementary education.

All education — as it now exists in most countries of Europe — may be divided into three stages — *elementary*, *scholastic*, and *academical;* or call it *primary*, *secondary*, and *tertiary*.

Elementary education has at last been made compulsory in most civilized countries. Unfortunately, however, it seems impossible to include under compulsory education anything beyond the very elements of knowledge — at least for the present; though I know from experience that, with proper management, a well-conducted elementary school can afford to provide instruction in extra subjects — such as natural science, modern languages, and political economy — and yet, with the present system of government grants, be self-supporting.[1]

The next stage above the elementary is *scholastic* education, as it is supplied in grammar schools, whether public or private. According as the pupils are intended either to go on to a university, or to enter at once on leaving school on the practical work of life, these schools are divided into two classes. In the one class, which in Germany are called *Real-schulen*, less Latin is taught, and no Greek, but more of mathematics, modern languages, and physical science; in the other, called *Gymnasia* on the Continent, classics form the chief staple of instruction.

It is during this stage that education, whether at private or public schools, exercises its strongest levelling influence. Little attention can be paid at large schools to individual tastes or talents. In Germany — even more, perhaps, than in England — it is the chief object of a good and conscientious master to have his class as uniform as possible at the end of the year; and he receives far more credit from the official examiner if his whole class marches well and keeps pace together, than if he can parade a few brilliant and forward boys, followed by a number of straggling laggards.

And as to the character of the teaching at school, how can it be otherwise than authoritative or dogmatic? The Sokratic method is very good if we can

[1] *Times*, January 25, 1879.

find the *viri Socratici* and leisure for discussion. But at school, which now may seem to be called almost in mockery σχολή, or leisure, the true method is, after all, that patronized by the great educators of the seventeenth and eighteenth centuries. Boys at school must turn their mind into a row of pigeon-holes, filling as many as they can with useful notes, and never forgetting how many are empty. There is an immense amount of positive knowledge to be acquired between the ages of ten and eighteen — rules of grammar, strings of vocables, dates, names of towns, rivers, and mountains, mathematical formulas, etc. All depends here on the receptive and retentive powers of the mind. The memory has to be strengthened, without being overtaxed, till it acts almost mechanically. Learning by heart, I believe, cannot be too assiduously practised during the years spent at school. There may have been too much of it when, as the Rev. H. C. Adams informs us in his "Wykehamica" (p. 357), boys used to say by heart 13,000 and 14,000 lines, when one repeated the whole of Virgil, nay, when another was able to say the whole of the English Bible by rote: "Put him on where you would, he would go fluently on, as long as any one would listen."

No intellectual investment, I feel certain, bears such ample and such regular interest as gems of English, Latin, or Greek literature deposited in the memory during childhood and youth, and taken up from time to time in the happy hours of solitude.

One fault I have to find with most schools, both in England and on the Continent. Boys do not read enough of the Greek and Roman classics. The majority of our masters are scholars by profession, and they are apt to lay undue stress on what they call accurate and minute scholarship, and to neglect wide and cursory reading. I know the arguments for minute accuracy, but I also know the mischief that is done by an exclusive devotion to critical scholarship before we have acquired a real familiarity with the principal works of classical literature. The time spent in our schools in learning the rules of grammar and syntax, writing exercises, and composing verses, is too large. Look only at our Greek and Latin grammars, with all their rules and exceptions, and exceptions on exceptions! It is too heavy a weight for any boy to carry; and no wonder that when one of the thousand small rules which they have learnt by heart is really wanted, it is seldom forthcoming. The end of classical teaching at school should be to make our boys acquainted, not only with the language, but with the literature and history, the ancient thought of the ancient world. Rules of grammar, syntax, or metre, are but means towards that end; they must never be mistaken for the end itself. A young man of eighteen, who has probably spent on an average ten years in learning Greek and Latin, ought to be able to read any of the ordinary Greek or Latin classics without much difficulty; nay, with a certain amount of pleasure. He might have to consult his dictionary now and then, or guess the meaning of certain words; he might also feel doubtful sometime whether certain forms came from ἵημι, I send, or εἶμι, I go, or εἰμί, I am, particularly if preceded by prepositions. In these matters the best scholars are least inclined to be pharisaical; and whenever I meet in the controversies of classical scholars the favorite phrase, "Every school-boy knows, or ought to know, this," I generally say to myself, "No, he ought not." Anyhow, those who wish to see the study of Greek and Latin retained in our public schools ought to feel convinced that it will certainly not be retained much longer, if it can be said with any truth that young men who leave school at eighteen are in many cases unable to read or to enjoy a classical text, unless they have seen it before.

Classical teaching, and all purely scholastic teaching, ought to be finished at school. When a young man goes to a University, unless he means to make scholarship his profession, he ought to be free to enter upon a new career. If he has not learnt by that time so much of Greek and Latin as is absolutely necessary in after-life for a lawyer, or a student of physical science, or even a clergyman, either he or his school is to blame. I do not mean to say that it would not be most desirable for every one during his University career to attend some lectures on classical literature, on ancient history, philosophy, or art. What is to be deprecated is, that the University should have to do the work which belongs properly to the school.

The best colleges at Oxford and Cambridge have shown by their matriculation examinations what the standard of classical knowledge ought to be at eighteen or nineteen. That standard can be reached by boys while still at school, as has been proved both by the so-called local examinations, and by the examinations of schools held under the Delegates appointed by the Universities. If, therefore, the University would reassert her old right, and make the first examination, called at Oxford Responsions, a general matriculation examination for admission to the University, not only would the public schools be stimulated to greater efforts, but the teaching of the University might assume, from the very beginning, that academic character which ought to distinguish it from mere school-boy work.

Academic teaching ought to be not merely a continuation, but in one sense a correction of scholastic teaching. While at school instruction must be chiefly dogmatic, at the University is it to be Sokratic? for I find no better name for that method which is to set a man free from the burden of purely traditional knowledge; to make him feel that the words which he uses are often empty, that the concepts he employs are, for the most part, mere bundles picked up at random; that even where he knows facts he does not know the evidence for them; and where he expresses opinions, they are mostly mere dogmas, adopted by him without examination.

But for the Universities, I should indeed fear that Mill's prophecies might come true, and that the intellect of Europe might drift into dreary monotony. The Universities always have been, and, unless they are diverted from their original purpose, always will be, the guardians of the freedom of thought, the protectors of individual spontaneity; and it was owing, I believe, to Mill's want of acquaintance with true academic teaching that he took so desponding a view of the generation growing up under his eyes.

When we leave school, our heads are naturally brimful of dogma — that is, of knowledge and opinions at second-hand. Such dead knowledge is extremely dangerous, unless it is sooner or later revived by the spirit of free inquiry. It does not matter whether our scholastic dogmas be true or false. The danger is the same. And why? Because to place either truth or error above the reach of argument is certain to weaken truth and to strengthen error. Secondly, because to hold as true on the authority of others anything which concerns us deeply, and which we could prove ourselves, produces feebleness, if not dishonesty. And, thirdly, because to feel unwilling or unable to meet objections by argument is generally the first step towards violence and persecution.

I do not think of religious dogmas only. They are generally the first to rouse inquiry, even during our school-boy days, and they are by no means the most difficult to deal with. Dogma often rages where we least expect it. Among scientific men the theory of evolution is at present becoming, or has become, a dogma. What is the result? No objections are listened to, no difficulties recognized, and a man like Virchow, himself the strongest supporter of evolution, who has the moral courage to say that the descent of man from any ape whatsoever is, as yet, before the tribunal of scientific zoölogy, "not proven," is howled down in Germany in a manner worthy of Ephesians and Galatians. But at present I am thinking not so much of any special dogmas, but rather of that dogmatic state of mind which is the almost inevitable result of the teaching at school. I think of the whole intellect, what has been called the *intellectus sibi permissus*, and I maintain it is the object of academic teaching to rouse that intellect out of its slumber by questions not less startling than when Galileo asked the world whether the sun was really moving and the earth stood still; or when Kant asked whether time and space were objects, or necessary forms of our sensuous intuition. Till our opinions have thus been tested and stood the test, we can hardly call them our own.

How true this is with regard to religion has been boldly expressed by Bishop Beveridge.

"Being conscious to myself," he writes in his "Private Thoughts on Religion," "how great an ascendant Christianity holds over me beyond the rest, as being that religion whereinto I was born and baptized; that which the supreme authority has enjoined and my parents educated me in; that which every one I meet withal highly approves of, and which I myself have, by a long-continued profession, made almost natural to me: I am resolved to be more jealous and suspicious of this religion than of the rest, and be sure not to entertain it any longer without being convinced, by solid and substantial arguments, of the truth and certainty of it."

This is bold and manly language from a Bishop, nearly two hundred years ago, and I certainly think that the time has come when some of the divinity lecturers at Oxford and Cambridge might well be employed in placing a knowledge of the sacred books of other religions within the reach of undergraduates. Many of the difficulties — most of them of our own making — with regard to the origin, the handing down, the later corruptions and misinterpretations of sacred texts, would find their natural solution, if it was shown how exactly the same difficulties arose and had to be dealt with by theologians of other creeds. If some — aye, if many — of the doctrines of Christianity were met with in other religions also, surely that would not affect their value, or diminish their truth; while nothing, I feel certain, would more effectually secure to the pure and simple teaching of Christ its true place in the historical development of the human mind than to place it side by side with the other religions of the world. In the series of translations of the "Sacred Books of the East," of which the first three volumes have just appeared,[1] I wished myself to include a new translation of the Old and New Testaments; and when that series is finished it will, I believe, be admitted that nowhere would these two books have had a grander setting, or have shone with a brighter light, than surrounded by the Veda, the Zendavesta, the Buddhist Tripitaka, and the Qur'ân.

But as I said before, I was not thinking of religious dogmas only, or even chiefly, when I maintained that the character of academic teaching must be Sokratic, not dogmatic. The evil of dogmatic teaching lies much deeper, and spreads much farther.

Think only of language, the work of other people, not of ourselves, which we pick up at random in our race through life. Does not every word we use require careful examination and revision? It is not enough to say that language assists our thoughts or colors them, or possibly obscures them. No language and thought are indivisible. It was not from poverty of expression that the Greeks called reason and language by the same word, λόγος. It was because they knew that, though we may distinguish between thought and speech, as we distinguish between force and function, it is as impossible to tear the one by violence away from the other as it is to separate the concave side of a lens from its convex side. This is something to learn and to understand, for, if, properly understood, will it supply the key to most of our intellectual puzzles, and serve as the safest thread through the whole labyrinth of philosophy.

1 *Sacred Books of the East*, edited by M. M., vols. i. to ix.; Clarendon Press, Oxford, 1879 and 1880.

"It is evident," as Hobbes remarks,[1] "that truth and falsity have no place but amongst such living creatures as use speech. For though some brute creatures, looking upon the image of a man in a glass, may be affected with it, as if it were the man himself, and for this reason fear it or fawn upon it in vain; yet they do not apprehend it as true or false, but only as like; and in this they are not deceived. Wherefore, as men owe all their true ratiocination to the right understanding of speech, so also they owe their errors to the misunderstanding of the same; and as all the ornaments of philosophy proceed only from man, so from man also is derived the ugly absurdity of false opinion. For speech has something in it like to a spider's web (as it was said of old of Solon's laws), for by contexture of words tender and delicate wits are ensnared or stopped, but strong wits break easily through them."

Let me illustrate my meaning by at least one instance.

Among the words which have proved spider's webs, ensnaring even the greatest intellects of the world from Aristotle down to Leibniz, the terms *genus*, *species*, and *individual* occupy a very prominent place. The opposition of Aristotle to Plato, of the Nominalists to the Realists, of Leibniz to Locke, of Herbart to Hegel, turns on the true meaning of these words. At school, of course, all we can do is to teach the received meaning of *genus* and *species;* and if a boy can trace these terms back to Aristotle's γένος and εἶδος, and show in what sense that philosopher used them, every examiner would be satisfied.

But the time comes when we have to act as our

[1] *Computation or Logic*, t. iii., viii., p. 36.

own examiners, and when we have to give an account to ourselves of such words as *genus* and *species*. Some people write, indeed, as if they had seen a *species* and a *genus* walking about in broad daylight; but a little consideration will show us that these words express subjective concepts, and that, if the whole world were silent, there would never have been a thought of a *genus* or a *species*. There are languages in which we look in vain for corresponding words; and if we had been born in the atmosphere of such a language, these terms and thoughts would not exist for us. They came to us, directly or indirectly, from Aristotle. But Aristotle did not invent them, he only defined them in his own way, so that, for instance, according to him, all living beings would constitute a *genus*, men a *species*, and Sokrates an *individual*.

No one would say that Aristotle had not a perfect right to define these terms, if those who use them in his sense would only always remember that they are thinking the thoughts of Aristotle, and not their own. The true way to shake off the fetters of old words, and to learn to think our own thoughts, is to follow them up from century to century, to watch their development, and in the end to bring ourselves face to face with those who first found and framed both words and thoughts. If we do this with *genus* and *species*, we shall find that the words which Aristotle defined — viz., γένος and εἶδος — had originally a very different and far more useful application than that which he gave to them. Γένος, *genus*, meant generation, and comprehended such living beings only as were believed to have a common origin, however they might differ in outward appearance, as, for instance, the spaniel and the bloodhound, or, according to Darwin, the ape and the man. Εἶδος or species, on the contrary, meant appearance, and comprehended all such things as had the same form or appearance, whether they had a common origin or not, as if we were to speak of a species of four-footed, two-footed, horned, winged, or blue animals.

That two such concepts, as we have here explained, had a natural justification we may best learn from the fact that exactly the same thoughts found expression in Sanskrit. There, too, we find *g*âti, generation, used in the sense of *genus*, and opposed to âk*ri*ti, appearance, used in the sense of *species*.

So long as these two words or thoughts were used independently (much as we now speak of a genealogical as independent of a morphological classification) no harm could accrue. A family, for instance, might be called a γένος, the *gens* or clan was a γένος, the nation (*gnatio*) was a γένος, the whole human kith and kin was a γένος; in fact, all that was descended from common ancestors was a true γένος. There is no obscurity of thought in this.

On the other side, taking εἶδος or species in its original sense, one man might be said to be like another in his εἶδος or appearance. An ape, too, might quite truly be said to have the same εἶδος or species or appearance as a man, without any prejudice as to their common origin. People might also speak of different εἴδη or forms or classes of things, such as different kinds of metals, or tools, or armor, without committing themselves in the least to any opinion as to their common descent.

Often it would happen that things belonging to the same γένος, such as the white man and the negro, differed in their εἶδος or appearance; often also that things belonged to the same εἶδος, such as eatables, differed in their γένος, as, for instance, meat and vegetables.

All this is clear and simple. The confusion began when these two terms, instead of being coördinate, were subordinated to each other by the philosophers of Greece, so that what from one point of view was called a *genus*, might from another be called a species, and *vice versâ*. Human beings, for instance, were now called a *species*, all living beings a *genus*, which may be true in logic, but is utterly false in what is older than logic — viz., language, thought, or fact. According to language, according to reason, and according to nature, all human beings constitute a γένος, or generation, so long as they are supposed to have common ancestors; but with regard to all living beings we can only say that they form an εἶδος — that is, agree in certain appearances, until it has been proved that even Mr. Darwin was too modest in admitting at least four or five different ancestors for the whole animal world.[1]

In tracing the history of these two words, γένος and εἶδος, you may see passing before your eyes almost the whole panorama of philosophy, from Plato's "ideas" down to Hegel's *Idee*. The question of *genera*, their origin and subdivision, occupied chiefly the attention of natural philosophers, who, after long controversies about the origin and classification of *genera* and *species*, seem at last, thanks to the clear sight of Darwin, to have arrived at the old truth which was prefigured in language — namely, that Nature knows nothing

1 Lectures on Mr. Darwin's "Philosophy of Language," *Fraser's Magazine*, June, 1873, p. 26.

but *genera*, or generations, to be traced back to a limited number of ancestors, and that the so-called *species* are only *genera*, whose genealogical descent is *as yet* more or less obscure.

But the question as to the nature of the εἶδος became a vital question in every system of philosophy. Granting, for instance, that women in every clime and country formed one species, it was soon asked what constituted a species? If all women shared a common form, what was that form? Where was it? So long as it was supposed that all women descended from Eve, the difficulty might be slurred over by the name of heredity. But the more thoughtful would ask even then how it was that, while all individual women came and went and vanished, the form in which they were cast remained the same?

Here you see how philosophical mythology springs up. The very question what εἶδος or species or form was, and where these things were kept, changed those words from predicates into subjects. Εἶδος was conceived as something independent and substantial, something within or above the individuals participating in it, something unchangeable and eternal. Soon there arose as many εἴδη or forms or types as there were general concepts. They were considered the only true realities of which the phenomenal world is only as a shadow that soon passeth away. Here we have, in fact, the origin of Plato's ideas, and of the various systems of idealism which followed his lead, while the opposite opinion that ideas have no independent existence, and that the one is nowhere found except in the many (τὸ ἓν παρὰ τὰ πολλά), was strenuously defended by Aristotle and his followers.[1]

[1] Prantl, *Geschichte der Logik*, vol. i. p. 121.

The same red thread runs through the whole philosophy of the Middle Ages. Men were cited before councils and condemned as heretics because they declared that *animal*, *man*, or *woman* were mere names, and that they could not bring themselves to believe in an ideal animal, an ideal man, an ideal woman as the invisible, supernatural, or metaphysical types of the ordinary animal, the individual man, the single woman. Those philosophers, called *Nominalists*, in opposition to the *Realists*, declared that all general terms were *names only*, and that nothing could claim reality but the individual.

We cannot follow this controversy farther, as it turns up again between Locke and Leibniz, between Herbart and Hegel. Suffice it to say that the knot, as it was tied by language, can be untied by the science of language alone, which teaches us that there is and can be no such thing as "a name only." That phrase ought to be banished from all works on philosophy. A name is and always has been the subjective side of our knowledge, but that subjective side is as impossible without an objective side as a key is without a lock. It is useless to ask which of the two is the more real, for they are real only by being, not two, but one. Realism is as one-sided as Nominalism. But there is a higher Nominalism, which might better be called the Science of Language, and which teaches us that, apart from sensuous perception, all human knowledge is by names and by names only, and that the object of names is always the general.

This is but one out of hundreds and thousands of cases to show how names and concepts which come to us by tradition must be submitted to very careful snuffing before they will yield a pure light. What I mean by academic teaching and academic study is exactly this process of snuffing, this changing of traditional words into living words, this tracing of modern thought back to ancient primitive thought, this living, as it were, once more, so far as it concerns us, the whole history of human thought ourselves, till we are as little afraid to differ from Plato or Aristotle as from Comte or Darwin.

Plato and Aristotle are, no doubt, great names; every school-boy is awed by them, even though he may have read very little of their writings. This, too, is a kind of dogmatism that requires correction. Now, at his University, a young student might chance to hear the following, by no means respectful, remarks about Aristotle, which I copy from one of the greatest English scholars and philosophers: "There is nothing so absurd that the old philosophers, as Cicero saith, who was one of them, have not some of them maintained; and I believe that scarce anything can be more absurdly said in natural philosophy than that which now is called Aristotle's Metaphysics; or more repugnant to government than much of that he hath said in his Politics; nor more ignorantly than a great part of his Ethics." I am far from approving this judgment, but I think that the shock which a young scholar receives on seeing his idols so mercilessly broken is salutary. It throws him back on his own resources; it makes him honest to himself. If he thinks the criticism thus passed on Aristotle unfair, he will begin to read his works with new eyes. He will not only construe his words, but try to reconstruct in his own mind the thoughts so carefully elaborated by that ancient philosopher. He will judge of their truth without being swayed by the authority of a great name, and probably in the end value what is valuable in Aristotle, or Plato, or any other great philosopher far more highly and honestly than if he had never seen them trodden under foot.

Do not suppose that I look upon the Universities as purely iconoclastic, as chiefly intended to teach us how to break the idols of the schools. Far from it! But I do look upon them as meant to supply a fresher atmosphere than we breathed at school, and to shake our mind to its very roots, as a storm shakes the young oaks, not to throw them down, but to make them grasp all the more firmly the hard soil of fact and truth! "*Stand upright on thy feet*" ought to be written over the gate of every college, if the epidemic of uniformity and sequacity which Mill saw approaching from China, and which since his time has made such rapid progress Westward, is ever to be stayed.

Academic freedom is not without its dangers; but there are dangers which it is safer to face than to avoid. In Germany — so far as my own experience goes — students are often left too much to themselves, and it is only the cleverest among them, or those who are personally recommended, who receive from the professors that individual guidance and encouragement which should and could be easily extended to all.

There is too much time spent in the German Universities in mere lecturing, and often in simply retailing to a class what each student might read in books in a far more perfect form. Lectures are useful if they teach us how to teach ourselves; if they stimulate; if they excite sympathy and curiosity; if they give advice that springs from personal experience; if they warn against wrong roads; if, in fact, they have less the character of a show-window than of a workshop. Half an hour's conversation with a tutor or a professor often does more than a whole course of lectures in giving the right direction and the right spirit to a young man's studies. Here I may quote the words of Professor Helmholtz, in full agreement with him. "When I recall the memory of my own University life," he writes, "and the impression which a man like Johannes Müller, the professor of physiology, made on us, I must set the highest value on the personal intercourse with teachers from whom one learns how thought works in independent heads. Whoever has come in contact but once with one or several first-class men will find his intellectual standard changed for life."

In English Universities, on the contrary, there is too little of academic freedom. There is not only guidance, but far too much of constant personal control. It is often thought that English undergraduates could not be trusted with that amount of academic freedom which is granted to German students, and that most of them, if left to choose their own work, their own time, their own books, and their own teachers, would simply do nothing. This seems to me unfair and untrue. Most horses, if you take them to the water, will drink; and the best way to make them drink is to leave them alone. I have lived long enough in English and in German Universities to know that the intellectual fibre is as strong and sound in the English as in the German youth. But if you supply a man, who wishes to learn swimming, with bladders — nay, if you insist on his using them — he will use them, but he will probably never learn to swim. Take them away, on the contrary, and depend on it, after a few aimless strokes and a few painful gulps, he will use his arms and his legs, and he will swim. If young men do not learn to use their arms, their legs, their muscles, their senses, their brain, and their heart too, during the bright years of their University life, when are they to learn it? True, there are thousands who never learn it, and who float happily on through life buoyed up on mere bladders. The worst that can happen to them is that some day the bladders may burst, and they may be left stranded or drowned. But these are not the men whom England wants to fight her battles. It has often been pointed out of late that many of those who during this century have borne the brunt of the battle in the intellectual warfare in England, have not been trained at our Universities, while others who have been at Oxford and Cambridge, and have distinguished themselves in after life, have openly declared that they attended hardly any lectures in college, or that they derived no benefit from them. What can be the ground of that? Not that there is less work done at Oxford than at Leipzig, but that the work is done in a different spirit. It is free in Germany; it has now become almost compulsory in England. Though an old professor myself, I like to attend, when I can, some of the professorial lectures in Germany; for it is a real pleasure to see hundreds of young faces listening to a teacher on the history of art, on modern history, on the science of language, or on philosophy, without any view to examinations, simply from love of the subject or of the teacher. No one who knows what the real joy of learning is, how it lightens all drudgery and draws away the mind from mean pursuits, can see without indignation that what ought to be the freest and happiest years in a man's life should often be spent between cramming and examinations.

And here I have at last mentioned the word, which to many friends of academic freedom, to many who dread the baneful increase of uniformity, may seem the cause of all mischief, the most powerful engine for intellectual levelling — *Examination.*

There is a strong feeling springing up everywhere against the tyranny of examinations, against the cramping and withering influence which they are supposed to exercise on the youth of England. I cannot join in that outcry. I well remember that the first letters which I ventured to address to the *Times*, in very imperfect English, were in favor of examinations. They were signed *La Carrière ouverte,* and were written before the days of the Civil Service Commission! I well remember, too, that the first time I ventured to speak, or rather to stammer, in public, was in favor of examinations. That was in 1857, at Exeter, when the first experiment was made, under the auspices of Sir T. Acland, in the direction of what has since developed into the Oxford and Cambridge Local Examinations. I have been an examiner myself for many years, I have watched the growth of that system in England from year to year, and, in spite of all that has been said and written of late against it, I confess I do not see how it would be possible to abolish it, and return to the old system of appointment by patronage.

But though I have not lost my faith in examinations, I cannot conceal the fact that I am frightened by the manner in which they are conducted, and by the results which they produce. As you are interested yourselves at this Midland Institute in the successful working of examinations, you will perhaps allow me in conclusion to add a few remarks on the safeguards necessary for the efficient working of examinations.

All examinations are a means to ascertain how pupils have been taught; they ought never to be allowed to become the end for which pupils are taught. Teaching with a view to them lowers the teacher in the eyes of his pupils; learning with a view to them is apt to produce shallowness and dishonesty.

Whatever attractions learning possesses in itself, and whatever efforts were formerly made by boys at school from a sense of duty, all this is lost if they once imagine that the highest object of all learning is to gain marks in a competition.

In order to maintain the proper relation between teacher and pupil, all pupils should be made to look to their teachers as their natural examiners and fairest judges, and therefore in every examination the report of the teacher ought to carry the greatest weight. This is the principle followed abroad in examining candidates at public schools; and even in their examination on leaving school, which gives them the right to enter the University, they know that their success depends far more on the work which they have done during the years at school, than on the work done on the few days of their examination. There are outside examiners appointed by Government to check the work done at schools and during the examinations; but the cases in which they have to modify or reverse the award of the master are extremely rare, and they are felt to reflect seriously on the competency or impartiality of the school authorities.

To leave examinations entirely to strangers reduces them to the level of lotteries, and fosters a cleverness in teachers and taught often akin to dishonesty. An examiner may find out what a candidate knows *not*, he can hardly ever find out all he knows; and even if he succeeds in finding out *how much* a candidate knows, he can seldom find out *how* he knows it. On these points the opinion of the masters who have watched their pupils for years is indispensable for the sake of the examiner, for the sake of the pupils, and for the sake of their teachers.

I know I shall be told that it would be impossible to trust the masters, and to be guided by their opinion, because they are interested parties. Now, first of all, there are far more honest men in the world than dishonest, and it does not answer to legislate as if all school-masters were rogues. It is enough that they should know that their reports would be scrutinized, to keep even the most reprobate of teachers from bearing false witness in favor of their pupils.

Secondly, I believe that unnecessary temptation is now being placed before all parties concerned in examinations. The proper reward for a good examination should be honor, not pounds, shillings, and pence. The mischief done by pecuniary rewards offered in the shape of scholarships and exhibitions at school and University, begins to be recognized very widely. To train a boy of twelve for a race against all England is generally to overstrain his faculties, and often to impair his usefulness in later life; but to make him feel that by his failure he will entail on his father the loss of a hundred a year, and on his teacher the loss of pupils, is simply cruel at that early age.

It is said that these scholarships and exhibitions enable the sons of poor parents to enjoy the privilege of the best education in England, from which they would otherwise be debarred by the excessive costliness of our public schools. But even this argument, strong as it seems, can hardly stand, for I believe it could be shown that the majority of those who are successful in obtaining scholarships and exhibitions at school or at the University are boys whose parents have been able to pay the highest price for their children's previous education. If all these prizes were abolished, and the funds thus set free used to lessen the price of education at school and in college, I believe that the sons of poor parents would be far more benefited than by the present system. It might also be desirable to lower the school fees in the case of the sons of poor parents, who were doing well at school from year to year; and, in order to guard against favoritism, an examination, particularly *vivâ voce*, before all the masters of a school, possibly even with some outside examiner, might be useful. But the present system bids fair to degenerate into mere horse-racing, and I shall not wonder if, sooner or later, the two-year olds entered for the race have to be watched by their trainer that they may not be overfed or drugged against the day of the race. It has come to this, that schools are bidding for clever boys in order to run them in the races, and in France, I read, that parents actually extort money from schools by threatening to take away the young racers that are likely to win the Derby.[1]

[1] L. Noiré, *Pädagogisches Skizzenbuch*, p. 157; "Todtes Wissen."

If we turn from the schools to the Universities we find here, too, the same complaints against over-examination. Now it seems to me that every University, in order to maintain its position, has a perfect right to demand two examinations, but no more: one for admission, the other for a degree. Various attempts have been made in Germany, in Russia, in France, and in England to change and improve the old academic tradition, but in the end the original, and, as it would seem, the natural system, has generally proved its wisdom and reasserted its right.

If a University surrenders the right of examining those who wish to be admitted, the tutors will often have to do the work of school-masters, and the professors can never know how high or how low they should aim in their public lectures; and the result will be a lowering of the standard at the Universities, and consequently at the public schools. Some Universities, on the contrary, like over-anxious mothers, have multiplied examinations so as to make quite sure, at the end of each term or each year, that the pupils confided to them have done at least some work. This kind of forced labor may do some good to the incorrigibly idle, but it does the greatest harm to all the rest. If there is an examination at the end of each year, there can be no freedom left for any independent work. Both teachers and taught will be guided by the same pole-star — examinations; no deviation from the beaten track will be considered safe, and all the pleasure derived from work done for its own sake, and all the just pride and joy, which those only know who have ever ventured out by themselves on the open sea of knowledge, must be lost.

We must not allow ourselves to be deceived by the brilliant show of examination papers.

It is certainly marvellous what an amount of knowledge candidates will produce before their examiners; but those who have been both examined and examiners know best how fleeting that knowledge often is, and how different from that other knowledge which has been acquired slowly and quietly, for its own sake, for our own sake, without a thought as to whether it would ever pay at examinations or not. A candidate, after giving most glibly the dates and the titles of the principal works of Cobbett, Gibbon, Burke, Adam Smith, and David Hume, was asked whether he had ever seen any of their writings, and he had to answer, No. Another who was asked which of the works of Pheidias he had seen, replied that he had only read the first two books. This is the kind of dishonest knowledge which is fostered by too frequent examinations. There are two kinds of knowledge, the one that enters into our very blood, the other which we carry about in our pockets. Those who read for examinations have generally their pockets cram full; those who work on quietly and have their whole heart in their work are often discouraged at the small amount of their knowledge, at the little life-blood they have made. But what they have learnt has really become their own, has invigorated their whole frame, and in the end they have often proved the strongest and happiest men in the battle of life.

Omniscience is at present the bane of all our knowledge. From the day he leaves school and enters the University a man ought to make up his mind that in many things he must either remain altogether ignorant, or be satisfied with knowledge at second-hand. Thus only can he clear the decks for action. And the sooner he finds out what his own work is to be, the more useful and delightful will be his life at the University and later. There are few men who have a passion for all knowledge; there is hardly one who has not a hobby of his own. Those so-called hobbies ought to be utilized, and not, as they are now, discouraged, if we wish our Universities to produce more men like Faraday, Carlyle, Grote, or Darwin. I do not say that in an examination for a University degree a minimum of what is now called general culture should not be insisted on; but in addition to that, far more freedom ought to be given to the examiner to let each candidate produce his own individual work. This is done to a far greater extent in Continental than in English Universities, and the examinations are therefore mostly confided to the members of the *Senatus Academicus*, consisting of the most experienced teachers, and the most eminent representatives of the different branches of knowledge in the University. Their object is not to find out how many marks each candidate may gain by answering a larger or smaller number of questions, and then to place them in order before the world like so many organ pipes. They want to find out whether a man, by the work he has done during his three or four University years, has acquired that vigor of thought, that maturity of judgment, and that special knowledge, which fairly entitle him to an academic degree, with or without special honors. Such a degree confers no material advantages;[1] it does not entitle its holder to any employment in Church or State; it does not vouch even for his being a fit person to be made an Archbishop or

[1] Mill *On Liberty*, p. 193.

Prime Minister. All this is left to the later struggle for life; and in that struggle it seems as if those who, after having surveyed the vast field of human knowledge, have settled on a few acres of their own and cultivated them as they were never cultivated before, who have worked hard and have tasted the true joy and happiness of hard work, who have gladly listened to others, but always depended on themselves, were, after all, the men whom great nations delighted to follow as their royal leaders in the onward march towards greater enlightenment, greater happiness, and greater freedom.

To sum up, no one can read Mill's Essay "On Liberty" at the present moment without feeling that even during the short period of the last twenty years the cause which he advocated so strongly and passionately, the cause of individual freedom, has made rapid progress — aye, has carried the day. In no country *may* a man be so entirely himself, so true to himself, and yet loyal to society, as in England.

But, although the enemy whose encroachments Mill feared most and resented most has been driven back and forced to keep within his own bounds — though such names as Dissenter and Nonconformist, which were formerly used in society as fatal darts, seem to have lost all the poison which they once contained — Mill's principal fears have nevertheless not been belied, and the blight of uniformity which he saw approaching with its attendant evils of feebleness, indifference, and sequacity, has been spreading more widely than ever.

It has ever been maintained that the very freedom which every individual now enjoys has been detrimental to the growth of individuality; that you must have an Inquisition if you want to see martyrs, that you must have despotism and tyranny to call forth heroes. The very measures which the friends of individual development advocated so warmly, compulsory education and competitive examinations, are pointed out as having chiefly contributed to produce that large array of pass-men, that dead level of uninteresting excellence, which is the *beau idéal* of a Chinese Mandarin, while it frightened and disheartened such men as Humboldt, Tocqueville, and John Stuart Mill himself.

There may be some truth in all this, but it is certainly not the whole truth. Education, as it has to be carried on, whether in elementary or in public schools, is no doubt a heavy weight which might well press down the most independent spirit; it is, in fact, neither more nor less than placing, in a systematized form, on the shoulders of every generation the ever-increasing mass of knowledge, experience, custom, and tradition that has been accumulated by former generations. We need not wonder, therefore, if in some schools all spring, all vigor, all joyousness of work is crushed out under that load of names and dates, of anomalous verbs and syntactic rules, of mathematical formulas and geometrical theories which boys are expected to bring up for competitive examinations.

But a remedy has been provided, and we are ourselves to blame if we do not avail ourselves of it to the fullest extent. Europe erected its Universities, and called them the homes of the Liberal Arts, and determined that between the mental slavery of the school and the physical slavery of busy life every man should have at least three years of freedom.

What Sokrates and his great pupil Plato had done for the youth of Greece,[1] these new academies were to do for the youth of Italy, France, England, Spain, and Germany; and, though with varying success, they have done it. The mediæval and modern Universities have been from century to century the homes of free thought. Here the most eminent men have spent their lives, not in retailing traditional knowledge, as at school, but in extending the frontiers of science in all directions. Here, in close intercourse with their teachers, or under their immediate guidance, generation after generation of boys fresh from school have grown up into men during the three years of their academic life. Here, for the first time, each man has been encouraged to dare to be himself, to follow his own tastes, to depend on his own judgment, to try the wings of his mind, and, lo, like young eagles thrown out of their nest, they could fly. Here the old knowledge accumulated at school was tested, and new knowledge acquired straight from the fountain-head. Here knowledge ceased to be a mere burden, and became a power invigorating the whole mind, like snow which during winter lies cold and heavy on the meadows, but when it is touched by the sun of spring melts away, and fertilizes the ground for a rich harvest.

That was the original purpose of the Universities; and the more they continue to fulfil that purpose, the more will they secure to us that real freedom from tradition, from custom, from mere opinion and superstition, which can be gained by independent study only; the more will they foster that "human

[1] Zeller, *Ueber den wissenschaftlichen Unterricht bei den Griechen*, 1878, p. 9.

development in its richest diversity" which Mill, like Humboldt, considered as the highest object of all society.

Such academic teaching need not be confined to the old Universities. There is many a great University that sprang from smaller beginnings than your Midland Institute. Nor is it necessary, in order to secure the real benefits of academic teaching, to have all the paraphernalia of a University, its colleges and fellowships, its caps and gowns. What is really wanted is the presence of men who, having done good work in their life, are willing to teach others how to work for themselves, how to think for themselves, how to judge for themselves. That is the true academic stage in every man's life, when he learns to work, not to please others, be they schoolmasters or examiners, but to please himself, when he works from sheer love of work, and for the highest of all purposes, the quest of truth. Those only who have passed through that stage know the real blessings of work. To the world at large they may seem mere drudges — but the world does not know the triumphant joy with which the true mountaineer, high above clouds and mountain walls that once seemed unsurpassable, drinks in the fresh air of the High Alps, and away from the fumes, the dust, and the noises of the city, revels alone, in freedom of thought, in freedom of feeling, and in the freedom of the highest faith.

II.

ON THE

PHILOSOPHY OF MYTHOLOGY.

A LECTURE DELIVERED AT THE ROYAL INSTITUTION IN 1871.

WHAT can be in our days the interest of mythology? What is it to us that Kronos was the son of Uranos and Gaia, and that he swallowed his children, Hestia, Demeter, Hera, Pluton, and Poseidon, as soon as they were born? What have we to do with the stories of Rhea, the wife of Kronos, who, in order to save her youngest son from being swallowed by his father, gave her husband a stone to swallow instead? And why should we be asked to admire the exploits of this youngest son, who, when he had grown up, made his father drink a draught, and thus helped to deliver the stone and his five brothers and sisters from their paternal prison? What shall we think if we read in the most admired of classic poets that these escaped prisoners became afterwards the great gods of Greece, gods believed in by Homer, worshipped by Sokrates, immortalized by Pheidias? Why should we listen to such horrors as that Tantalos killed his own son, boiled him, and placed him before the gods to eat? or that the gods collected his limbs, threw them into a cauldron, and thus restored Pelops to life, *minus*, however, his shoulder, which Demeter had eaten in a fit of absence, and which had therefore to be replaced by a shoulder made of ivory?

Can we imagine anything more silly, more savage, more senseless, anything more unworthy to engage our thoughts, even for a single moment? We may pity our children that, in order to know how to construe and understand the master-works of Homer and Virgil, they have to fill their memory with such idle tales; but we might justly suppose that men who have serious work to do in this world would banish such subjects forever from their thoughts.

And yet, how strange, from the very childhood of philosophy, from the first faintly-whispered Why? to our own time of matured thought and fearless inquiry, mythology has been the ever-recurrent subject of anxious wonder and careful study. The ancient philosophers, who could pass by the petrified shells on mountain-tops and the fossil trees buried in their quarries without ever asking the question how they came to be there, or what they signified, were ever ready with doubts and surmises when they came to listen to ancient stories of their gods and heroes. And, more curious still, even modern philosophers cannot resist the attraction of these ancient problems. That stream of philosophic thought which, springing from Descartes (1596–1650), rolled on through the seventeenth and eighteenth centuries in two beds — the *idealistic*, marked by the names of Malebranche (1638–1715), Spinoza (1632–1677), and Leibniz (1646–1716); and the *sensualistic*, marked by the names of Locke (1632–1704), David Hume (1711–1776), and Condillac (1715–1780), till the two arms united again in Kant (1724–1804), and the full stream was carried on by Schelling (1775–1854), and

Hegel (1770–1831), — this stream of modern philosophic thought has ended where ancient philosophy began — in a Philosophy of Mythology, which, as you know, forms the most important part of Schelling's final system, of what he called himself his *Positive Philosophy*, given to the world after the death of that great thinker and poet, in the year 1854.

I do not mean to say that Schelling and Aristotle looked upon mythology in the same light, or that they found in it exactly the same problems; yet there is this common feature in all who have thought or written on mythology, that they look upon it as something which, whatever it may mean, does certainly not mean what it seems to mean; as something that requires an explanation, whether it be a system of religion, or a phase in the development of the human mind, or an inevitable catastrophe in the life of language.

According to some, mythology is history changed into fable; according to others, fable changed into history. Some discover in it the precepts of moral philosophy enunciated in the poetical language of antiquity; others see in it a picture of the great forms and forces of nature, particularly the sun, the moon, and the stars, the changes of day and night, the succession of the seasons, the return of the years — all this reflected by the vivid imagination of ancient poets and sages.

Epicharmos, for instance, the pupil of Pythagoras, declared that the gods of Greece were not what, from the poems of Homer, we might suppose them to be — personal beings, endowed with superhuman powers, but liable to many of the passions and frailties of human nature. He maintained that these gods were really the Wind, the Water, the Earth, the Sun, the Fire, and the Stars. Not long after his time, another philosopher, Empedokles, holding that the whole of nature consisted in the mixture and separation of the four elements, declared that Zeus was the element of Fire, Here the element of Air, Aidoneus or Pluton the element of Earth, and Nestis the element of Water. In fact, whatever the free thinkers of Greece discovered successively as the first principles of Being and Thought, whether the air of Anaximenes, or the fire of Herakleitos, or the Nous or Mind of Anaxagoras, was readily identified with Zeus and the other divine persons of Olympian mythology. Metrodoros, the contemporary of Anaxagoras, went even farther. While Anaxagoras would have been satisfied with looking upon Zeus as but another name of his Nous, the highest intellect, the mover, the disposer, the governor of all things, Metrodoros resolved not only the persons of Zeus, Here, and Athene, but likewise those of human kings and heroes — such as Agamemnon, Achilles, and Hektor — into various combinations and physical agencies, and treated the adventures ascribed to them as natural facts hidden under a thin veil of allegory.

Sokrates, it is well known, looked upon such attempts at explaining all fables allegorically as too arduous and unprofitable: yet he, too, as well as Plato, pointed frequently to what they called the *hypónoia*, the under-current, or, if I may say so, the under-meaning of ancient mythology.

Aristotle speaks more explicitly: —

"It has been handed down," he says, "by early and very ancient people, and left to those who came after, in the form of myths, that these (the first principles of the world) are the gods, and that the divine embraces the whole of nature. The rest has been added mythically, in order to persuade the many, and in order to be used in support of laws and other interests. Thus they say that the gods have a human form, and that they are like to some of the other living beings, and other things consequent on this, and similar to what has been said. If one separated out of these fables, and took only that first point, namely, that they believed the first essences to be gods, one would think that it had been divinely said, and that while every art and every philosophy was probably invented ever so many times and lost again, these opinions had, like fragments of them, been preserved until now. So far only is the opinion of our fathers, and that received from our first ancestors, clear to us."

I have quoted the opinions of these Greek philosophers, to which many more might have been added, partly in order to show how many of the most distinguished minds of ancient Greece agreed in demanding an interpretation, whether physical or metaphysical, of Greek mythology, partly in order to satisfy those classical scholars, who, forgetful of their own classics, forgetful of their own Plato and Aristotle, seem to imagine that the idea of seeing in the gods and heroes of Greece anything beyond what they appear to be in the songs of Homer, was a mere fancy and invention of the students of Comparative Mythology.

There were, no doubt, Greeks, and eminent Greeks too, who took the legends of their gods and heroes in their literal sense. But what do these say of Homer and Hesiod? Xenophanes, the contemporary of Pythagoras, holds Homer and Hesiod responsible for the popular superstitions of Greece. In this he agrees with Herodotus, when he declares that these two poets made the theogony for the Greeks, and gave to the gods their names, and assigned to them their honors and their arts, and described their appearances. But he then continues in a very different strain from the pious historian.[1] "Homer," he says,[2] "and Hesiod ascribed to the gods whatever is disgraceful and scandalous among men, yea, they declared that the gods had committed nearly all unlawful acts, such as theft, adultery, and fraud." "Men seem to have created their gods, and to have given to them their own mind, voice, and figure. The Ethiopians made their gods black and flat-nosed; the Thracians red-haired and blue-eyed." This was spoken about 500 B. C. Herakleitos, about 460 B. C., one of the boldest thinkers of ancient Greece, declared that Homer deserved to be ejected from public assemblies and flogged; and a story is told that Pythagoras (about 540 B. C.) saw the soul of Homer in Hades, hanging

[1] Her. ii. 53, οὗτοι δέ εἰσι οἱ ποιήσαντες θεογονίην Ἕλλησι, καὶ τοῖσι θεοῖσι τὰς ἐπωνυμίας δόντες καὶ τιμάς τε καὶ τέχνας διελόντες, καὶ εἴδεα αὐτῶν σημήναντες.

[2] Πάντα θεοῖς ἀνέθηκαν Ὅμηρός θ' Ἡσίοδός τε
ὅσσα παρ' ἀνθρώποισι ὀνείδεα καὶ ψόγος ἐστίν.
ὡς πλεῖστ' ἐφθέγξαντο θεῶν ἀθεμίστια ἔργα,
κλέπτειν μοιχεύειν τε καὶ ἀλλήλους ἀπατεύειν.

Sext. Emp. *adv. Math.* 1289 ; ix. 193.

δοκέουσι θεοὺς γεγενῆσθαι
τὴν σφετέρην τ' αἴσθησιν ἔχειν φωνήν τε δέμας τε.—
'Αλλ' εἴτοι χεῖράς γ' εἶχον βόες ἠὲ λέοντες
ἢ γράψαι χείρεσσι καὶ ἔργα τελεῖν ἅπερ ἄνδρες,
καί κε θεῶν ἰδέας ἔγραφον καὶ σώματ' ἐποίουν
τοιαῦθ' οἷόν περ καὐτοὶ δέμας εἶχον ὁμοῖον,
ἵπποι μέν θ' ἵπποισι, βόες δέ τε βουσὶν ὁμοῖα.

Clem. Alex. *Strom.* v. p. 601, c.

Ὡς φησιν Ξενοφάνης· Αἰθίοπές τε μέλανας σιμούς τε, Θρᾷκές τε πυῤῥοὺς καὶ γλαυκούς. Clem. Alex. *Strom.* vii. p. 711, *B. Historia Philosophiæ*, ed. Ritter et Preller, cap. iii.

on a tree and surrounded by serpents, as a punishment for what he had said of the gods. And what can be stronger than the condemnation passed on Homer by Plato? I shall read an extract from the "Republic," from the excellent translation lately published by Professor Jowett: —

"But what fault do you find with Homer and Hesiod, and the other great story-tellers of mankind?"

"A fault which is most serious," I said: "the fault of telling a lie, and a bad lie."

"But when is this fault committed?"

"Whenever an erroneous representation is made of the nature of gods and heroes — like the drawing of a limner which has not the shadow of a likeness to the truth."

"'Yes,' he said, 'that sort of thing is certainly very blamable; but what are the stories which you mean?'

"'First of all,' I said, 'there was that greatest of all lies in high places, which the poet told about Uranos, and which was an immoral lie too — I mean what Hesiod says that Uranos did, and what Kronos did to him. The fact is that the doings of Kronos, and the sufferings which his son inflicted upon him, even if they were true, ought not to be lightly told to young and simple persons; if possible, they had better be buried in silence. But if there is an absolute necessity for their mention, a very few might hear them in a mystery, and then let them sacrifice not a common (Eleusinian) pig, but some huge and unprocurable victim; this would have the effect of very greatly reducing the number of the hearers.'

"'Why, yes,' said he, 'these stories are certainly objectionable.'

"'Yes, Adeimantos, they are stories not to be narrated in our state; the young man should not be told that in committing the worst of crimes he is far from doing anything outrageous, and that he may chastise his father when he does wrong in any manner that he likes, and in this will only be following the example of the first and greatest of the gods.'

"'I quite agree with you,' he said; 'in my opinion those stories are *not fit to be repeated*.'

"'Neither, if we mean our future guardians to regard the habit of quarrelling as dishonorable, should anything be said of the wars in heaven, and of the plots and fightings of the gods against one another, which are quite untrue. Far be it from us to tell them of the battles of the giants, and embroider them on garments; or of all the innumerable other quarrels of gods and heroes with their friends and relations. If they would only believe us, we would tell them that quarrelling is unholy, and that never up to this time has there been any quarrel between citizens; this is what old men and old women should begin by telling children, and the same when they grow up. And these are the sort of fictions which the poets should be required to compose. But the narrative of Hephaestos binding Here his mother, or how, on another occasion, Zeus sent him flying for taking her part when she was being beaten — such tales must not be admitted in our state, whether they are supposed to have an allegorical meaning or not. For the young man cannot judge what is allegorical and what is literal, and anything that he receives into his mind at that age is apt to become indelible and unalterable; and therefore the tales which they first hear should be models of virtuous thoughts.'"

To those who look upon mythology as an ancient form of religion, such freedom of language as is here used by Xenophanes and Plato, must seem startling. If the Iliad were really the Bible of the Greeks, as it has not unfrequently been called, such violent invectives would have been impossible. For let us bear in mind that Xenophanes, though he boldly denied the existence of all the mythological deities, and declared his belief in One God, "neither in form nor in thought like unto mortals,"[1] was not therefore considered a heretic. He never suffered for uttering his honest convictions: on the contrary, as far as we know, he was honored by the people among whom he lived and taught. Nor was Plato ever punished on account of his unbelief, and though he, as well as his master, Sokrates, became obnoxious to the dominant party at Athens, this was due to political far more than to theological motives. At all events, Plato, the pupil, the friend, the apologist of Sokrates, was allowed to teach at Athens to the end of his life, and few men commanded greater respect in the best ranks of Greek society.

But, although mythology was not religion in our sense of the word, and although the Iliad certainly never enjoyed among Greeks the authority either of the Bible, or even of the Veda among the Brahmans, or the Zend Avesta among the Parsis, yet I would not deny altogether that in a certain sense the mythology of the Greeks belonged to their religion. We must only be on our guard, here as everywhere else, against the misleading influence of words. The word

[1] Εἷς θεὸς ἕν τε θεοῖσι καὶ ἀνθρώποισι μέγιστος,
οὔ τι δέμας θνητοῖσι ὁμοίιος οὐδὲ νόημα.
Clem. Alex. *Strom.* v. p. 601, c.

Religion has, like most words, had its history ; it has grown and changed with each century, and it cannot, therefore, have meant with the Greeks and Brahmans what it means with us. Religions have sometimes been divided into *national* or *traditional*, as distinguished from *individual* or *statutable* religion. The former are, like languages, home-grown, autochthonic, without an historical beginning, generally without any recognized founder, or even an authorized code; the latter have been founded by historical persons, generally in antagonism to traditional systems, and they always rest on the authority of a written code. I do not consider this division as very useful [1] for a scientific study of religion, because in many cases it is extremely difficult, and sometimes impossible, to draw a sharp line of demarcation, and to determine whether a given religion should be considered as the work of one man, or as the combined work of those who came before him, who lived with him, nay, even of those who came after him. For our present purpose, however, for showing at once the salient difference between what the Greeks and what we ourselves should mean by Religion, this division is very serviceable. The Greek religion was clearly a national and traditional religion, and, as such, it shared both the advantages and disadvantages of this form of religious belief; the Christian religion is an historical and, to a great extent, an individual religion, and it possesses the advantage of an authorized code and of a settled system of faith. Let it not be supposed, however, that between traditional and individual religions the advantages are all on one, the disadvantages on the other side. As long as the immemorial religions of

[1] See *Introduction to the Science of Religion*, p. 139.

the different branches of the human race remained in their natural state, and were not pressed into the service of political parties or an ambitious priesthood, they allowed great freedom of thought and a healthy growth of real piety, and they were seldom disgraced by an intolerant or persecuting spirit. They were generally either honestly believed, or, as we have just seen, honestly attacked, and a high tone of intellectual morality was preserved, untainted by hypocrisy, equivocation, or unreasoning dogmatism. The marvellous development of philosophy in Greece, particularly in ancient Greece, was chiefly due, I believe, to the absence of an established religion and an influential priesthood; and it is impossible to overrate the blessing which the fresh, pure, invigorating, and elevating air of that ancient Greek philosophy has conferred on all ages, not excepting our own. I shudder at the thought of what the world would have been without Plato and Aristotle, and I tremble at the idea that the youth of the future should ever be deprived of the teaching and the example of these true prophets of the absolute freedom of thought. Unfortunately, we know but little of the earliest fathers of Greek philosophy; we have but fragments, and those not always trustworthy, nor easily intelligible, of what they taught on the highest questions that can stir the heart of man. We have been accustomed to call the oracular sayings of men like Thales, Pythagoros, Xenophanes, or Herakleitos, philosophy, but there was in them as much of religion as in the songs of Homer and Hesiod. Homer and Hesiod were great powers, but their poems were not the only feeders of the religious life of Greece. The stream of ancient wisdom and philosophy flowed parallel with the stream of legend and poetry; and both were meant to support the religious cravings of the soul. We have only to attend without prejudice to the utterances of these ancient prophets, such as Xenophanes and Herakleitos, in order to convince ourselves that these men spoke with authority to the people,[1] that they considered themselves the equals of Homer and Hesiod, nay, their betters, and in no way fettered by the popular legends about gods and goddesses. While modern religions assume in general a hostile attitude towards philosophy, ancient religions have either included philosophy as an integral part, or they have at least tolerated its growth in the very precincts of their temples.

After we have thus seen what limitations we must place on the meaning of the word Religion, if we call mythology the religion of the ancient world, we may now advance another step.

We have glanced at the principal interpretations which have been proposed by the ancients themselves of the original purpose and meaning of mythology. But there is one question which none, either of the ancient or of the modern interpreters of mythology, has answered, or even asked, and on which, nevertheless, the whole problem of mythology seems to turn. If mythology is history changed into fable, why was it so changed? If it is fable represented as history, why were such fables invented? If it contains precepts of moral philosophy, whence their immoral disguise? If it is a picture of the great forms and forces of nature, the same question still returns, why were

[1] Empedokles, *Carmina*, v. 411 (*Fragm. Philos. Græc.* vol. i. p. 12): —

ὦ φίλοι, οἶδα μὲν οὖν ὅτ' ἀληθείη παρὰ μύθοις
οὓς ἐγὼ ἐξερέω · μάλα δ' ἀργαλέη γὲ τέτυκται
ἀνδράσι καὶ δύσζηλος ἐπὶ φρένα πίστιος ὁρμή.

these forms and forces represented as heroes and heroines, as nymphs and shepherds, as gods and goddesses? It is easy enough to call the sun a god, or the dawn a goddess, after these predicates have once been framed. But how were these predicates framed? How did people come to know of gods and goddesses, heroes and nymphs, and what meaning did they originally connect with these terms? In fact, the real question which a philosophy of mythology has to answer is this — Is the whole of mythology an invention, the fanciful poetry of a Homer or Hesiod, or is it a growth? Or, to speak more definitely, Was mythology a mere accident, or was it inevitable? Was it only a false step, or was it a step that could not have been left out in the historical progress of the human mind?

The study of the history of language, which is only a part of the study of the history of thought, has enabled us to give a decisive answer to this question. Mythology is inevitable, it is natural, it is an inherent necessity of language, if we recognize in language the outward form and manifestation of thought: it is, in fact, the dark shadow which language throws on thought, and which can never disappear till language becomes altogether commensurate with thought, which it never will. Mythology, no doubt, breaks out more fiercely during the early periods of the history of human thought, but it never disappears altogether. Depend upon it, there is mythology now as there was in the time of Homer, only we do not perceive it, because we ourselves live in the very shadow of it, and because we all shrink from the full meridian light of truth. We are ready enough to see that if the ancients called their kings and heroes Διογενεῖς, sprung of Zeus, that expression, intended originally to convey the highest praise which man can bestow on man, was apt to lapse into mythology. We easily perceive how such a conception, compatible in its origin with the highest reverence for the gods, led almost inevitably to the growth of fables, which transferred to divine beings the incidents of human paternity and sonship. But we are not so ready to see that it is our fate, too, to move in allegories which illustrate things intellectual by visions exhibited to the fancy. In our religion, too, the conceptions of paternity and sonship have not always been free from all that is human, nor are we always aware that nearly every note that belongs to human paternity and sonship must be taken out of these terms, before they can be pronounced safe against mythological infection. Papal decisions on immaculate conception are of no avail against that mythology. The mind must become immaculate and rise superior to itself; or it must close its eyes and shut its lips in the presence of the Divine.

If then we want to understand mythology, in the ordinary and restricted sense of the word, we must discover the larger circle of mental phenomena to which it belongs. Greek mythology, is but a small segment of mythology; the religious mythologies of all the races of mankind are again but a small segment of mythology. Mythology, in the highest sense, is the power exercised by language on thought in every possible sphere of mental activity; and I do not hesitate to call the whole history of philosophy, from Thales down to Hegel, an uninterrupted battle against mythology, a constant protest of thought against language. This will require some explanation.

Ever since the time of Wilhelm von Humboldt, all who have seriously grappled with the highest problems of the Science of Language have come to the conviction that thought and language are inseparable, that language is as impossible without thought as thought is without language; that they stand to each other somewhat like soul and body, like power and function, like substance and form. The objections which have been raised against this view arise generally from a mere misunderstanding. If we speak of language as the outward realization of thought, we do not mean language as deposited in a dictionary, or sketched in a grammar; we mean language as an act, language as being spoken, language as living and dying with every word that is uttered. We might perhaps call this speech, as distinguished from language.

Secondly, though if we speak of language, we mean chiefly phonetic articulate language, we do not exclude the less perfect symbols of thought, such as gestures, signs, or pictures. They, too, are language in a certain sense, and they must be included in language before we are justified in saying that discursive thought can be realized in language only. One instance will make this clear. We hold that we cannot think without language. But can we not count without language? We certainly can. We can form the conception of *three* without any spoken word, by simply holding up three fingers. In the same manner, the hand might stand for five, both hands for ten, hands and feet for twenty.[1] This is how people who possessed no organs of speech would speak; this is how the deaf and dumb *do* speak. Three fingers

[1] *Daily Life and Origin of the Tasmanians*, by J. Bonwick, 1870, p. 143.

are as good as three strokes, three strokes are as good as three clicks of the tongue, three clicks of the tongue are as good as the sound *three*, or *trois*, or *drei*, or *shalosh* in Hebrew, or *san* in Chinese. All these are signs, more or less perfect, but being signs, they fall under the category of language; and all we maintain is, that without some kind of sign, discursive thought is impossible, and that in that sense, language, or λόγος, is the only possible realization of human thought.

Another very common misunderstanding is this: people imagine that, if it be impossible to think, except in language, language and thought must be one and the same thing. But a true philosophy of language leads to the very opposite result. Every philosopher would say that matter cannot exist without form, nor form without matter, but no philosopher would say that therefore it is impossible to distinguish between form and matter. In the same way, though we maintain that thought cannot exist without language nor language without thought, we do distinguish between thought and language, between the inward and the outward λόγος, between the substance and the form. Nay, we go a step beyond. We admit that language necessarily reacts on thought, and we see in this reaction, in this refraction of the rays of language, the real solution of the old riddle of mythology.

You will now see why these somewhat abstruse disquisitions were necessary for our immediate purpose, and I can promise those who have hitherto followed me on this rather barren and rugged track, that they will now be able to rest, and command, from the point of view which we have reached, the whole panorama of the mythology of the human mind.

We saw just now that the names of numbers may most easily be replaced by signs. Numbers are simple analytical conceptions, and for that very reason they are not liable to mythology: name and conception being here commensurate, no misunderstanding is possible. But as soon as we leave this department of thought, mythology begins. I shall try by at least one example to show how mythology not only pervades the sphere of religion or religious tradition, but infects more or less the whole realm of thought.

When man wished for the first time to grasp and express a distinction between the body and something else within him distinct from the body, an easy name that suggested itself was *breath*. The breath seemed something immaterial and almost invisible, and it was connected with the life that pervaded the body, for as soon as the breath ceased, the life of the body became extinct. Hence the Greek name ψυχή,[1]

1 The word ψυχή is clearly connected in Greek with ψύχω, which meant originally blowing, and was used either in the sense of cooling by blowing, or breathing by blowing. In the former acceptation it produced ψύχος, coldness; ψυχρός, cold; ψυχάω, I cool; in the latter ψυχή, breath, then life, then soul. So far the purely Greek growth of words derived from ψύχω is clear. But ψύχω itself is difficult. It seems to point to a root *spu*, meaning to blow out, to spit; Lat. *spuo*, and *spuma*, foam; Goth. *speivan;* Gr. πτύω, supposed to stand for σπιύω. Hesychius mentions ψύττει = πτύει, ψυττόν = πτύελον. (Pott, *Etym. Forsch.* No. 355.) Curtius connects this root with Gr. φυ, in φῦσα, blowing, bellows, φυσάω, to blow, φυσιάω, to snort, ποι-φύσσω, to blow, and with Lat. *spirare* (i. e. spoisare). See E. B. Tylor, "The Religion of Savages," *Fortnightly Review*, 1866, p. 73.

Stahl, who rejected the division of life and mind adopted by Bacon, and returned to the Aristotelian doctrine, falls back on Plato's etymology of ψυχή as φυσέχη, from φύσιν ἔχειν or ὀχεῖν, *Crat.* 400 B. In a passage of his *Theoria Medica Vera* (Halæ, 1708), pointed out to me by Dr. Rolleston, Stahl says: "Invenio in lexico græco antiquiore post alios, et Budæum imprimis, iterum iterumque reviso, nomenclaturam nimis quam fugitive allegatam; φυσέχη, poetice, pro ψυχή. Incidit animo suspicari, an non verum primum nomen animæ antiquissimis Græcis fuerit hoc φυσέχη, quasi ἔχων τὸ φύειν, e cuius vocis pronunciatione deflectente, uti vere familiariter solet vocalium, inprimis sub accentibus, fugitiva enunciatione, sensim which originally meant breath, was chosen to express at first the principle of life, as distinguished from the decaying body, afterwards the incorporeal, the immaterial, the undecaying, the immortal part of man — his soul, his mind, his Self. All this was very natural. When a person dies, we too say that he has given up the ghost, and ghost, too, meant originally spirit, and spirit meant breath.

A very instructive analogous case is quoted by Mr. E. B. Tylor from a compendium of the theology of the Indians of Nicaragua, the record of question and answer in an inquest held by Father Francisco de Bobadilla in the early days of the Spanish conquest. Asked, among other things, concerning death, the Indians said: "Those who die in their houses go underground, but those who are killed in war go to serve the gods (*teotes*). When men die, there comes forth from their mouth something which resembles a person, and is called *julio* (Aztec *yuli*, 'to live'). This being is like a person, but does not die, and the corpse remains here." The Spanish ecclesiastics inquired whether those who go on high keep the same body, features, and limbs as here below; to which the Indians answered, "No, there is only the heart." "But," said the Spaniards, "as the hearts are torn out" (they meant in the case of warriors who fell into the hands of the enemy), "what happens then?" Hereupon the Indians replied: "It is not precisely the heart, but that which is in them, and makes them

natum sit φυσ-χή φσυχή, denique ad faciliorem pronunciationem in locum φσυχή, ψυχή. Quam suspicionem fovere mihi videtur illud, quod vocabuli ψυχῆs, pro anima, nulla idonea analogia in lingua græca occurrat; nam quæ a ψῦχω ducitur, cum verus huius et directus significatus notorie sit refrigero, indirectus autem magis, spiro, nihil certe hæc ad animam puto." (P. 44.)

live, and which quits the body when they die;" and again they said, "It is not their heart which goes up on high, but that which makes them live, that is, the breath coming out from their mouth, which is called *julio*." "Then," asked the Spaniards, "does this heart, *julio*, or soul, die with the body?" "When the deceased has lived well," replied the Indians, "the *julio* goes up on high with our gods; but when he has lived ill, the *julio* perishes with the body, and there is an end of it."

The Greeks expressed the same idea by saying that the *ψυχή* had left the body,[1] had fled through the mouth, or even through a bleeding wound,[2] and had gone into Hades, which meant literally no more than the place of the Invisible (Ἀίδης). That the breath had become invisible was matter of fact; that it had gone to the house of Hades, was mythology springing spontaneously from the fertile soil of language.

The primitive mythology was by no means necessarily religious. In the very case which we have chosen, philosophical mythology sprang up by the side of religious mythology. The religious mythology consisted in speaking of the spirits of the departed as ghosts, as mere breath and air, as fluttering about the gates of Hades, or ferried across the Styx in the boat of Charon.[3]

1 ἀνδρὸςδὲ ψυχὴ πάλιν ἐλθεῖν οὔτεν λεϊστὴ,
οὔθ' ἑλετὴ, ἐπεὶ ἄρ κεν ἀμείψεται ἕρκος ὀδόντων.
Il. ix. 408.

2 διὰ δ' ἔντερα χαλκὸς ἄφυσσεν
δηώσας· ψυχὴ δὲ κατ' οὐταμένην ὠτειλὴν
ἔσσυτ' ἐπειγομένη·
Il. xiv. 517.

3 "Ter frustra compressa manu effugit imago,
Par levibus ventis volucrique simillima somno."
Virg. *Æn.* ii. 792.

The philosophical mythology, however, that sprang from this name was much more important. We saw that *Psyche*, meaning originally the breathing of the body, was gradually used in the sense of vital breath, and as something independent of the body; and that at last, when it had assumed the meaning of the immortal part of man, it retained that character of something independent of the body, thus giving rise to the conception of a soul, not only as a being without a body, but in its very nature opposed to body. As soon as that opposition had been established in language and thought, philosophy began its work in order to explain how two such heterogeneous powers could act on each other — how the soul could influence the body, and how the body could determine the soul. Spiritualistic and materialistic systems of philosophy arose, and all this in order to remove a self-created difficulty, in order to join together again what language had severed, the living body and the living soul. The question whether there is a soul or spirit, whether there is in man something different from the mere body, is not at all affected by this mythological phraseology. We certainly can distinguish between body and soul, but as long as we keep within the limits of human knowledge, we have no right to speak of the living soul as a breath, or of spirits and ghosts as fluttering about like birds or fairies. The poet of the nineteenth century says: —

> "The spirit does but mean the breath,
> I know no more."

And the same thought was expressed by Cicero two thousand years ago: "Whether the soul is air or fire, I do not know." As men, we only know of embodied spirits, however ethereal their bodies may be conceived to be, but of spirits, separate from body, without form or frame, we know as little as we know of thought without language, or of the Dawn as a goddess, or of the Night as the mother of the Day.

Though breath, or spirit, or ghost are the most common names that were assigned through the metaphorical nature of language to the vital, and afterwards to the intellectual, principle in man, they were by no means the only possible names. We speak, for instance, of the *shades* of the departed, which meant originally their shadows. Those who first introduced this expression — and we find it in the most distant parts of the world [1] — evidently took the shadow as the nearest approach to what they wished to express; something that should be incorporeal, yet closely connected with the body. The Greek εἴδωλον, too, is not much more than the shadow, while the Latin *manes* meant probably in the beginning no more than the Little Ones, the Small Folk.[2] But the curious part, as showing again the influence of language on thought, an influence more powerful even than the evidence of the senses, is this, that people who speak of the life or soul as the shadow of the body, have brought themselves to believe that a dead body casts no shadow, because the shadow has departed from it; that it becomes, in fact, a kind of Peter Schlemihl.[3]

Let us now return to mythology in the narrower sense of the word. One of the earliest objects that

1 See E. B. Tylor, *Fortnightly Review*, 1866, p. 74.

2 *Im-manis*, originally "not small," came to mean enormous or monstrous. See Preller, *Römische Mythologie*, p. 72 *seq.*

3 *Unkulunkulu; or the Tradition of Creation as existing among the Amazulu and other Tribes of South Africa*, by the Rev. J. Callaway, M. D. Natal, 1868. Part I. p. 91.

would strike and stir the mind of man, and for which a sign or a name would soon be wanted, is surely the Sun. It is very hard for us to realize the feelings with which the first dwellers on the earth looked upon the sun, or to understand fully what they meant by a morning prayer, or a morning sacrifice. Perhaps there are few people here present who have watched a sunrise more than once or twice in their lives; few people who have ever known the true meaning of a morning prayer, or a morning sacrifice. But think of man at the very dawn of time: forget for a moment, if you can, after having read the fascinating pages of Mr. Darwin, forget what man is supposed to have been before he was man; forget it, because it does not concern us here whether his bodily form and frame were developed once for all in the mind of a Creator, or gradually in the creation itself, which from the first monad or protoplasm to the last of the primates, or man, is not, I suppose, to be looked on as altogether causeless, meaningless, purposeless; think of him only as man (and man means the thinker), with his mind yet lying fallow, though full of germs — germs of which I hold as strongly as ever no trace has ever, no trace will ever, be discovered anywhere but in man; think of the Sun awakening the eyes of man from sleep, and his mind from slumber! Was not the Sunrise to him the first wonder, the first beginning of all reflection, all thought, all philosophy? was it not to him the first revelation, the first beginning of all trust, of all religion? To us that wonder of wonders has ceased to exist, and few men now would even venture to speak of the sun as Sir John Herschel has spoken, calling him "the Almoner of the Almighty, the delegated dispenser to us of light and warmth, as well as the centre of attraction, and as such, the immediate source of all our comforts, and, indeed, of the very possibility of our existence on earth." [1]

Man is a creature of habit, and wherever we can watch him, we find that before a few generations have passed he has lost the power of admiring what is regular, and that he can see signs and wonders only in what is irregular. Few nations only have preserved in their ancient poetry some remnants of the natural awe with which the earliest dwellers on the earth saw that brilliant being slowly rising from out the darkness of the night, raising itself by its own might higher and higher, till it stood triumphant on the arch of heaven, and then descended and sank down in its fiery glory into the dark abyss of the heaving and hissing sea. In the hymns of the Veda the poet still wonders whether the sun will rise again; he asks how he can climb the vault of heaven? why he does not fall back? why there is no dust on his path? And when the rays of the morning rouse him from sleep and call him back to new life; when he sees the sun, as he says, stretching out his golden arms to bless the world and rescue it from the terrors of darkness, he exclaims, "Arise, our life, our spirit has come back! the darkness is gone, the light approaches!"

For so prominent an object in the primeval picture-gallery of the human mind, a sign or a name must have been wanted at a very early period. But how was this to be achieved? As a mere sign, a circle would have been sufficient, such as we find in

[1] See J. Samuelson, *Views of the Deity, Traditional and Scientific*, p. 144. Williams & Norgate, 1871.

the hieroglyphics of Egypt, in the graphic system of China, or even in our own astronomical tables. If such a sign was fixed upon, we have a beginning of language in the widest sense of the word, for we have brought the Sun under the general concept of roundness, and we have found a sign for this concept which is made up of a large number of single sensuous impressions. With such definite signs mythology has little chance; yet the mere fact that the sun was represented as a circle would favor the idea that the sun was round; or, as ancient people, who had no adjective as yet for round or *rotundus*,[1] would say, that the sun was a wheel, a *rota*. If, on the contrary, the round sign reminded the people of an eye, then the sign of the sun would soon become the eye of heaven, and germs of mythology would spring up even from the barren soil of such hieroglyphic language.

But now, suppose that a real name was wanted for the sun, how could that be achieved?

We know that all words are derived from roots, that these roots express general concepts, and that, with few exceptions, every name is founded on a general concept under which the object that has to be named can be ranged. How these roots came to be, is a question into which we need not enter at

1 "It has already been implied that the Aborigines of Tasmania had acquired very limited powers of abstraction or generalization. They possessed no words representing abstract ideas; for each variety of gum-tree and wattle-tree, etc., etc., they had a name, but they had no equivalent for the expression, 'a tree;' neither could they express abstract qualities, such as hard, soft, warm, cold, long, short, round, etc.; for 'hard' they would say 'like a stone;' for 'tall' they would say 'long legs,' etc.; for 'round' they said 'like a ball,' 'like the moon,' and so on, usually suiting the action to the word, and confirming by some sign the meaning to be understood." Milligan, *Vocabulary of the Dialects of some of the Aboriginal Tribes of Tasmania*, p. 34. Hobart Town, 1866.

present. Their origin and growth form a problem of psychology rather than of philology, and each science must keep within its proper bounds. If a name was wanted for snow, the early framers of language singled out one of the general predicates of snow, its whiteness, its coldness, or its liquidity, and called the snow the white, the cold, or the liquid, by means of roots conveying the general idea of whiteness, coldness, or liquidity. Not only Nix, nivis, but Niobe[1] too, was a name of the snow, and meant the melting; the death of her beautiful children by the arrows of Apollon and Artemis represents the destruction of winter by the rays of the sun. If the sun itself was to be named, it might be called the brilliant, the awakener, the runner, the ruler, the father, the giver of warmth, of fertility, of life, the scorcher, the destroyer, the messenger of death, and many other names; but there was no possibility of naming it,

[1] If Signor Ascoli blames me for deriving *Niobe* with other names for snow from the root *snu*, instead of from the root *snigh*, this can only be due to an oversight. I am responsible for the derivation of Niobe, and for the admission of a secondary root *snyu* or *nyu*, and so far I may be either right or wrong. But Signor Ascoli ought to have known that the derivation of Gothic *snáiv-s*, Old High-German *snêo*, or *snê*, gen. *snêwe-s*, Lithuanian *snéga-s*, Slav. *snjeg*, Hib. *sneachd*, from the root *snu*, rests on the authority of Bopp (*Glossarium*, 1847, s. v. snu; see also Grimm, *Deutsche Grammatik*, ii. p. 700). He ought likewise to have known that in 1852 Professor Schweizer-Siedler, in his review of Bötticher's *Arica* (Kuhn's *Zeitschrift*, i. p. 479), had pointed out that *snigh* may be considered as a secondary root by the side of *snu* and *snâ* (cf. σμάω, σμήχω; ψάω, ψήχω; νάω, νήχω). The real relation of *snu* to *snigh* had been explained as early as 1842 by Benfey, *Wurzellexicon*, ii. p. 54; and Signor Ascoli was no doubt aware of what Professor Curtius had written on the relation of *snigh* to *snu* (*Grūndzüge der Griechischen Etymologie*, p. 297). Signor Ascoli has certainly shown with greater minuteness than his predecessors that not only Zend *snizh* and Lithuanian *snêga-s*, but likewise Gothic *snaiv-s*, Greek νίφει, Latin nix, nĭv-is, and ninguis, may be derived from *snigh*; but if from *snigh*, a secondary development of the root *snu*, we can arrive at νίφ-α, and at νίβα, the other steps that lead on to Niobe will remain just the same.

except by laying hold of one of its characteristic features, and expressing that feature by means of one of the conceptual or predicative roots.

Let us trace the history of at least one of these names. Before the Aryan nations separated, before there was a Latin, a Greek, or a Sanskrit language, there existed a root *svar* or *sval*, which meant to beam, to glitter, to warm. It exists in Greek, σέλας, splendor; σελήνη, moon; in Anglo-Saxon, as *swélan*, to burn, to sweal; in modern German, *schwül*, oppressively hot. From it we have in Sanskrit the noun *svar*, meaning sometimes the sky, sometimes the sun; and exactly the same word has been preserved in Latin, as *sol;* in Gothic as *sauil;* in Anglo-Saxon, as *sol.* A secondary form of *svar* is the Sanskrit *sûrya* for *svârya*, the sun, which is the same word as the Greek ἥλιος.

All these names were originally mere predicates; they meant bright, brilliant, warm. But as soon as the name *svar* or *sûrya* was formed, it became, through the irresistible influence of language, the name, not only of a living, but of a male being. Every noun in Sanskrit must be either a masculine or a feminine (for the neuter gender was originally confined to the nominative case), and as *sûryas* had been formed as a masculine, language stamped it once for all as the sign of a male being, as much as if it had been the name of a warrior or a king. In other languages where the name for sun is a feminine, and the sun is accordingly conceived as a woman, as a queen, as the bride of the moon, the whole mythology of the love-making of the heavenly bodies is changed.

You may say that all this shows, not so much the influence of language on thought, as of thought on language; and that the sexual character of all words reflects only the peculiarities of a child's mind, which can conceive of nothing except as living, as male or female. If a child hurts itself against a chair, it beats and scolds the chair. The chair is looked upon not as *it*, but as *he;* it is the naughty chair, quite as much as a boy is a naughty boy. There is some truth in this, but it only serves to confirm the right view of the influence of language on thought; for this tendency, though in its origin intentional, and therefore the result of thought, became soon a mere rule of tradition in language, and it then reacted on the mind with irresistible power. As soon, in fact, as *sûryas* or ἥλιος appears as a masculine, we are in the very thick of mythology. We have not yet arrived at Helios as a god — that is a much later stage of thought, which we might describe almost in the words of Plato at the beginning of the seventh book of the "Republic," "And after this, he will reason that the sun is he who gives the seasons and the years, and is the guardian of all that is in the visible world, and in a certain way the cause of all things which he and his fellows have been accustomed to behold." We have not yet advanced so far, but we have reached at least the first germs of a myth. In the Homeric hymn to Helios, Helios is not yet called an immortal, but only ἐπιείκελος ἀθανάτοισι, like unto immortals, yet he is called the child of Euryphaessa, the son of Hyperion, the grandson of Uranos and Gæa.[1]

[1] At the end of the hymn the poet says: —

χαῖρε, ἄναξ, πρόφρων δὲ βίον θυμήρε' ὄπαζε·
ἐκ σέο δ' ἀρξάμενος κλήσω μερόπων γένος ἀνδρῶν
ἡμιθέων, ὧν ἔργα θεοὶ θνητοῖσιν ἔδειξαν.

This would seem to imply that the poet looked upon Helios as a half-god, almost as a hero, who had once lived on earth.

All this is mythology; it is ancient language going beyond its first intention.

Nor is there much difficulty in interpreting this myth. Helios, the sun, is called the son of Hyperīon, sometimes Hyperīon himself. This name Hyperīon is derived from the preposition ὑπέρ, the Latin *super*, which means above. It is derived by means of the suffix -ιων, which originally was not a patronymic, but simply expressed belonging to. So if Helios was called Hyperion, this simply meant he who dwells on high, and corresponds to Latin *Summanus* or *Superior*, or *Excelsior*. If, on the contrary, Helios is called Hyperionides, this, too, which meant originally no more than he who comes from, or belongs to those who dwell on high,[1] led to the myth that he was the descendant of Hyperion; so that in this case, as in the case of Zeus Kronīon, the son really led to the conception of his father. Zeus Kronīon meant originally no more than Zeus the eternal, the god of ages, the ancient of days; but -ίων becoming usual as a patronymic suffix, Kronion was supposed to mean the son of Kronos. Kronos, the father, was created in order to account for the existence of the name Kronion. If Hyperīon is called the son of Euryphaessa, the wide-shining, this requires no commentary; for even at present a poet might say that the sun is born of the wide-shining dawn. You see the spontaneous generation of mythology with every new name that is formed. As not only the sun, but also the moon and the dawn could be called dwellers on high, they, too, took the name of Hyperionis or Hyperionides; and hence Homer called Selene, the Moon, and Eos, the Dawn, sisters of Helios, and

[1] Corssen, *Ueber Steigerungsendungen*, Kuhn's *Zeitschrift*, iii. p. 299.

daughters of Hyperion and Euryphaessa, the Dawn doing service twice, both as mother, Euryphaessa, and as daughter, Eos. Nay, according to Homer, Euryphaessa, the Dawn, is not only the wife, but also the sister of Helios. All this is perfectly intelligible, if we watch the growth of language and mythology; but it leads, of course, to the most tragic catastrophes as soon as it is all taken in a literal sense.

Helios is called ἀκάμας, the never-tiring; πανδερκής, the all-seeing; φαέθων, the shining; and also φοῖβος, the brilliant. This last epithet φοῖβος has grown into an independent deity Phœbus, and it is particularly known as a name of Apollon, Phoibos Apollon; thus showing what is also known from other sources, that in Apollo, too, we have one of the many mythic disguises of the sun.

So far all is clear, because all the names which we have to deal with are intelligible, or, at all events, yield to the softest etymological pressure. But now if we hear the story of Phoibos Apollon falling in love with Daphne, and Daphne praying to her mother, the Earth, to save her from Phoibos; and if we read how either the earth received her in her lap, and then a laurel tree sprang up where she had disappeared, or how she herself was changed into a laurel tree, what shall we think of this? It is a mere story, it might be said, and why should there be any meaning in it? My answer is, because people do not tell such stories of their gods and heroes, unless there is some sense in them. Besides, if Phoibos means the sun, why should not Daphne have a meaning too? Before, therefore, we can decide whether the story of Phoibos and Daphne is a mere invention, we must try to find out what can have been the meaning of the word Daphne.

In Greek it means a laurel,[1] and this would explain the purely Greek legend that Daphne was changed into a laurel tree. But who was Daphne? In order to answer this question, we must have recourse to etymology, or, in other words, we must examine the history of the word. Etymology, as you know, is no longer what it used to be; and though there may still be a classical scholar here and there who crosses himself at the idea of a Greek word being explained by a reference to Sanskrit, we naturally look to Sanskrit as the master-key to many a lock which no Greek key will open. Now Daphne, as I have shown, can be traced back to Sanskrit Ahanâ, and Ahanâ in Sanskrit means the dawn. As soon as we know this, everything becomes clear. The story of Phoibos and Daphne is no more than a description of what every one may see every day; first, the appearence of the Dawn in the eastern sky, then the rising of the Sun as if hurrying after his bride, then the gradual fading away of the bright Dawn at the touch of the fiery rays of the sun, and at last her death or disappearance in the lap of her mother, the Earth. All this seems to me as clear as daylight, and the only objection that could be raised against this reading of the ancient myth would be, if it could be proved, that Ahanâ does not mean Dawn, and that Daphne cannot be traced back to Ahanâ, or that *Helios* does not mean the Sun.

I know there is another objection, but it seems to me so groundless as hardly to deserve an answer. Why, it is asked, should the ancient nations have told

[1] See *Selected Essays*, vol. i. p. 399.

these endless stories about the Sun and the Dawn, and why should they have preserved them in their mythology? We might as well ask why the ancient nations should have invented so many irregular verbs, and why they should have preserved them in their grammar. A fact does not cease to be a fact, because we cannot at once explain it. As far as our knowledge goes at present, we are justified in stating that the Aryan nations preserved not only their grammatical structure, and a large portion of their dictionary, from the time which preceded their separation, but that they likewise retained the names of some of their deities, some legends about their gods, some popular sayings and proverbs, and in these, it may be, the seeds of parables, as part of their common Aryan heirloom. Their mythological lore fills, in fact, a period in the history of Aryan thought, half-way between the period of language and the period of literature, and it is this discovery which gives to mythology its importance in the eyes of the student of the most ancient history and psychology of mankind.

And do not suppose that the Greeks, or the Hindus, or the Aryan nations in general, were the only people who possessed such tales. Wherever we look, in every part of the world, among uncivilized as well as a civilized people, we find the same kind of stories, the same traditions, the same myths.

I shall give one story from the extreme North, another from the extreme South.

Among the Esquimaux of Repulse Bay, on the west side of Hudson's Bay, on the Arctic Circle, Mr. John Rae picked up the following story:—

"Many years ago, a great Esquimaux Conqueror

gained so much power that he was able to rise unto the heavens, taking with him on one occasion a sister, a very beautiful girl, and some fire. He added much fuel to the fire, and thus formed the Sun. For some time he and his sister lived in great harmony, but after a time he became very cruel, and ill-treated his sister in many ways. She bore it at first with great patience, until at last he threw fire at her, and scorched one side of her face. This spoiling of her beauty was beyond endurance; she therefore ran away from him, and formed the Moon. Her brother then began, and still continues to chase her; but although he sometimes got near, he has not yet overtaken her, nor ever will.

"When it is New Moon, the burnt side of the face is towards us; at Full Moon it is the reverse."

There are dialectic varieties in the Mythology of the Esquimaux as of the Greeks and Hindus, and, with a change of gender between Sun and Moon, the same story occurs among other tribes in the following form: —

"There was a girl at a party, and some one told his love for her by shaking her shoulders, after the manner of the country. She could not see who it was in the dark hut, so she smeared her hands with soot, and when he came back she blackened his cheek with her hand. When a light was brought she saw that it was her brother and fled. He ran after her, followed her, and as she came to the end of the earth, he sprang out into the sky. Then she became the sun, and he the moon, and this is why the moon is always chasing the sun through the heavens, and why the moon is sometimes dark as he turns his blackened cheek towards the earth." [1]

[1] *The Childhood of the World*, by E. Clodd, p. 62.

We now turn to the South, and here, among the lowest of the low, among the Hottentots, who are despised even by their black neighbors, the Zulus, we find the following gem of a fable, beaming with mingled rays of religion and philosophy: —

"The Moon, it is said, sent once an insect to men, saying, "Go thou to men, and tell them, As I die, and dying live, so ye shall also die, and dying live." The insect started with the message, but whilst on his way was overtaken by the hare, who asked: "On what errrand art thou bound?" The insect answered, "I am sent by the Moon to men, to tell them that as she dies and dying lives, they also shall die and dying live." The hare said, "As thou art an awkward runner, let me go" (to take the message). With these words he ran off, and when he reached men, he said, "I am sent by the Moon to tell you, As I die, and dying perish, in the same manner ye also shall die and come wholly to an end." Then the hare returned to the Moon, and told her what he had said to men. The Moon reproached him angrily, saying, "Darest thou tell the people a thing which I have not said?" With these words she took up a piece of wood, and struck him on the nose. Since that day the hare's nose is slit."

Of this story, too, there are various versions and in one of them the end is as follows: —

"The hare, having returned to the Moon, was questioned as to the message delivered, and the Moon, having heard the true state of the case, became so enraged with him that she took up a hatchet to split his head; falling short, however, of that, the hatchet fell upon the upper lip of the hare, and cut it severely. Hence it is that we see the "hare-lip."

The hare, being duly incensed at having received such treatment, raised his claws, and scratched the Moon's face; and the dark parts which we now see on the surface of the Moon are the scars which she received on that occasion."[1]

The Finns, Lapps, and Esthonians do not seem a very poetical race, yet there is poetry even in their smoky huts, poetry surrounded with all the splendor of an arctic night, and fragrant with the perfume of moss and wild flowers. Here is one of their legends: —

"Wanna Issi had two servants, Koit and Ämmarik, and he gave them a torch which Koit should light every morning, and Ämmarik should extinguish in the evening. In order to reward their faithful services, Wanna Issi told them they might be man and wife, but they asked Wanna Issi that he would allow them to remain forever bride and bridegroom. Wanna Issi assented, and henceforth Koit handed the torch every evening to Ämmarik, and Ämmarik took it and extinguished it. Only during four weeks in summer they remain together at midnight;

[1] *Reynard the Fox in South Africa, or Hottentot Fables and Tales*, by W. H. I. Bleek, 1864, p. 69. Dr. Theophilus Hahn, *Die Sprache der Nama*, 1870, p. 59. As a curious coincidence, it may be mentioned that in Sanskrit, too, the Moon is called *sasânka*, *i. e.* "having the marks of a hare," the black marks in the moon being taken for the likeness of the hare. Another coincidence is that the Namaqua Hottentots will not touch hare's flesh (see Sir James E. Alexander's *Expedition of Discovery into the Interior of Africa*, vol. i. p. 269), because the hare deceived men, while the Jews abstain from it, because the hare is supposed to chew the cud (Lev. xi. 6).

A similar tradition on the meaning of death occurs among the Zulus, but as they do not know of the Moon as a deity, the message that men are not to die, or that they are to die, is sent there by Unkulunkulu, the ancestor of the human race, and thus the whole story loses its point. See Dr. Callaway, *Unkulunkulu*, p. 4; and Gray, *Polynesian Mythology*, pp. 16-58.

Koit hands the dying torch to Ämmarik, but Ämmarik does not let it die, but lights it again with her breath. Then their hands are stretched out, and their lips meet, and the blush of the face of Ämmarik colors the midnight sky."

This myth requires hardly any commentary; yet as long as it is impossible to explain the names, Wanna Issi, Koit, and Ämmarik, it might be said that the story was but a love story, invented by an idle Lapp, or Finn, or Esthonian. But what if Wanna Issi in Esthonian means the Old Father, and if Koit means the Dawn? Can we then doubt any longer that Ämmarik[1] must be the Gloaming and that their meeting in the summer reflects those summer evenings when, particularly in the North, the torch of the sun seems never to die, and when the Gloaming is seen kissing the Dawn?

I wish I could tell you some more of these stories which have been gathered from all parts of the world, and which, though they may be pronounced childish and tedious by some critics, seem to me to glitter with the brightest dew of nature's own poetry, and to contain those very touches that make us feel akin, not only with Homer or Shakespeare, but even with Lapps, and Finns, and Kaffirs.

I cannot resist, however, the temptation of inserting here a poetical rendering of the story of Koit and Ämmarik, sent to me from the New World, re-

[1] According to a letter just received from an Esthonian lady, *ämmarik* does mean the gloaming in the language of the common people of Esthonia. Bertram (*Ilmatar*, Dorpat, 1870, p. 265) remarks that *Koit* is the dawn, *Koido täht*, the morning-star, also called *eha täht*. *Ämarik*, the ordinary name for the dawn, is used as the name for the evening twilight, or the gloaming in the well-known story, published by Fählmann (*Verhandlungen der gelehrten Estnischen Gesellschaft zu Dorpat*, vol. i.) In Finnish *hämärä* is twilight in general.

marking only that instead of Lapland, Esthonia is really the country that may claim the original story.

A LEGEND OF LAPLAND.

"Two servants were in Wanna Issi's pay;
A blazing torch their care;
Each morning Koit must light it till its ray
Flamed through the air;

"And every evening Ämmarik's fair hand
Must quench the waning light;
Then over all the weary, waiting land
Fell the still night.

"So passed the time; then Wanna Issi said,
'For faithful service done,
Lo, here reward! To-morrow shall ye wed,
And so be one.'

"'Not so,' said Koit; 'for sweeter far to me
The joy that neareth still;
Then grant us ever fast betrothed to be.'
They had their will.

"And now the blazing lustre to transfer
Himself, is all his claim;
Warm from her lover's hand it comes to her,
To quench the flame.

"Only for four times seven lengthening days,
At midnight, do they stand
Together, while Koit gives the dying blaze
To Ämmarik's hand.

"O wonder then! She lets it not expire,
But lights it with her breath —
The breath of love, that, warm with quickening fire,
Wakes life from death.

"Then hands stretch out, and touch, and clasp on high,
Then lip to lip is pressed,
And Ämmarik's blushes tinge the midnight sky
From east to west."

ANNA C. BRACKETT.

If people cannot bring themselves to believe in

solar and celestial myths among the Hindus and Greeks, let them study the folk-lore of the Semitic and Turanian races. I know there is, on the part of some of our most distinguished scholars, the same objection against comparing Aryan to non-Aryan myths, as there is against any attempt to explain the features of Sanskrit or Greek by a reference to Finnish or Bask. In one sense that objection is well founded, for nothing would create greater confusion than to ignore the genealogical principle as the only safe one in a scientific classification of languages, of myths, and even of customs. We must first classify our myths and legends, as we classify our languages and dialects. We must first of all endeavor to explain what wants explanation in one member of a family by a reference to other members of the same family, before we allow ourselves to glance beyond. But there is in a comparative study of languages and myths not only a philological, but also a philosophical, and, more particularly, a psychological interest, and though even in this more general study of mankind the frontiers of language and race ought never to disappear, yet they can no longer be allowed to narrow or intercept our view. How much the student of Aryan mythology and ethnology may gain for his own progress by allowing himself a wider survey over the traditions and customs of the whole human race, is best known to those who have studied the works of Klemm, Waitz, Bastian, Sir John Lubbock, Mr. Tylor, and Dr. Callaway. What is prehistoric in language among the Aryan nations, is frequently found as still historic among Turanian races. The same applies with regard to religions, myths, legends, and customs. Among Finns and Lapps, among Zulus and Maoris, among Khonds and Karens, we sometimes find the most startling analogies to Aryan traditions, and we certainly learn, again and again, this one important lesson, that as in language, so in mythology, there is nothing which had not originally a meaning, that every name of the gods and heroes had a beginning, a purpose, and a history.

Jupiter was no more called Jupiter by accident, than the Polynesian *Maui*, the Samoyede *Num*, or the Chinese *Tien*.[1] If we can discover the original meaning of these names, we have reached the first ground of their later growth. I do not say that, if we can explain the first purpose of the mythological names, we have solved the whole riddle of mythology, but I maintain that we have gained firm ground. I maintain that every true etymology gives us an historical fact, because the first giving of a name was an historical fact, and an historical fact of the greatest importance for the later development of ancient ideas. Think only of this one fact, which no one would now venture to doubt, that the supreme deity of the Greeks, the Romans, the Germans, is called by the same name as the supreme deity of the earliest Aryan settlers in India. Does not this one fact draw away the curtain from the dark ages of antiquity, and open before our eyes an horizon which we can hardly measure by years? The Greek *Zeus* is the same word as the Latin *Ju* in *Jupiter*, as the German *Tiu;* and all these were merely dialectic varieties of the Vedic *Dyaus*.[2] Now *dyaus* in Sanskrit is the name of the sky, if used as a feminine; if used as a masculine,

[1] See *Lectures on the Science of Religion*, pp. 194, 200.

[2] See my *Lectures on the Science of Language* (10th ed.), vol. ii. p 468.

as it is still in the Veda, it is the sky as a man or as a god — it is Zeus, the father of gods and men. You know, of course, that the whole language of ancient India is but a sister dialect of Greek, Latin, of German, Keltic, and Slavonic, and that if the Greek says *es-ti*, he is, if the Roman says *est*, the German *ist*, the Slave *yesté*, the Hindu, three thousand years ago, said *as-ti*, he is. This *as-ti* is a compound of a root *as*, to be, and the pronoun *ti*. The root meant originally *to breathe*, and dwindled down after a time to the meaning of *to be*. All this must have happened before a single Greek or German reached the shores of Europe, and before a single Brahman descended into the plains of India. At that distant time we must place the gradual growth of language and ideas, of a language which we are still speaking, of ideas which we are still thinking; and at the same time only can we explain the framing of those names which were the first attempts at grasping supernatural powers, which became in time the names of the deities of the ancient world, the heroes of mythology, the chief actors in many a legend, nay, some of which have survived in the nursery tales of our own time.[1]

My time, I see, is nearly over, but before I finish, I feel that I have a duty to perform from which I ought not to shrink. Some of those who have honored me with their presence to-night may recollect that about a year ago a lecture was delivered in this very room by Professor Blackie, in which he tried to throw discredit on the scientific method of the interpretation of popular myths, or on what I call Com-

[1] See a most interesting essay, *Le Petit Poucet* (Tom Thumb), by Gaston Paris.

parative Mythology. Had he confined his remarks to the subject itself, I should have felt most grateful for his criticisms, little minding the manner in which they were conveyed — for a student of language knows what words are made of. Nor, had his personal reflections concerned myself alone, should I have felt called upon to reply to them thus publicly, for it has always seemed to me that unless we protest against unmerited praise, we have no right to protest against unmerited abuse. I believe I can appeal to all here present, that during the many years I have had the honor to lecture in this Institution, I have *not once* allowed myself to indulge in any personal remarks, or attacked those who, being absent, cannot defend themselves. Even when I had to answer objections, or to refute false theories, I have always most carefully avoided mentioning the names of living writers. But as Professor Blackie has directed his random blows, not against myself, but against a friend of mine, Mr. Cox, the author of a work on Aryan Mythology, I feel that I must for once try to get angry, and return blow for blow. Professor Blackie speaks of Mr. Cox as if he had done nothing beyond repeating what I had said before. Nothing can be more unfair. My own work in Comparative Mythology has consisted chiefly in laying down some of the general principles of that science, and in the etymological interpretation of some of the ancient names of gods, goddesses, and heroes. In fact, I have made it a rule never to interpret or to compare the legends of India, Greece, Italy, or Germany, except in cases where it was possible, first of all, to show an identity or similarity in the Sanskrit, Greek, Latin, or German names of the principal actors. Mr. Cox having convinced himself that the method which I have followed in mythology rests on sound and truly scientific principles, has adopted most, though by no means all, of my etymological interpretations. Professor Blackie, on the contrary, without attempting any explanation of the identity of mythological names in Greek and Sanskrit which must be either disproved or explained, thunders forth the following sentence of condemnation: "Even under the scientific guidance of a Bopp, a Bott, a Grimm, and a Müller, a sober man may sometimes, even in the full blaze of the new sun of comparative philology, allow himself to drink deep draughts, if not of *maundering madness*, at least of *manifest hallucination*."

If such words are thrown at my head, I pick them up chiefly as etymological curiosities, and as striking illustrations of what Mr. Tylor calls "survivals in culture," showing how the most primitive implements of warfare, rude stones and unpolished flints, which an ethnologist would suppose to be confined to prehistoric races, to the red Indians of America or the wild Picts of Caledonia, turn up again most unexpectedly at the present day in the very centre of civilized life. All I can say is, that if, as a student of Comparative Mythology, I have been drinking deep draughts of maundering madness, I have been drinking in good company. In this respect Mr. Cox has certainly given me far more credit than I deserve. I am but one out of many laborers in this rich field of scientific research, and he ought to have given far greater prominence to the labors of Grimm, Burnouf, Bopp, and, before all, of my learned friend, Professor Kuhn.

But while, with regard to etymology, Mr. Cox contents himself with reporting the results of other scholars, he stands quite independent in his own treatment of Comparative Mythology. Of this Professor Blackie seems to have no suspicion whatever. The plan which Mr. Cox follows is to collect the coincidences in the legends themselves, and to show how in different myths the same story with slight variations is told again and again of different gods and heroes. In this respect his work is entirely original and very useful; for although these coincidences may be explained in different ways, and do not afford a proof of a common historical origin of the mythologies of India, Greece, Italy, and Germany, they are all the more interesting from a purely psychological point of view, and supply important material for further researches. Mr. Tylor has lately worked with great success in the same rich mine; extending the limits of mythological research far beyond the precincts of the Aryan world, and showing that there are solar myths wherever the sun shines. I differ from Mr. Cox on many points, as he differs from me. I shall certainly keep to my own method of never attempting an interpretation or a comparison, except where the ground has first been cleared of all uncertainty by etymological research, and where the names of different gods and heroes have been traced back to a common source. I call this the *nominalistic* as opposed to the *realistic* method of Comparative Mythology, and it is the former only that concerns the student of the Science of Language. I gratefully acknowledge, however, the help which I have received from Mr. Cox's work, particularly as suggesting new clusters of myths that might be disentangled by etymological analysis.

But not only has Professor Blackie failed to perceive the real character of Mr. Cox's researches, but he has actually charged him with holding opinions which both Mr. Cox and myself have repeatedly disavowed, and most strenuously opposed. Again and again have we warned the students of Comparative Mythology that they must not expect to be able to explain everything. Again and again have we pointed out that there are irrational elements in mythology, and that we must be prepared to find grains of local history on which, as I said,[1] the sharpest tools of Comparative Mythology must bend or break. Again and again have we shown that historical persons[2] — not only Cyrus and Charlemagne, but Frederick Barbarossa and even Frederick the Great — have been drawn into the vortex of popular mythology. Yet these are the words of Professor Blackie: "The cool way in which Max Müller and his English disciple, Mr. Cox, assume that there are no human figures and historical characters in the whole gallery of heroes and demi-gods in the Greek Mythology, is something very remarkable."

I readily admit that some of the etymologies which I have proposed of mythological names are open to criticism; and if, like other scholars, Professor Blackie had pointed out to me any cases where I might seem to him to have offended against Grimm's law or other

1 *Selected Essays*, vol. i. p. 478: "Here then we see that mythology does not always create its own heroes, but that it lays hold of real history, and coils itself round it so closely that it is difficult, nay, almost impossible, to separate the ivy from the oak, the lichen from the granite to which it clings. And here is a lesson which comparative mythologists ought not to neglect. They are naturally bent on explaining everything that can be explained; but they should bear in mind that there may be elements in every mythological riddle which resist etymological analysis, for the simple reason that their origin was not etymological, but historical."

2 *Lectures on the Science of Language*, vol. ii. p. 581.

phonetic rules, I should have felt most grateful; but if he tells me that the Greek Erinys should not be derived from the Sanskrit Saranyû, but from the Greek verb ἐριννύειν, to be angry, he might as well derive *critic* from *to criticise;*[1] and if he maintains that a name may have two or three legitimate etymologies, I can only answer that we might as well say that a child could have two or three legitimate mothers.

I have most reluctantly entered upon these somewhat personal explanations, and I should not have done so if I alone had been concerned in Professor Blackie's onslaught. I hope, however, that I have avoided anything that could give just offence to Professor Blackie, even if he should be present here tonight. Though he abuses me as a German, and laughs at the instinctive aversion to external facts and the extravagant passion for self-evolved ideas as national failings of all Germans (I only wonder that the story of the camel and the inner consciousness did not come in), yet I know that for many years German poetry and German scholarship have had few more ardent admirers, and German scholars few more trusty friends, than Professor Blackie. Nationality, it seems to me, has as little to do with scholarship as with logic. On the contrary, in every nation he that will work hard and reason honestly may be sure to

[1] Professor Blackie quotes Pausanias in support of this etymology. He says: "The account of Pausanias (viii. 25, 26), according to which the terrible impersonation of conscience, or the violated moral law, is derived from ἐριννύειν, an old Greek verb originally signifying to be angry, has sufficient probability, not to mention the obvious analogy of 'Αραί, another name sometimes given to the awful maids (σεμναί), from ἀρά, an imprecation." If Professor Blackie will refer to Pausanias himself, he will find that the Arcadians assigned a very different cause to the anger of Demeter, which is supposed to have led to the formation of her new name Erinys.

discover some grains of truth. National jealousies and animosities have no place in the republic of letters, which is, and I trust always will be, the true international republic of all friends of work, of order, and of truth.

III.

ON FALSE ANALOGIES

IN

COMPARATIVE THEOLOGY.

VERY different from the real similarities that can be discovered in nearly all the religions of the world, and which, owing to their deeply human character, in no way necessitate the admission that one religion borrowed from the other, are those minute coincidences between the Jewish and the Pagan religions which have so often been discussed by learned theologians, and which were intended by them as proof positive, either that the Pagans borrowed their religious ideas direct from the Old Testament, or that some fragments of a primeval revelation, granted to the ancestors of the whole race of mankind, had been preserved in the temples of Greece and Italy.

Bochart, in his "Geographia Sacra," considered the identity of Noah and Saturn so firmly established as hardly to admit of the possibility of a doubt. The three sons of Saturn — Jupiter, Neptune, and Pluto — he represented as having been originally the three sons of Noah: Jupiter being Ham; Neptune, Japhet; and Shem, Pluto. Even in the third generation the two families were proved to have been one, for Phut, the son of Ham, or of Jupiter Hammon, could be no other than Apollo Pythius; Canaan no other than

Mercury; and Nimrod no other than Bacchus, whose original name was supposed to have been Bar-chus, the son of Cush. G. J. Vossius, in his learned work, "De Origine et Progressu Idolatriæ" (1688), identified Saturn with Adam, Janus with Noah, Pluto with Ham, Neptune with Japhet, Minerva with Naamah, Vulcan with Tubal Cain, Typhon with Og. Huet, the friend of Bochart, and the colleague of Bossuet, went still farther; and in his classical work, the "Demonstratio Evangelica," he attempted to prove that the whole theology of the heathen nations was borrowed from Moses, whom he identified not only with ancient law-givers, like Zoroaster and Orpheus, but with gods and demi-gods, such as Apollo, Vulcan, Faunus, and Priapus.

All this happened not more than two hundred years ago; and even a hundred years ago, nay, even after the discovery of Sanskrit and the rise of Comparative Philology, the troublesome ghost of Huet was by no means laid at once. On the contrary, as soon as the ancient language and religion of India became known in Europe, they were received by many people in the same spirit. Sanskrit, like all other languages, was to be derived from Hebrew, the ancient religion of the Brahmans from the Old Testament.

There was at that time an enthusiasm among Oriental scholars, particularly at Calcutta, and an interest for Oriental antiquities in the public at large, of which we in these days of apathy for Eastern literature can hardly form an adequate idea. Everybody wished to be first in the field, and to bring to light some of the treasures which were supposed to be hidden in the sacred literature of the Brahmans. Sir William Jones, the founder of the Asiatic Society at Calcutta, published in the first volume of the "Asiatic Researches" his famous essay, "On the Gods of Greece, Italy, and India;" and he took particular care to state that his essay, though published only in 1788, had been written in 1784. In that essay he endeavored to show that there existed an intimate connection, not only between the mythology of India and that of Greece and Italy, but likewise between the legendary stories of the Brahmans and the accounts of certain historical events as recorded in the Old Testament. No doubt, the temptation was great. No one could look down for a moment into the rich mine of religious and mythological lore that was suddenly opened before the eyes of scholars and theologians, without being struck by a host of similarities, not only in the languages, but also in the ancient traditions of the Hindus, the Greeks, and the Romans; and if at that time the Greeks and Romans were still supposed to have borrowed their language and their religion from Jewish quarters, the same conclusion could hardly be avoided with regard to the language and the religion of the Brahmans of India.

The first impulse to look in the ancient religion of India for reminiscences of revealed truth seems to have come from missionaries rather than from scholars. It arose from a motive, in itself most excellent, of finding some common ground for those who wished to convert and those who were to be converted. Only, instead of looking for that common ground where it really was to be found — namely, in the broad foundations on which all religions are built up: the belief in a divine power, the acknowledgment of sin, the habit of prayer, the desire to offer sacrifice, and the hope of a future life — the students of Pagan religion as well as Christian missionaries were bent on discovering more striking and more startling coincidences, in order to use them in confirmation of their favorite theory that some rays of a primeval revelation, or some reflection of the Jewish religion, had reached the uttermost ends of the world. This was a dangerous proceeding — dangerous because superficial, dangerous because undertaken with a foregone conclusion; and very soon the same arguments that had been used on one side in order to prove that all religious truth had been derived from the Old Testament were turned against Christian scholars and Christian missionaries, in order to show that it was not Brahmanism and Buddhism which had borrowed from the Old and New Testament, but that the Old and the New Testament had borrowed from the more ancient religions of the Brahmans and Buddhists.

This argument was carried out, for instance, in Holwell's "Original Principles of the Ancient Brahmans," published in London as early as 1779, in which the author maintains that "the Brahmanic religion is the first and purest product of supernatural revelation," and "that the Hindu scriptures contain to a moral certainty the original doctrines and terms of restoration delivered from God himself, by the mouth of his first created Birmah, to mankind, at his first creation in the form of man."

Sir William Jones[1] tells us that one or two missionaries in India had been absurd enough, in their zeal for the conversion of the Gentiles, to urge "that the Hindus were even now almost Christians, be-

[1] *Asiatic Researches,* i. p. 272; *Life of Sir W. Jones,* vol. ii. p. 240 *seq.*

cause their Brahma, Vishnu, and Mahesa were no other than the Christian Trinity;" a sentence in which, he adds, we can only doubt whether folly, ignorance, or impiety predominates.

Sir William Jones himself was not likely to fall into that error. He speaks against it most emphatically. "Either," he says, "the first eleven chapters of Genesis — all due allowance being made for a figurative Eastern style — are true, or the whole fabric of our national religion is false; a conclusion which none of us, I trust, would wish to be drawn. But it is not the truth of our national religion as such that I have at heart; it is truth itself; and if any cool, unbiassed reasoner will clearly convince me that Moses drew his narrative through Egyptian conduits from the primeval fountains of Indian literature, I shall esteem him as a friend for having weeded my mind from a capital error, and promise to stand amongst the foremost in assisting to circulate the truth which he has ascertained."

But though he speaks so strongly against the uncritical proceedings of those who would derive anything that is found in the Old Testament from Indian sources, Sir William Jones himself was really guilty of the same want of critical caution in his own attempts to identify the gods and heroes of Greece and Rome with the gods and heroes of India. He begins his essay,[1] "On the Gods of Greece, Italy, and India," with the following remarks: —

"We cannot justly conclude, by arguments preceding the proof of facts, that one idolatrous people must have borrowed their deities, rites, and tenets from another, since gods of all shapes and dimensions

[1] *Asiatic Researches*, i. p. 221.

may be framed by the boundless powers of imagination, or by the frauds and follies of men, in countries never connected; but when features of resemblance, too strong to have been accidental, are observable in different systems of polytheism, without fancy or prejudice to color them and improve the likeness, we can scarce help believing that some connection has immemorially subsisted between the several nations who have adopted them. It is my design in this essay to point out such a resemblance between the popular worship of the old Greeks and Italians and that of the Hindus; nor can there be any room to doubt of a great similarity between their strange religions and that of Egypt, China, Persia, Phrygia, Phœnice, and Syria; to which, perhaps, we may safely add some of the southern kingdoms, and even islands of America; while the Gothic system which prevailed in the northern regions of Europe was not merely similar to those of Greece and Italy, but almost the same in another dress, with an embroidery of images apparently Asiatic. From all this, if it be satisfactorily proved, we may infer a general union or affinity between the most distinguished inhabitants of the primitive world at the time when they deviated, as they did too early deviate, from the rational adoration of the only true God."

Here, then, in an essay written nearly a hundred years ago by Sir W. Jones, one of the most celebrated Oriental scholars in England, it might seem as if we should find the first outlines of that science which is looked upon as but of to-day or yesterday — the outlines of Comparative Mythology. But in such an expectation we are disappointed. What we find is merely a superficial comparison of the mythology of

India and that of other nations, both Aryan and Semitic, without any scientific value, because carried out without any of those critical tests which alone keep Comparative Mythology from running riot. This is not intended as casting a slur on Sir W. Jones. At his time the principles which have now been established by the students of the science of language were not yet known, and as with words, so with the names of deities, similarity of sound, the most treacherous of all sirens, was the only guide in such researches.

It is not pleasant to have to find fault with a man possessed of such genius, taste, and learning as Sir W. Jones, but no one who is acquainted with the history of these researches will be surprised at my words. It is the fate of all pioneers, not only to be left behind in the assault which they had planned, but to find that many of their approaches were made in a false direction, and had to be abandoned. But as the authority of their names continues to sway the public at large, and is apt to mislead even painstaking students and to entail upon them repeated disappointments, it is necessary that those who know should speak out, even at the risk of being considered harsh or presumptuous.

A few instances will suffice to show how utterly baseless the comparisons are which Sir W. Jones instituted between the gods of India, Greece, and Italy. He compares the Latin Janus with the Sanskrit deity Ga*n*esa. It is well known that Janus is connected with the same root that has yielded the names of Jupiter, Zeus, and Dyaus, while Ga*n*esa is a compound, meaning lord of hosts, lord of the companies of gods.

Saturnus is supposed to have been the same as Noah, and is then identified by Sir W. Jones with the Indian Manu Satyavrata, who escaped from the flood. Ceres is compared with the goddess *S*ri, Jupiter or Diespiter with Indra or Divaspati; and though etymology is called a weak basis for historical inquiries, the three syllables Jov in Jovis, Zeu in Zeus, and Siv in Siva are placed side by side, as possibly containing the same root, only differently pronounced. Now the s of Siva is a palatal s, and no scholar who has once looked into a book on Comparative Philology need be told that such an s could never correspond to a Greek Zeta or a Latin J.

In K*r*ish*n*a, the lovely shepherd-god, Sir W. Jones recognizes the features of Apollo Nomius, who fed the herds of Admetus, and slew the dragon Python; and he leaves it to etymologists to determine whether Gopâla — *i. e.*, the cow-herd — may not be the same word as Apollo. We are also assured, on the authority of Colonel Vallancey, that K*r*ish*n*a in Irish means the sun, and that the goddess Kâlî, to whom human sacrifices were offered, as enjoined in the Vedas (?) was the same as Hekate. In conclusion, Sir W. Jones remarks, "I strongly incline to believe that Egyptian priests have actually come from the Nile to the Gangâ and Yamunâ, and that they visited the *S*armans of India, as the sages of Greece visited them, rather to acquire than to impart knowledge."

The interest that had been excited by Sir William Jones's researches did not subside, though he himself did not return to the subject, but devoted his great powers to more useful labors. Scholars, both in India and in Europe, wanted to know more of the ancient religion of India. If Jupiter, Apollo, and Janus had once been found in the ancient pantheon of the Brahmans; if the account of Noah and the deluge could be traced back to the story of Manu Satyavrata, who escaped from the flood, more discoveries might be expected in this newly-opened mine, and people rushed to it with all the eagerness of gold-diggers. The idea that everything in India was of extreme antiquity had at that time taken a firm hold on the minds of all students of Sanskrit; and, as there was no one to check their enthusiasm, everything that came to light in Sanskrit literature was readily accepted as more ancient than Homer, or even than the Old Testament.

It was under these influences that Lieutenant Wilford, a contemporary of Sir William Jones at Calcutta, took up the thread which Sir William Jones had dropped, and determined at all hazards to solve the question which at that time had excited a world-wide interest. Convinced that the Brahmans possessed in their ancient literature the originals, not only of Greek and Roman mythology, but likewise of the Old Testament history, he tried every possible means to overcome their reserve and reticence. He related to them, as well as he could, the principal stories of classical mythology, and the leading events in the history of the Old Testament; he assured them that they would find the same things in their ancient books, if they would but look for them; he held out the hopes of ample rewards for any extracts from their sacred literature containing the histories of Adam and Eve, of Deukalion and Prometheus; and at last he succeeded. The coyness of the Pandits yielded; the incessant demand created a supply; and for several years essay after essay appeared in the "Asiatic Researches," with extracts from Sanskrit MSS., containing not only the names of Deukalion, Prometheus, and other heroes and deities of Greece, but likewise the names of Adam and Eve, of Abraham and Sarah, and all the rest.

Great was the surprise, still greater the joy, not only in Calcutta, but in London, at Paris, and all the universities of Germany. The Sanskrit MSS. from which Lieutenant Wilford quoted, and on which his theories were based, had been submitted to Sir W. Jones and other scholars; and though many persons were surprised, and for a time even incredulous, yet the fact could not be denied that all was found in these Sanskrit MSS. as stated by Lieutenant Wilford. Sir W. Jones, then President of the Asiatic Society, printed the following declaration at the end of the third volume of the "Asiatic Researches": —

"Since I am persuaded that the learned essay on Egypt and the Nile has afforded you equal delight with that which I have myself received from it, I cannot refrain from endeavoring to increase your satisfaction by confessing openly that I have at length abandoned the greatest part of the natural distrust and incredulity which had taken possession of my mind before I had examined the sources from which our excellent associate, Lieutenant Wilford, has drawn so great a variety of new and interesting opinions. Having lately read again and again, both alone and with a Pandit, the numerous original passages in the Purâ*n*as, and other Sanskrit books, which the writer of the dissertation adduces in support of his assertions, I am happy in bearing testimony to his perfect good faith and general accuracy, both in his extracts and in the translation of them."

Sir W. Jones then proceeds himself to give a translation of some of these passages. "The following translation," he writes, "of an extract from the Padma-purâ*n*a is minutely exact": —

"1. To Satyavarman, the sovereign of the whole earth, were born three sons; the eldest, Sherma; then Charma; and thirdly, Jyapeti.

"2. They were all men of good morals, excellent in virtue and virtuous deeds, skilled in the use of weapons to strike with, or to be thrown, brave men, eager for victory in battle.

"3. But Satyavarman, being continually delighted with devout meditation, and seeing his sons fit for dominion, laid upon them the burden of government,

"4. Whilst he remained honoring and satisfying the gods, and priests, and kine. One day, by the act of destiny, the king, having drunk mead,

"5. Became senseless, and lay asleep naked; then was he seen by Charma, and by him were his two brothers called.

"6. To whom he said: What now has befallen? In what state is this our sire? By those two was he hidden with clothes, and called to his senses again and again.

"7. Having recovered his intellect, and perfectly knowing what had passed, he cursed Charma, saying, Thou shalt be the servant of servants:

"8. And since thou wast a laugher in their presence, from laughter shalt thou acquire a name. Then he gave to Sherma the wide domain on the south of the snowy mountains.

"9. And to Jyapeti he gave all on the north of the snowy mountains; but he, by the power of religious contemplation, obtained supreme bliss."

After this testimony from Sir W. Jones — wrung from him, as it would seem, against his own wish and will — Lieutenant Wilford's essays became more numerous and more startling every year.

At last, however, the coincidences became too great. The MSS. were again carefully examined; and then it was found that a clever forgery had been committed, that leaves had been inserted in ancient MSS., and that on these leaves the Pandits, urged by Lieutenant Wilford to disclose their ancient mysteries and traditions, had rendered in correct Sanskrit verse all that they had heard about Adam and Abraham from their inquisitive master. Lieutenant (then Colonel) Wilford did not hesitate for one moment to confess publicly that he had been imposed upon; but in the meantime the mischief had been done, his essays had been read all over Europe, they retained their place in the volumes of the "Asiatic Researches," and to the present day some of his statements and theories continue to be quoted authoritatively by writers on ancient religion.

Such accidents, and, one might almost say, such misfortunes, will happen, and it would be extremely unfair were we to use unnecessarily harsh language with regard to those to whom they have happened. It is perfectly true that at present, after the progress that has been made in an accurate and critical study of Sanskrit, it would be unpardonable if any Sanskrit scholar accepted such passages as those translated by Sir W. Jones as genuine. Yet it is by no means certain that a further study of Sanskrit will not lead to similar disenchantments, and deprive many a book in Sanskrit literature which now is considered as very ancient of its claims to any high antiquity. Certain portions of the Veda even, which, as far as our knowledge goes at present, we are perfectly justified in referring to the tenth or twelfth century before our era, may some day or other dwindle down from their high estate, and those who have believed in their extreme antiquity will then be held up to blame or ridicule, like Sir W. Jones or Colonel Wilford. This cannot be avoided, for science is progressive, and does not acknowledge, even in the most distinguished scholars, any claims to infallibility. One lesson only may we learn from the disappointment that befell Colonel Wilford, and that is to be on our guard against anything which in ordinary language would be called "too good to be true."

Comparative Philology has taught us again and again that when we find a word exactly the same in Greek and Sanskrit, we may be certain that it cannot be the same word; and the same applies to Comparative Mythology. The same god or the same hero cannot have exactly the same name in Sanskrit and Greek, for the simple reason that Sanskrit and Greek have deviated from each other, have both followed their own way, have both suffered their own phonetic corruptions; and hence, if they do possess the same word, they can only possess it either in its Greek or its Sanskrit disguise. And if that caution applies to Sanskrit and Greek, members of the same family of language, how much more strongly most it apply to Sanskrit and Hebrew! If the first man were called in Sanskrit Âdima, and in Hebrew Adam, and if the two were really the same word, then Hebrew and Sanskrit could not be members of two different families of speech, or we should be driven to admit that Adam was borrowed by the Jews from the Hindus for it is in Sanskrit only that âdima means the first, whereas in Hebrew it has no such meaning.

The same remark applies to a curious coincidence pointed out many years ago by Mr. Ellis in his "Polynesian Researches" (London, 1829, vol. ii. p. 38). We there read: —

"A very generally received Tahitian tradition is that the first human pair were made by Taaroa, the principal deity formerly acknowledged by the nation. On more than one occasion I have listened to the details of the people respecting his work of creation. They say that, after Taaroa had formed the world, he created man out of araea, red earth, which was also the food of man until bread first was made. In connection with this some relate that Taaroa one day called for the man by name. When he came, he caused him to fall asleep, and, while he slept, he took out one of his *ivi*, or bones, and with it made a woman, whom he gave to the man as his wife, and they became the progenitors of mankind. This," Mr. Ellis continues, "always appeared to me a mere recital of the Mosaic account of creation, which they had heard from some European, and I never placed any reliance on it, although they have repeatedly told me it was a tradition among them before any foreigners arrived. Some have also stated that the woman's name was *Ivi*, which would be by them pronounced as if written *Eve*. *Ivi* is an aboriginal word, and not only signifies a bone, but also a widow, and a victim slain in war. Notwithstanding the assertion of the natives, I am disposed to think that *Ivi*, or *Eve*, is the only aboriginal part of the story, as far as it respects the mother of the human race. Should more careful and minute inquiry confirm the truth of this declaration, and prove that their account was in existence among them prior to their intercourse with Europeans, it will be the most remarkable and valuable oral tradition of the origin of the human race yet known."

In this case, I believe the probability is that the story of the creation of the first woman from the bone of a man [1] existed among the Tahitians before their intercourse with Christians, but I need hardly add that the similarity between the Polynesian name for bone, *ivi*, even when it was used as the name of the first woman, and the English corruption of the Hebrew חַוָּה, Chāvah, Eve, could be the result of accident only. Whatever Chāvah meant in Hebrew, whether life or living or anything else, it never meant bone, while the Tahitian *ivi*, the Maori *wheva*,[1] meant bone, and bone only.

These principles and these cautions were hardly thought of in the days of Sir William Jones and Colonel Wilford, but they ought to be thought of at present. Thus, before Bopp had laid down his code of phonetic laws, and before Burnouf had written his works on Buddhism, one cannot be very much surprised that Buddha should have been identified with Minos and Lamech; nay, that even the Babylonian deity Belus, and the Teutonic deity Wodan or Odin, should have been supposed to be connected with the founder of Buddhism in India. As Burnouf said in his "Introduction à l'Histoire du Buddhisme," p. 70: "On avait même fait du Buddha une planète; et je

1 See *Introduction to the Science of Religion*, p. 48.

2 The Rev. W. W. Gill tells me that the Maori word for bone is *iwi*, but he suspects a foreign origin for the fable founded on it.

ne sais pas si quelques savants ne se plaisent pas encore aujourd'hui à retrouver ce sage paisible sous les traits du belliqueux Odin." But we did not expect that we should have to read again, in a book published in 1869, such statements as these:[1] —

"There is certainly a much greater similarity between the Buddhism of the Topes and the Scandinavian mythology than between it and the Buddhism of the books; but still the gulf between the two is immense; and if any traces of the doctrines of the gentle ascetic (Buddha) ever existed in the bosom of Odin or his followers, while dwelling near the roots of the Caucasus, all that can be said is, that they suffered fearful shipwreck among the rocks of the savage superstitions of the North, and sank, never again to appear on the surface of Scandinavian mythology. If the two religions come anywhere in con-

[1] *Tree and Serpent Worship*, by James Fergusson. London, 1868. Very similar opinions had been advocated by Rajendralal Mitra, in a paper published in 1858 in the *Journal of the Royal Asiatic Society*, "Buddhism and Odinism, illustrated by extracts from Professor Holmboe's Memoir on the *Traces du Buddhisme en Norvège*." How much mischief is done by opinions of this kind when they once find their way into the general public, and are supported by names which carry weight, may be seen by the following extracts from the *Pioneer* (July 30, 1878), a native paper published in India. Here we read that the views of Holmboe, Rajendralal Mitra, and Fergusson, as to a possible connection between Buddha and Wodan, between Buddhism and Wodenism, have been adopted and preached by an English bishop, in order to convince his hearers, who were chiefly Buddhists, that the religion of the gentle ascetic came originally, if not from the Northeast of Scotland, at all events from the Saxons. "Gotama Buddha," he maintained, "was a Saxon," coming from "a Saxon family which had penetrated into India." And again: "The most convincing proof to us Anglo-Indians lies in the fact that the Purâ*n*as named Varada and Matsy distinctly assert that the White Island in the West — meaning England — was known in India as Sacana, having been conquered at a very early period by the Sacas or Saks." After this the bishop takes courage, and says: "Let me call your attention to the Pâli word Nibban, called in Sanskirt Nirvâ*n*a. In the Anglo-Saxon you have the identical word — Nabban, meaning "not to have," or "to be without a thing."

tact, it is at their base, for underlying both there existed a strange substratum of Tree and Serpent Worship; on this the two structures seem to have been raised, though they afterwards diverged into forms so strangely dissimilar" (p. 34).

Or again (p. 32): —

"We shall probably not err far if we regard these traces of serpent worship as indicating the presence in the Northeast of Scotland of the head of that column of migration, or of propagandism, which, under the myth of Wodenism, we endeavored in a previous chapter to trace from the Caucasus to Scandinavia."

"The arbors under which two of the couples are seated are curious instances of that sort of summer-house which may be found adorning tea-gardens in the neighborhood of London to the present day. It is scenes like these that make us hesitate before asserting that there could not possibly be any connection between Buddhism and Wodenism" (p. 140).

"One of the most tempting nominal similarities connected with this subject is suggested by the name of Mâyâ. The mother of Buddha was called Mâyâ. The mother of Mercury was also Maia, the daughter of Atlas. The Romans always called Wodin, Mercury, and *dies Mercurii* and *Wodensday* alike designated the fourth day of the week. . . . . These and other similarities have been frequently pointed out and insisted upon, and they are too numerous and too distinct not to have some foundation in reality" (p. 186, note).

Statements like these cannot be allowed to pass unnoticed or uncontradicted, particularly if supported by the authority of a great name; and after having spoken so freely of the unscientific character of the mythological comparisons instituted by scholars like Sir William Jones and Lieutenant Wilford, who can no longer defend themselves, it would be mere cowardice to shrink from performing the same unpleasant duty in the case of a living writer, who has shown that he knows how to wield the weapons both of defence and attack.

It is perfectly true that the mother of Buddha was called Mâyâ, but it is equally true that the Sanskrit Mâyâ cannot be the Greek Maiā. It is quite true, also, that the fourth day of the week is called *dies Mercurii* in Latin, and Wednesday in English; nay, that in Sanskirt the same day is called Budha-dina or Budha-vâra. But the origin of all these names falls within perfectly historical times, and can throw no light whatever on the early growth of mythology and religion.

First of all, we have to distinguish between Budha and Buddha. The two names, though so like each other, and therefore constantly mistaken one for the other, have nothing in common but their root. Buddha with two d's, is the participle of budh, and means awakened, enlightened.[1] It is the name given to those who have reached the highest stage of human wisdom, and it is known most generally as the title of Gotama, *S*âkya-muni, the founder of Buddhism, whose traditional era dates from 543 B.C. Budha, on the contrary, with one d, means simply knowing, and it became in later times, when the Hindus received from the Greeks a knowl-

[1] See *Buddhaghosha's Parables*, translated by Captain Rogers, with an Introduction containing Buddha's Dhammapada, translated from Pâli, by M. M., 1870, p. 110, note.

edge of the planets, the name of the planet Mercury.

It is well known that the names of the seven days of the week are derived from the names of the planets,[1] and it is equally well known that in Europe the system of weeks and week-days is comparatively of very modern origin. It was not a Greek, nor a Roman, nor a Hindu, but a Jewish or Babylonian invention. The Sabbath (Sabbata) was known and kept at Rome in the first century B. C. with many superstitious practices. It is mentioned by Horace, Ovid, Tibullus (*dies Saturni*), Persius, Juvenal. Ovid calls it a day "*rebus minus apta gerendis.*" Augustus (Suet. "Aug." c. 76) evidently imagined that the Jews fasted on their Sabbath, for he said, "Not even a Jew keeps the fast of the Sabbath so strictly as I have kept this day." In fact, Josephus ("Contra Apion." ii. 39) was able to say that there was no town, Greek or not Greek, where the custom observing the seventh day had not spread.[2] It is

[1] Hare, "On the Names of the Days of the Week (*Philol. Museum*, Nov. 1831); Ideler, *Handbuch der Chronologie*, p. 177; Grimm, *Deutsche Mythologie*, p. 111.

[2] A writer in the *Index* objects to my representation of what Josephus said with regard to the observance of the seventh day in Greek and barbarian towns. He writes: —

WASHINGTON, *Nov.* 9, 1872.

"The article by Max Müller in the *Index* of this week contains, I think, one error, caused doubtless by his taking a false translation of a passage from Josephus instead of the original. 'In fact,' says Professor Müller, 'Josephus (*Contra Apion.* ii. 39) was able to say that there was no town, Greek or not Greek, where the custom of observing the seventh day had not spread.' Mr. Wm. B. Taylor, in a discussion of the Sabbath question with the Rev. Dr. Brown, of Philadelphia, in 1853 (*Obligation of the Sabbath*, p. 120), gives this rendering of the passage: 'Nor is there anywhere any city of the Greeks, nor a single barbarian nation, whither the institution of the Hebdomade (*which we mark by resting*) has not travelled;' then in a note Mr. Taylor gives the original Greek of part of the passage,

curious that we find the seventh day, the Sabbath, even under its new Pagan name, as *dies Saturni* or *Kronike*, mentioned by Roman and Greek writers, before the names of the other days of the week made their appearance. Tibullus speaks of the day of Saturn, *dies Saturni;* Julius Frontinus (under Nerva, 96–98) says that Vespasian attacked the Jews on the day of Saturn, *dies Saturni;* and Justin Martyr (died 165) states that Christ was crucified the day before the day of Kronos, and appeared to his disciples the day after the day of Kronos. He does not use the names of Friday and Sunday. Sunday, as *dies Solis*, is mentioned by Justin Martyr ("Apolog."

and adds: 'Josephus does not say that the Greek and barbarian rested, but that *we* [the Jews] observe it by rest.'

"The corrected translation only adds strength to Max Müller's position in regard to the very limited extent of Sabbath observance in ancient times; and Mr. Taylor brings very strong historical proof to maintain the assertion (p. 24) that 'throughout all history we discover no trace of a Sabbath among the nations of antiquity.'"

It seems to me that if we read the whole of Josephus's work, *On the Antiquity of the Jews*, we cannot fail to perceive that what Josephus wished to show towards the end of the second book was that other nations had copied or were trying to copy the Jewish customs. He says: Ὑφ' ἡμῶν τε διηνέχθησαν οἱ νόμοι καὶ τοῖς ἄλλοις ἅπασιν ἀνθρώποις, ἀεὶ καὶ μᾶλλον αὐτῶν ζῆλον ἐμπεποιήκασι. He then says that the early Greek philosophers, though apparently original in their theoretic speculations, followed the Jewish laws with regard to practical and moral precepts. Then follows this sentence: Οὐ μὴν ἀλλὰ καὶ πλήθεσιν ἤδη πολὺς ζῆλος γέγονεν ἐκ μακροῦ τῆς ἡμετέρας εὐσεβείας, οὐ δ' ἔστιν οὐ πόλις Ἑλλήνων οὐδητισουν οὐδὲ βάρβαρος, οὐδὲ ἓν ἔθνος, ἔνθα μὴ τὸ τῆς ἑβδομάδος, ἣν ἀργοῦμεν ἡμεῖς, ἔθος οὐ διαπεφοίτηκε, καὶ αἱ νηστεῖαι καὶ λύχνων ἀνακαύσεις καὶ πολλὰ τῶν εἰς βρῶσιν ἡμῖν οὐ νενομισμένων παρατετήρηται. Μιμεῖσθαι δὲ πειρῶνται καὶ τὴν πρὸς ἀλλήλους ἡμῶν ὁμόνοιαν, κ.τ.λ. Standing where it stands, the sentence about the ἑβδομάς can only mean that "there is no town of Greeks nor of barbarians, nor one single people, where the custom of the seventh day, on which we rest, has not spread, and where fastings, and lighting of lamps, and much of what is forbidden to us with regard to food are not observed. They try to imitate our mutual concord also, etc." Hebdomas, which originally meant the week, is here clearly used in the sense of the seventh day, and though Josephus may exaggerate, what he says is certainly "that there was no town, Greek or not Greek, where the custom of observing the seventh day had not spread."

i. 67), and by Tertullian (died 220), the usual name of that day amongst Christians being the Lord's-day, Κυριακή, *dominica* or *dominicus.* Clemens of Alexandria (died 220) seems to have been the first who used the names of Wednesday and Friday, Ἑρμοῦ καὶ Ἀφροδίτης ἡμέρα.

It is generally stated, on the authority of Cassius Dio, that the system of counting by weeks and week-days was first introduced in Egypt, and that at his time, early in the third century, the Romans had adopted it, though but recently. Be this as it may, it would seem that, if Tibullus could use the name of *dies Saturni* for Saturday, the whole system of week-days must have been settled and known at Rome in his time. Cassius Dio tells us that the names were assigned to each day διὰ τεσσάρων, by fours; or by giving the first hour of the week to Saturn, then giving one hour to each planet in succession, till the twenty-fifth hour became again the first of the next day. Both systems lead to the same result, as will be seen from the following table: —

Planets.	*Latin.*	*French.*	*Sanskrit.*
1 Saturn 1	Dies Saturni	Samedi (dies sabbati)	*S*ani-vāra
2 Jupiter 6	" Solis	Dimanche (dominicus)	Ravi-vāra
3 Mars 4	" Lunæ	Lundi	Soma-vāra
4 Sun 2	" Martis	Mardi	Bhauma-vāra
5 Venus 7	" Mercurii	Mercredi	Budha-vāra
6 Mercury 5	" Jovis	Jeudi	B*ri*haspati-vāra
7 Moon 3	" Veneris	Vendredi	*S*ukra-vāra

	Old Norse.	*Anglo-Saxon.*	*English.*
1 Saturn 1	laugardagr (washing day)	sätres däg	Saturday
2 Jupiter 6	sunnudagr	sunnan däg	Sunday
3 Mars 4	mânadagr	monan däg	Monday
4 Sun 2	tysdagr	tives däg	Tuesday
5 Venus 7	odhinsdagr	vôdenes däg	Wednesday
6 Mercury 5	thôrsdagr	thunores däg	Thursday
7 Moon 3	friadagr	frige däg	Friday

Planets.	*Old-High German.*	*Middle-High German.*	*German.*
1 Saturn 1	sambaztag (sunnûn âband)	samztac (sunnen âbent)	Samstag (Sonnabend)
2 Jupiter 6	sunnûn dag	sunnen tac	Sonntag
3 Mars 4	mânin tac (?)	mân tac	Montag
4 Sun 2	ziuwes tac (cies dac)	zies tac (eritic)	Dienstag
5 Venus 7	wuotanes tac (?) (mittawecha)	mittwoch	Mittwoch
6 Mercury 5	donares tac	donres tac	Donnerstag
7 Moon 3	fria dag	frîtac	Freitag

After the names of the week-days had once been settled, we have no difficulty in tracing their migration towards the East and towards the West. The Hindus had their own peculiar system of reckoning days and months, but they adopted at a later time the foreign system of counting by weeks of seven days, and assigning a presiding planetary deity to each of the seven days, according to the system described above. As the Indian name of the planet Mercury was Budha, the *dies Mercurii* was naturally called Budha-vâra but never Buddha-vâra; and the fact that the mother of Mercury was called Maia, and the mother of Buddha Mâyâ, could, therefore, have had no bearing whatever on the name assigned to the Indian Wednesday.[1] The very Buddhists, in Ceylon, distinguish between buddha, the enlightened, and budha, wise, and call Wednesday the day of Budha, not of Buddha.[2] Whether the names of the planets were formed in India independently, or after Greek models, is difficult to settle. The name of Budha, the knowing or the clever, given to the planet Mercury, seems, however, inexplicable except on the latter hypothesis.

[1] Grimm, *Deutsche Mythologie*, p. 118, note.

[2] In Singalese Wednesday is Badâ, in Tamil Budau. See Kennet, in *Indian Antiquary*, 1874, p. 90; D'Alwis, *Journal of Ceylon Branch of the Royal Asiatic Society*, 1870, p. 17.

Having traced the origin of the Sanskrit name of the *dies Mercurii*, Budha-vâra, let us now see why the Teutonic nations, though perfectly ignorant of Buddhism, called the same day the day of Wodan.

That the Teutonic nations received the names of the week-days from their Greek and Roman neighbors admits of no doubt. For commercial and military arrangements between Romans and Germans some kind of *lingua franca* must soon have sprung up, and in it the names of the week-days must have found their place. There would have been little difficulty in explaining the meaning of Sun-day and Mon-day to the Germans, but in order to make them understand the meaning of the other names, some explanations must have been given on the nature of the different deities, in order to enable the Germans to find corresponding names in their own language. A Roman would tell his German friend that *dies Veneris* meant the day of a goddess who represented beauty and love, and on hearing this the German would at once have thought of his own goddess of love, *Freyja*, and have called the *dies Veneris* the day of *Freyja* or Friday.[1]

If *Jupiter* was described as the god who wields the thunderbolt, his natural representative in German would be *Donar*,[2] the Anglo-Saxon *Thunar*, the Old Norse *Thor;* and hence the *dies Jovis* would be called the day of *Thor*, or Thursday. If the fact that Jupiter was the king of the gods had been mentioned, his proper representative in German would, no doubt, have been *Wuotan* or *Odin*.[3] As it was, *Wuotan* or

1 Grimm, *Deutsche Mythologie*, p. 276.
2 *Ibid.* p. 151.
3 *Ibid.* p. 120.

Odin was chosen as the nearest approach to *Mercury*, the character which they share in common, and which led to their identification, being most likely their love of travelling through the air,[1] also their granting wealth and fulfilling the wishes of their worshippers, in which capacity Wuotan is known by the name of *Wunsch*[2] or *Wish*. We can thus understand how it happened that father and son changed places, for while *Mercurius* is the son of *Jupiter*, *Wuotan* is the father of *Donar*. *Mars*, the god of war, was identified with the German *Tiu* or *Ziu*, a name which, though originally the same as *Zeus* in Greek or Dyaus in Sanskrit, took a peculiarly national character among the Germans, and became their god of war.[3]

There remained thus only the *dies Saturni*, the day of Saturn, and whether this was called so in imitation of the Latin name, or after an old German deity of a similar name and character, is a point which for the present we must leave unsettled.

What, however, is not unsettled is this, that if the Germans, in interpreting these names of Roman deities as well as they could, called the *dies Mercurii*, the same day which the Hindus had called the day of Budha (with one *d*), their day of *Wuotan*, this was not because "the doctrines of the gentle ascetic existed in the bosom of Odin or his followers, while dwelling near the roots of the Caucasus," but for very different and much more tangible reasons.

But, apart from all this, by what possible process

1 Grimm, *Deutsche Mythologie*, pp. 137–148.

2 *Ibid.* p. 126. Oski in Icelandic, the god Wish, one of the names of the highest god.

3 Tacit. *Hist.* iv. 64: "Communibus Diis et præcipuo Deorum Marti grates agimus."

could Buddha and Odin have ever been brought together in the flesh? In the history of ancient religions, Odin belongs to the same stratum of mythological thought as Dyaus in India, *Zeus* in Greece, *Jupiter* in Italy. He was worshipped as the supreme deity during a period long anterior to the age of the Veda and of Homer. His travels in Greece, and even in Tyrkland,[1] and his half-historical character as a mere hero and a leader of his people, are the result of the latest Euhemerism. Buddha, on the contrary, is not a mythological, but a personal and historical character, and to think of a meeting of Buddha and Odin, or even of their respective descendants, at the roots of Mount Caucasus, would be like imagining an interview between Cyrus and Odin, between Mohammed and Aphrodite.

A comparative study of ancient religions and mythologies, as will be seen from these instances, is not a subject to be taken up lightly. It requires not only an accurate acquaintance with the minutest details of comparative philology, but a knowledge of the history of religions which can hardly be gained without a study of original documents. As long, however, as researches of this kind are carried on for their own sake, and from a mere desire of discovering truth, without any ulterior objects, they deserve no blame, though, for a time, they may lead to erroneous results. But when coincidences between different religions and mythologies are searched out simply in support of preconceived theories, whether by the friends or enemies of religion, the sense of truth, the very life of all science, is sacrified, and serious mischief will follow without fail. Here we have a right, not

[1] Grimm, *l. c.* p. 148.

only to protest, but to blame. There is on this account a great difference between the books we have hitherto examined, and a work lately published in Paris by M. Jacolliot, under the sensational title of "La Bible dans l'Inde, Vie de Jeseus Christna." If this book had been written with the pure enthusiasm of Lieutenant Wilford, it might have been passed by as a mere anachronism. But when one sees how its author shuts his eyes against all evidence that would tell against him, and brings together, without any critical scruples, whatever seems to support his theory that Christianity is a mere copy of the ancient religion of India, mere silence would not be a sufficient answer. Besides, the book has lately been translated into English, and will be read, no doubt, by many people who cannot test the evidence on which it professes to be founded. We learn that M. Jacolliot was some years ago appointed President of the Court of Justice at Chandernagore, and that he devoted the leisure left him from the duties of his position to studying Sanskrit and the holy books of the Hindus. He is said to have put himself in communication with the Brahmans, who had obtained access to a great number of MSS. carefully stored up in the depths of the pagodas. "The purport of his book is" (I quote from a friendly critic), "that our civilization, our religion, our legends, our gods, have come to us from India, after passing in succession through Egypt, Persia, Judea, Greece, and Italy." This statement, we are told, is not confined to M. Jacolliot, but has been admitted by almost all Oriental scholars. The Old and New Testaments are found again in the Vedas, and the texts quoted by M. Jacolliot in support of his theory are said to leave it without doubt. Brahma created Adima (in Sanskrit, the first man) and gave him for companion Heva (in Sanskrit, that which completes life). He appointed the island of Ceylon for their residence. What follows afterwards is so beautifully described that I may be pardoned for quoting it. Only I must warn my readers, lest the extract should leave too deep an impression on their memory, that what M. Jacolliot calls a simple translation from Sanskrit is, as far as I can judge, a simple invention of some slightly mischievous Brahman, who, like the Pandits of Lieutenant Wilford, took advantage of the zeal and credulity of a French judge: —

"Having created the Man and the Woman (*simultaneously*, not one after the other), and animated them with the divine afflatus — the Lord said unto them: 'Behold, your mission is to people this beautiful Island [Ceylon], where I have gathered together everything pleasant and needful for your subsistence — the rest of the Earth is as yet uninhabitable, but should your progeny so increase as to render the bounds of paradise too narrow a habitation, let them inquire of me by sacrifice and I will make known my will.'

"And thus saying, the Lord disappeared. . . . .

"Then Adam and Eve dwelt together for a time in perfect happiness; but ere long a vague disquietude began to creep upon them. . . . . The Spirit of Evil, jealous of their felicity and of the work of Brahma, inspired them with disturbing thoughts; — 'Let us wander through the Island,' said Adam to his companion, 'and see if we may not find some part even more beautiful than this.' . . . .

"And Eve followed her husband . . . . wandering for days and for months; . . . . but as they advanced the woman was seized with strange and inexplicable terrors: 'Adam,' said she, "let us go no farther: it seems to me that we are disobeying the Lord; have we not already quitted the place which he assigned us for a dwelling and forbade us to leave?'

"'Fear not,' replied Adam; 'this is not that fearful wilderness of which he spake to us.' . . . .

"And they wandered on. . . . .

"Arriving at last at the extremity of the Island, they beheld a smooth and narrow arm of the sea, and beyond it a vast and apparently boundless country, connected with their Island only by a narrow and rocky pathway arising from the bosom of the waters.

"The two wanderers stood amazed: the country before them was covered with stately trees, birds of a thousand colors flitting amidst their foliage.

". . . . 'Behold, what beautiful things!' cried Adam, 'and what good fruit such trees must produce; . . . let us go and taste them, and if that country is better than this, we will dwell there.'

"Eve, trembling, besought Adam to do nothing that might irritate the Lord against them. "Are we not well here? Have we not pure water and delicious fruits? Wherefore seek other things?'

"'True,' replied Adam, 'but we will return; what harm can it be to visit this unknown country that presents itself to our view?' . . . . And as he approached the rocks, Eve, trembling, followed.

"Placing his wife upon his shoulders, he proceeded to cross the space that separated him from the object of his desires, but no sooner did he touch the shore than trees, flowers, fruits, birds, all that they had perceived from the opposite side, in an instant vanished amidst terrific clamor; . . . . the rocks by which they had crossed sunk beneath the waters, a few sharp peaks alone remaining above the surface, to indicate the place of the bridge which had been destroyed by Divine displeasure.

"The vegetation which they had seen from the opposite shore was but a delusive mirage raised by the Spirit of Evil to tempt them to disobedience.

"Adam fell, weeping, upon the naked sands, ... but Eve throwing herself into his arms, besought him not to despair; . . . . 'let us rather pray to the Author of all things to pardon us.' . . . .

"And as she spake there came a voice from the clouds, saying,

"'Woman! *thou* hast only sinned from love to thy husband, whom I commanded thee to love, and thou hast hoped in me.

"'I therefore pardon thee — and I pardon him also for *thy* sake: . . . . but ye may no more return to paradise, which I had created for your happiness; . . . . through your disobedience to my commands the Spirit of Evil has obtained possession of the Earth. . . . . Your children reduced to labor and to suffer by your fault will become corrupt and forget me. . . . .

"'But I will send Vish*n*u, who will be born of a woman, and who will bring to all the hope of a reward in another life, and the means by prayer of softening their sufferings.'"

The translator from whom I have quoted exclaims at the end, as well he might: —

"What grandeur and what simplicity is this Hindu legend! and at the same time how simply logical! . . . . Behold here the veritable Eve — the true woman."

But much more extraordinary things are quoted

by M. Jacolliot, from the Vedas and the commentaries.

On p. 63 we read that Manu, Minos, and Manes, had the same name as Moses; on p. 73, the Brahmans who invaded India are represented as the successors of a great reformer called Christna. The name of Zoroaster is derived from the Sanskrit Sûryastara (p. 110), meaning "he who spreads the worship of the Sun." After it has been laid down (p. 116) that Hebrew was derived from Sanskrit, we are assured that there is little difficulty in deriving Jehovah from Zeus.[1] Zeus, Jezeus, Jesus, and Isis are all declared to be the same name, and later on (p. 130) we learn that "at present the Brahmans who officiate in the pagodas and temples give this title of Jeseus — *i. e.* the pure essence, the divine emanation — to Christna only, who alone is recognized as the Word, the truly incarnated, by the worshippers of Vish*n*u and the freethinkers among the Brahmans."

We are assured that the Apostles, the poor fishermen of Galilee, were able to read the Veda (p. 356); and it was their greatest merit that they did not reject the miraculous accounts of the Vedic period, because the world was not yet ripe for freedom of thought. Kristna, or Christna, we read on p. 360, signified in Sanskrit, sent by God, promised by God, holy; and as the name of Christ or *Christos* is not Hebrew, whence could it have been taken except from Krishna, the son of Devakî, or, as M. Jacolliot writes, Devanaguy?

It is difficult, nay, almost impossible, to criticise or refute such statements, and yet it is necessary to

[1] P. 125. "Pour quiconque s'est occupé d'études philologiques, Jéhova dérivé de Zeus est facile à admettre."

do so; for such is the interest, or I should rather say the feverish curiosity, excited by anything that bears on ancient religion, that M. Jacolliot's book has produced a very wide and very deep impression. It has been remarked with some surprise that Vedic scholars in Europe had failed to discover these important passages in the Veda which he has pointed out, or, still worse, that they had never brought them to the knowledge of the public. In fact, if anything was wanting to show that a general knowledge of the history of ancient religion ought to form part of our education, it was the panic created by M. Jacolliot's book. It is simply the story of Lieutenant Wilford over again, only far less excusable now than a hundred years ago. Many of the words which M. Jacolliot quotes as Sanskrit are not Sanskrit at all; others never have the meaning which he assigns to them; and as to the passages from the Vedas (including our old friend the Bhagaveda-gîta), they are not from the Veda, they are not from any old Sanskrit writer — they simply belong to the second half of the nineteenth century. What happened to Lieutenant Wilford has happened again to M. Jacolliot. He tells us the secret himself: —

"One day," he says (p. 280), "when we were reading the translation of Manu, by Sir W. Jones, a note led us to consult the Indian commentator, Kullûka Bha*tt*a, when we found an allusion to the sacrifice of a son by his father prevented by God himself after he had commanded it. We then had only one *idée fixe* — namely, to find again in the dark mass of the religious books of the Hindu, the original account of that event. We should never have succeeded but for 'the complaisance' of a Brahman with whom we were reading Sanskrit, and who, yielding to our request, brought us from the library of his pagoda the works of the theologian Ramatsariar, which have yielded us such precious assistance in this volume."

As to the story of the son offered as a sacrifice by his father, and released at the command of the gods, M. Jacolliot might have found the original account of it from the Veda, both text and translation, in my "History of Ancient Sanskrit Literature." He would soon have seen that the story of *S*una*h*sepa being sold by his father in order to be sacrificed in the place of an Indian prince, has very little in common with the intended sacrifice of Isaac by Abraham. M. Jacolliot has, no doubt, found out by this time that he has been imposed upon; and if so, he ought to follow the example of Colonel Wilford, and publicly state what has happened. Even then, I doubt not that his statements will continue to be quoted for a long time, and that Adima and Heva, thus brought to life again, will make their appearance in many a book and many a lecture-room.

Lest it be supposed that such accidents happen to Sanskrit scholars only, or that this fever is bred only in the jungles of Indian mythology, I shall mention at least one other case which will show that this disease is of a more general character, and that want of caution will produce it in every climate.

Before the discovery of Sanskrit, China had stood for a long time in the place which was afterwards occupied by India. When the ancient literature and civilization of China became first known to the scholars of Europe, the Celestial Empire had its admirers and prophets as full of enthusiasm as Sir W. Jones and Lieutenant Wilford, and there was nothing, whether Greek philosophy or Christian morality, that was not supposed to have had its first origin among the sages of China. The proceedings of the Jesuit missionaries in China were most extraordinary. They had themselves admitted the antiquity of the writings of Confucius and Lao-tse, both of whom lived in the sixth century B. C.[1] But in their zeal to show that the sacred books of the Chinese contained numerous passages borrowed from the Bible, nay, even some of the dogmas of the later Church, they hardly perceived that, taking into account the respective dates of these books, they were really proving that a kind of anticipated Christianity had been accorded to the ancient sages of the Celestial Empire. The most learned advocate of this school was Father Prémare. Another supporter of the same view, Montucci,[2] speaking of Lao-tse's Tao-te-king, says: —

"We find in it so many sayings clearly referring to the triune God, that no one who has read this book can doubt that the mystery of the most holy Trinity was revealed to the Chinese more than five centuries before the advent of Christ. Everybody, therefore, who knows the strong feeling of the Chinese for their own teachers, will admit that nothing more efficient could be found in order to fix the dogmas of the Christian religion in the mind of the Chinese than the demonstration that these dogmas agree with their own books. The study, therefore, and the translation of this singular book (the Tao-te-king) would prove most useful to the missionaries, in order to bring to a happy issue the desired gathering in of the Apostolic harvest."

[1] Stanislas Julien, *Le Livre de la Voie et de la Vertu.* Paris, 1842, p. iv.

[2] Montucci, *De studiis sinicis.* Berolini, 1808.

What followed is so extraordinary that, though it has often been related, it deserves to be related again, more particularly as the whole problem which was supposed to have been solved once for all by M. Stanislas Julien, has of late been opened again by Dr. von Strauss, in the "Journal of the German Oriental Society," 1869.

There is a passage at the beginning of the fourteenth chapter of the Tao-te-king in which Father Amyot felt certain that the three Persons of the Trinity could be recognized. He translated it: —

"He who is as it were visible but cannot be seen is called Khi.

"He whom we cannot hear, and who does not speak to our ear, is called Hi.

"He who is as it were tangible, but cannot be touched, is called Wei."

Few readers, I believe, would have been much startled by this passage, or would have seen in it what Father Amyot saw. But more startling revelations were in store. The most celebrated Chinese scholar of his time, Abel Rémusat, took up the subject; and after showing that the first of the three names had to be pronounced, not Khi, but I, he maintained that the three syllables I Hi Wei, were meant for Je-ho-vah. According to him, the three characters employed in this name have no meaning in Chinese; they are only signs of sounds foreign to the Chinese language; and they were intended to render the Greek Ἰαῶ, the name which, according to Diodorus Siculus, the Jews gave to their God. Rémusat goes on to remark that Lao-tse had really rendered this Hebrew name more accurately than the Greeks, because he had preserved the aspiration of the second syllable, which was lost in Greek. In fact, he entertained no doubt that this word, occurring in the work of Lao-tse, proves an intellectual communication between the West and China, in the sixth century B. C.

Fortunately, the panic created by this discovery did not last long. M. Stanislas Julien published in 1842 a complete translation of this difficult book; and here all traces of the name of Jehovah have disappeared.

"The three syllables," he writes, "which Abel Rémusat considered as purely phonetic and foreign to the Chinese language, have a very clear and intelligible meaning, and have been fully explained by Chinese commentators. The first syllable, I, means without color; the second, Hi, without sound or voice; the third, Wei, without body. The proper translation therefore is: —

"You look (for the Tao, the law) and you see it not: it is colorless.

"You listen and you hear it not: it is voiceless.

"You wish to touch it and you reach it not: it is without body."

Until, therefore, some other traces can be discovered in Chinese literature proving an intercourse between China and Judæa in the sixth century B. C., we can hardly be called upon to believe that the Jews should have communicated this one name, which they hardly trusted themselves to pronounce at home, to a Chinese philosopher; and we must treat the apparent similarity between I-Hi-Wei and Jehovah as an accident, which ought to serve as a useful warning, though it need in no way discourage a careful and honest study of Comparative Theology.

ON SPELLING.

THE remarks which I venture to offer in these pages on the corrupt state of the present spelling of English, and on the advantages and disadvantages connected with a reform of English orthography, were written in fulfillment of a promise of very long standing. Ever since the publication of the Second Volume of my "Lectures on the Science of Language," in 1863, where I had expressed my sincere admiration for the courage and perseverance with which Mr. Isaac Pitman and some of his friends (particularly Mr. A. J. Ellis, for six years his most active associate) had fought the battle of a reform in English spelling, Mr. Pitman had been requesting me to state more explicitly than I had done in my "Lectures" my general approval of his life-long endeavors. He wished more particularly that I should explain why I, though by profession an etymologist, was not frightened by the specter of phonetic spelling, while such high authorities as Archbishop Trench and Dean Alford had declared that phonetic spelling would necessarily destroy the historical and etymological character of the English language.

If I ask myself why I put off the fulfillment of my

promise from year to year, the principal reason I find is, that really I had nothing more to say than what, though in few words, I had said before. Every thing that can be said on this subject has been said, and well said, not only by Mr. Pitman, but by a host of writers and lecturers, among whom I might mention Mr. Alexander J. Ellis, Dr. Latham, Professors Haldeman, Whitney, and Hadley, Mr. Withers, Mr. E. Jones, Dr. J. H. Gladstone, and many others. The whole matter is no longer a matter for argument; and the older I grow, the more I feel convinced that nothing vexes people so much, and hardens them in their unbelief and in their dogged resistance to reforms, as undeniable facts and unanswerable arguments. Reforms are carried by Time, and what generally prevails in the end, are not logical deductions, but some haphazard and frequently irrational motives. I do not say, therefore, with Dean Swift, that "there is a degree of corruption wherein some nations, as bad as the world is, will proceed to an amendment; till which time particular men should be quiet." On the contrary, I feel convinced that practical reformers, like Mr. Pitman, should never slumber nor sleep. They should keep their grievances before the public in season and out of season. They should have their lamps burning, to be ready whenever the right time comes. They should repeat the same thing over and over again, undismayed by indifference, ridicule, contempt, and all the other weapons which the lazy world knows so well how to employ against those who venture to disturb its peace.

I myself, however, am not a practical reformer; least of all in a matter which concerns Englishmen only—namely, the spelling of the English language. I should much rather, therefore, have left the fight to others, content with being merely a looker-on. But when I was on the point of leaving England my conscience smote me. Though I had not actually given a pledge, I remembered how, again and again, I had said to Mr. Pitman that I would much rather keep than make a promise; and though overwhelmed with other work at the time, I felt that before my departure I ought, if possible, to satisfy Mr. Pitman's demands. The article was written; and though my own plans have since been changed, and I remain at Oxford, it may as well be published in discharge of a debt which has been for some time heavy on my conscience.

What I wish most strongly to impress on my readers is that I do not write as an advocate. I am not an agitator for phonetic reform in England. My interest in the matter is, and always has been, purely theoretical and scientific. Spelling and the reform of spelling are problems which concern every student of the science of language. It does not matter whether the language be English, German, or Dutch. In every written language the problem of reforming its antiquated spelling must sooner or later arise; and we must form some clear notion whether any thing can be done to remove or alleviate a complaint inherent in the very life of language. If my friends tell me that the idea of a reform of spelling is entirely Quixotic, that it is a mere waste of time to try to influence a whole nation to surrender its historical orthography and to write phonetically, I bow to their superior wisdom as men of the world. But as I am not a man of the world, but rather an observer of the world, my interest in the subject, my convictions as to what is right and wrong, remain just the same. It is the duty of scholars and philosophers not to shrink from holding and expressing what men of the world call Quixotic opinions; for, if I read the history of the world rightly, the victory of reason over unreason, and the whole progress of our race, have generally been achieved by such fools as ourselves "rushing in where angels fear to tread," till, after a time, the track becomes beaten, and even angels are no longer afraid. I hold, and have confessed, much more Quixotic theories on language than this belief—that what has been done before by Spaniards and Dutchmen—what is at this very moment being done by Germans, namely, to reform their corrupt spelling—may be achieved even by Englishmen and Americans.

I have expressed my belief that the time will come when not only the various alphabets and systems of spelling, but many of the languages themselves which are now spoken in Europe, to say nothing of the rest of the world, will have to be improved away from the face of the earth and abolished. Knowing that nothing rouses the ire of a Welshman or a Gael so much as to assert the expediency, nay, necessity, of suppressing the teaching of their languages at school, it seems madness to hint that it would be a blessing to every child born in Holland, in Portugal, or in Denmark—nay, in Sweden and even in Russia—if, instead of learning a language which is for life a barrier between them and the rest of mankind, they were at once to learn one of the great historical languages which confer intellectual and social fellowship with the whole world. If, as a first step in the right direction, four languages only, namely, English, French, German, Italian (or possibly Spanish) were taught at school, the saving of time—and what is more precious than time?—would be infinitely greater than what has been effected by railways and telegraphs. But I know that no name in any of the doomed languages would be too strong to stigmatize such folly. We should be told that a Japanese only could conceive such an idea; that for a people deliberately to give up its language was a thing never heard of before; that a nation would cease to be a nation if it changed its language; that it would, in fact, commit "the happy despatch," *à la Japonaise.* All this may be true, but I hold that language is meant to be an instrument of communication, and that in the struggle for life, the most efficient instrument of communication must certainly carry the day, as long as natural selection, or, as we formerly called it, reason, rules the world.

The following figures may be of use in forming an opinion as to the fates of the great languages of Europe:*-

Portuguese is spoken in		
Portugal, by	3,980,000	
Brazil, by	10,000,000	
		13,980,000
Italian, by		27,524,238
French, in France, Belgium, Switzerland, etc., by .		40,188,000
Spanish, in		
Spain, by	16,301,000	
South America, by	27,408,082	
		43,709,082

* See W. E. A. Axon's "The Future of the English Language," the "Almanach de Gotha," and De Candolle's "Histoire des Sciences," 1873.

Russian, by		51,370,000
German, by		55,789,000
English, in		
Europe, by	31,000,000	
America, by	45,000,000	
Australia, etc., by	2,000,000	
the Colonies, by	1,050,000	
		79,050,000

According to De Candolle, the population doubles in

England, in	56 years
America, among the German races, in	25 "
Italy, in	135 "
Russia, in	100 "
Spain, in	112 "
South America, in	27½ "
Germany, in	100 "
France, in	140 "

Therefore, in 200 years (barring accidents)

Italian will be spoken by		53,370,000
French will be spoken by		72,571,000
German will be spoken by		157,480,000
Spanish will be spoken in		
Europe, by	36,938,338	
South America, by	468,347,904	
		505,286,242
English will be spoken in		
Europe, by	178,846,153	
United States, and British Dependencies, by	1,658,440,000	
		1,837,286,153

But I shall say no more on this, for as it is, I know I shall never hear the end of it, and shall go down to posterity, if for nothing else, at least for this the most suicidal folly in a student of languages; a folly comparable only to that of Leibniz, who actually conceived the possibility of one universal language.

To return, however, to the problem to the solution of which Mr. Pitman has devoted the whole of his active life, let me say again that my interest in it is purely philological; or, if you like, historical. The problem which has to be solved in England and the United States of America is not a new one, nor an isolated one. It occurs again and again in the history of language; in fact, it must occur. When languages are reduced to writing, they are at first written phonetically, though always in a very rough-and-ready manner. One dialect, that of the dominant, the literary, or priestly character, is generally selected; and the spelling, once adopted, becomes in a very short time traditional and authoritative. What took place thousands of years ago, we can see taking place, if we like, at the present moment. A missionary from the island of Mangaia, the Rev. W. Gill, first introduced the art of writing among his converts. He learned their language, at least one dialect of it, he translated part of the Bible into it, and adopted, of necessity, a phonetic spelling. That dialect is gradually becoming the recognized literary language of the whole island, and his spelling is taught at school. Other dialects, however, continue to be spoken, and they may in time influence the literary dialect. For the present, however, the missionary dialect, as it is called by the natives themselves, and the missionary spelling, rule supreme, and it will be some time before a spelling reform is wanted out there.

Among the more ancient nations of Europe, not only does the pronunciation of language maintain its inherent dialectic variety, and fluctuate through the prevalence of provincial speakers, but the whole body of a language changes, while yet the spelling, once adopted in public documents, and taught to children, remains for a long time the same. In early times, when literature was in its infancy, when copies of books could easily be counted, and when the *norma scribendi* was in the hands of a few persons, the difficulty of adapting the writing to the ever-varying pronunciation of a language was comparatively small. We see it when we compare the Latin of early Roman inscriptions with the Latin of Cicero. We know from Cicero himself that when he settled among the patricians of Rome, he had on some small points to change both his pronunciation and his spelling of Latin. The reform of spelling was a favorite subject with Roman scholars, and even emperors were not too proud to dabble in inventing new letters and diacritical signs. The difficulty, however, never assumes serious proportions. The small minority of people who were able to read and write, pleased themselves as best they could; and, by timely concessions, prevented a complete estrangement between the written and the spoken language.

Then came the time when Latin ceased to be Latin, and the vulgar dialects, such as Italian, French, and Spanish took its place. At that time the spelling was again phonetic, though here and there tinged by reminiscences of Latin spelling. There was much variety, but considering how limited the literary intercourse must have been between different parts of France, Spain, or Italy, it is surprising that on the whole there should have been so much uniformity in the spelling of these modern dialects. A certain local and individual freedom of spelling, however, was retained; and we can easily detect in mediæval MSS. the spelling of literate and illiterate writers, the hand of the learned cleric, the professional clerk, and the layman.

[A style of spelling will now be introduced which has received the name of Semiphonotypy. It requires no new letter: "Ɒ ɒ" for the vowel in *but, son,* are made from "D p" by a pen-knife. The short vowels, diphthongs, and consonants are all written phonetically, except an occasional "n" = "ŋ" before *k* and *g*, and "th" = both "ŧ" and "đ;" leaving only the long vowels in the old spelling. Six syllables out of seven are thus written as in full phonotypy. The italic and script forms of "ɒ" are "*ɒ*" (a turned italic "*a*") and *ɒ*]

The great event hwich formz a deseisiv epok in the histori ov speling iz the introdɒkshon ov printing. With printed buks, and partikiularli with printed Beibelz, skaterd over the kɒntri, the speling of wɒrdz bekame rijid, and universali beinding. Sɒm langwejez, sɒch az Italian, wer more fortiunate than ɒtherz in having a more rashonal sistem ov speling tu start with. Sɒm, agen, leik Jerman, wer abel tu make teimli konseshonz, hweil ɒtherz, sɒch az Spanish, Dɒch, and French, had Akademiz tu help them at kritikal periodz ov their histori. The most ɒnfortiunate in all theze respekts woz Inglish. It started with a Latin alfabet, the pronɒnsiashon ov hwich woz ɒnseteld, and hwich had tu be apleid tu a Tiutonik langwej. After this ferst fonetik kompromeiz it had tu pas through a konfiúzd sistem ov speling, half Sakson, half Norman; half fonetik, half tradishonal. The histori ov the speling, and even ov the pronɒnsiashon, ov Inglish, in its pasej from Anglo-Sakson tu midel and modern Inglish, haz lateli been stʊdid with great sʊkses bei Mr. Ellis and Mr. Sweet. Ei mʊst refer tu their buks "On Erli Inglish Pronʊnsiashon," and "On the Histori ov Inglish Soundz," hwich kontain a welth ov ilʊstrashon, almost bewildering. And even after Inglish reachez the period ov printing, the konfiuzhon iz bei no meanz terminated; on the kontrari, for a teim it iz greater than ever. Hou this kame tu pas haz been wel ilʊstrated bei Mr. Marsh in hiz ekselent "Lektiurz on the Inglish Langwej," p. 687, *seq.** Hwot we nou kall the establisht sistem ov Inglish orthografi may, in the main, be trast bak tu Jonson'z Dikshonari, and tu the stil more kaprishʊs sway ekserseizd bei larj printing ofisez and pʊblisherz. It iz true that the evil ov printing karid tu a serten ekstent its own remedi. If the speling bekame ʊnchanjabel, the langwej itself, too, woz, bei meanz ov a printed literatiur, chekt konsiderabli in its natiural growth and its dealektik vareieti. Nevertheles Inglish haz chanjed sins the invenshon ov printing; Inglish iz chanjing, though bei imperseptibel degreez, even nou; and if we kompare Inglish az spoken with Inglish az riten, they seem almost leik two diferent langwejez; az diferent az Latin iz from Italian.

This, no dout, iz a nashonal misfortiun, bʊt it iz inevitabel. Litel az we perseive it, langwej iz, and alwayz mʊst be, in a state ov fermentashon; and hwether within hʊndredz or thouzandz ov yearz, all

*The pronoun *it* woz speld in eight diferent wayz bei Tyndale, thʊs, *hyt, hytt, hit, hitt, it, itt, yt, ytt.* Anʊther author speld *tongue* in the folowing wayz: *tung, tong, tunge, tonge, tounge.* The wʊrd *head* woz variʊsli speld *hed, heede, hede, hefode.* The spelingz *obay, survay, pray, vail, vain,* ar often uzed for *obey, survey, prey, veil, vein.*

living langwejez mɒst be prepared tu enkounter the difikɒlti hwich in Ingland starez ɒs in the fase at prezent. "Hwot shal we do?" ask our frendz. "Ther iz our hole nashonal literatiur," they say, "our leibrariz aktiuali bɒrsting with buks and nuizpaperz. Ar all theze tu be thrown away? Ar all valiuabel buks tu be reprinted? Ar we ourselvz tu ɒnlern hwot we hav lernd with so mɒch trɒbel, and hwot we hav taught tu our children with greater trɒbel stil? Ar we tu sakrifeiz all that iz historikal in our langwej, and sink doun tu the low level ov the *Fonetik Nuz?*" Ei kud go on mɒltipleiing theze kwestionz til even thoze men ov the wɒrld who nou hav onli a shrɒg ov the shoulder for the reformerz ov speling shud say, "We had no eidea hou strong our pozishon reali iz."

Bɒt with all thát, the problem remainz ɒnsolvd. Hwot ar peopel tu do hwen langwej and pronɒnsiashon chanje, hweil their speling iz deklared tu bè ɒnchanjabel? It iz, ei believ, hardli nesesari that ei shud prove hou korɒpt, efete, and ɒterli irrashonal the prezent sistem ov speling iz, for nowɒn seemz inkleind tu denei all thát. Ei shal onli kwote, therefor, the jɒ̣jment ov wɒn man, the late Bishop Thirlwall, a man who never uzed ekzajerated langwej. "Ei luk," he sez "ɒpon the establisht sistem, if an aksidental kɒstom may be so kalld, az a mas ov anomaliz, the growth ov ignorans and chans, ekwali repɒgnant tu gud taste and tu komon sens. Bɒt ei am aware that the pɒblik kling tu theze anomaliz with a tenasiti proporshond tu their absɒrditi, and ar jelɒs ov all enkroachment on ground konsekrated tu the free play ov bleind kaprise."

It may be useful, houever, tu kwote the testimonialz ov a fiu praktikal men in order tu show that this sistem ov speling haz reali bekɒm wɒn ov the greatest nashonal misfortiunz, swolowing ɒp milionz ov mɒni everi year and bleiting all atempts at nashonal ediukashon. Mr. Edward Jones, a skoolmaster ov great eksperiens, having then siuperintendens ov the Heibernian Skoolz, Liverpool, rote, in the year 1868:

"The Gɒvernment haz for the last twenti yearz taken ediukashon ɒnder its kare. They diveided the sɒbjekts ov instrɒkshon intu siks gradez. The heiest point that woz atempted in the Gɒvernment Skoolz woz that a piupil shud be abel tu read with tolerabel eaze and ekspreshon a pasej from a niuzpaper, and tu spel the same with a tolerabel amount ov akiurasi."

Let ɒs luk at the rezɒlts az they apear in the report ov the Komíti ov Kounsil on Ediukashon for 1870–71:

Skoolz or Departments ɒnder separate hed teacherz in Ingland and Walez inspekted diuring the year 31st Augɒst, 1870,		15,287
Sertifikated asistant, and piupil teacherz emploid in theze skoolz		28,033
Skolarz in daili averej atendans throughout the year		1,168,981
Skolarz prezent on the day ov inspekshon		1,473,883
Skolarz prezented for ekzaminashon:		
Ɒnder ten yearz ov aje	473,444	
Over ten yearz ov aje	292.144	
		765,588
Skolarz prezented for Standard VI.:		
Ɒnder ten yearz ov aje	227	
Over ten yearz ov aje	32,953	
		33,180
Skolarz who past in Standard VI.:		
1. Reading a short paragraf from a niuzpaper		30,985
2. Reiting the same from diktashon		27.989
3. Arithmetik		22,839

Therfor, les than wʋn skolar for each teacher, and les than two skolarz for each skool inspekted, reacht Standard VI.

In 1873 the state ov thingz, akording tu the ofishal retʋrnz ov the Ediukashon Department, woz mʋch the same. Ferst ov all, ther ought tu hav been at skool 4,600,000 children between the ajez ov three and therteen. The nʋmber ov children on the rejister ov inspekted skoolz woz 2,218,598. Out ov thát number, about 200,000 leav skool aniuali, their ediukashon beïng sʋpozed tu be finisht. Out ov theze 200,000, neinti per sent. leav without reaching the 6th Standard, eighti per sent. without reaching the 5th, and siksti per sent. without reaching the 4th Standard.

The report for 1874–75 showz an inkreas ov children on the buks, bʋt the proporshon ov children pasing in the varis standardz iz sʋbstanshali the same. (See "Popiular Ediukashon," bei E. Jones, B.A., an eks-skoolmaster, 1875.) It iz kalkiulated that for sʋch rezʋlts az theze the kʋntri, hwether bei taksashon or bei volʋntari kontribiushonz, payz nearli £3,500,000 aniuali.

Akording tu the same authoriti, Mr. E. Jones, it nou takes from siks tu seven yearz tu lern the arts ov reading and speling with a fair degree ov intelijens —thát iz, about 2,000 ourz; and tu meni meindz the difikʋltiz ov orthografi ar insʋrmountabel. The bʋlk ov the children pas through the Gʋvernment skoolz without having akweird the abiliti tu read with eaze and intelijens.

"An averej cheild," sez anʋther skoolmaster, "begining skool at seven, ought tu be abel tu read the

Niu Testament fluentli at eleven or twelv yearz ov aje, and at therteen or fourteen ought tu be abel tu read a gud leading artikel with eaze and ekspreshon." That iz, with seven ourz a week for forti weeks for feiv yearz, a cheild rekweirz 1,400 ourz' wɒrk, tu be abel tu read the Niu Testament.

After a kareful ekzaminashon ov yɒng men and wimen from therteen tu twenti yearz ov aje in the faktoriz ov Birmingham, it woz proved that onli 4½ per sent. wer abel tu read a simpel sentens from an ordinari skool-buk with intelijens and akiurasi.

This apleiz tu the lower klasez. Bɒt with regard tu the heier klasez the kase seemz almost wɒrs; for Dr. Morell, in hiz "Maniual ov Speling," aserts that out ov 1,972 failiurz in the Sivil Servis Ekzaminashonz 1,866 kandidates wer plɒkt for speling.

So mɒch for the piupilz. Amɒng the teacherz themselvz it woz found in Amerika that out ov wɒn hɒndred komon wɒrdz the best speler amɒng the eighti or neinti teacherz ekzamind faild in wɒn, sɒm preiz-takerz faild in four or feiv, and sɒm ɒtherz mist over forti. The Depiuti State Siuperintendent deklared that on an averej the teacherz ov the State wud fail in speling tu the ekstent ov 25 per sent.

Hwot, houever, iz even more seriɒs than all this iz not the great waste ov teim in lerning tu read, and the almost komplete failiur in nashonal ediukashon, bɒt the aktiual mischef dɒn bei sɒbjekting yɒng meindz tu the illojikal and tediɒs drɒjeri ov lerning tu read Inglish az speld at prezent. Everithing they hav tu lern in reading (or pronɒnsiashon) and speling iz irrashonal; wɒn rule kontradikts the ɒther, and each statement haz tu be aksepted simpli on authoriti, and with a komplete disregard ov all thoze rashonal instinkts which lei dormant in the cheild, and ought tu be awakend bei everi keind ov helthi ekserseiz.

Ei nó ther ar personz who kan defend enithing, and who hold that it iz diu tu this veri disiplin that the Inglish karakter iz hwot it iz; that it retainz respekt for authoriti; that it dɒz not rekweir a reazon for everithing; and that it dɒz not admit that hwot iz inkonseivabel iz therefor imposibel. Even Inglish orthodoksi haz been trast bak tu thát hiden sourse, bekauz a cheild akɒstomd tu believe that t-h-o-u-g-h iz *tho*, and that t-h-r-o-u-g-h iz *throo*, wud afterwardz believe enithing. It may be so; stil ei dout hwether even sɒch objekts wud jɒstifei sɒch meanz. Lord Lytton sez, "A more leiing, round-about, pɒzel-heded deluzhon than thát bei hwich we konfiúz the klear instinkts ov truth in our akɒrsed sistem ov speling woz never konkokted bei the father ov fols·hud. . . . Hou kan a sistem ov ediukashon flɒrish that beginz bei so monstrɒs a fols·hud, hwich the sens ov hearing sɒfeisez tu kontradikt?"

Though it may seem a wɒrk ov siupererogashon tu bring forward stil more fakts in sɒport ov the jeneral kondemnashon past on Inglish speling, a fiu ekstrakts from a pamflet bei Mr. Meiklejohn, late Asistant-Komishoner ov the Endoud Skoolz Komishon for Skotland, may here feind a plase.

"Ther ar therteen diferent wayz ov reprezenting the sound ov long *o*:—*note, boat, toe, yeoman, soul, row, sew, hautboy, beau, owe, floor, oh! O!*"

And agen (p. 16),

"Double-you-aitch-eye-see-aitch	is	*which*
Tea-are-you-tea-aitch . .	"	*truth*
Bee-o-you-gee-aitch . .	"	*bough*

See-are-eh-bee . . .	"	*crab*
Bee-ee-eh-see-aitch . . .	"	*beach*
Oh-you-gee-aitch-tee . .	"	*ought*
Oh-enn-see-ee . . .	"	*once*

"Or, tu sɒm ɒp the hole indeitment agenst the kɒlprit: 1. Out ov the twenti-siks leterz, onli eight ar true, fikst, and permanent kwolitiz—thát iz, are true both tu eí and ear. 2. Ther ar therti-eight distinkt soundz in our spoken langwej; and ther ar about 400 distinkt simbolz (simpel and kompound) tu reprezent theze therti-eight soundz. In ɒther wɒrdz, ther ar 400 servants tu do the wɒrk ov therti-eight. 3. Ov the twenti-siks leterz, fifteen hav akweird a habit ov heiding themselvz. They ar riten and printed; bɒt the ear haz no akount ov them; sɒch ar *w* in *wrong*, and *gh* in *right*. 4. The vouel soundz ar printed in diferent wayz; a long *o*, for ekzampel, haz therteen printed simbolz tu reprezent it. 5. Fourteen vouel soundz hav 190 printed simbolz atácht tu their servis. 6. The singel vouel *e* haz feiv diferent fɒnkshonz; it ought onli tu hav wɒn. 7. Ther ar at least 1,300 wɒrdz in hwich the simbol and the sound ar at varians —in hwich the wɒrd iz not sounded az it iz printed. 8. Ov theze 1,300, 800 ar monosilabelz—the komonest wɒrdz, and sɒpozed tu be eazier for children. 9. The hole langwej ov kɒntri children leiz within theze wɒrdz; and meni agrikɒltiural laborerz go from the kradel tu the grave with a stok ov no more than 500 wɒrdz."

The kwestion, then, that wil hav tu be anserd sooner or later iz this:—Kan this ɒnsistematik sistem ov speling Inglish be aloud tu go on for ever? Iz everi Inglish cheild, az kompared with ɒther children, tu be mɒlkted in two or three yearz ov hiz leif in order tu lern it? Ar the lower klasez tu go through skool without lerning tu read and reit their own langwej intelijentli? And iz the kɒntri tu pay milionz everi year for this ɒter failiur ov nashonal ediukashon? Ei do not believ that sɒch a state ov thingz wil be aloud tu kontiniu for ever, partikiularli az a remedi iz at hand—a remidi that haz nou been tested for twenti or therti yearz, and that haz anserd ekstremli wel. Ei mean Mr. Pitman'z sistem ov fonetik reiting, az apleid tu Inglish. Ei shal not enter here intu eni miniút diskɒshon ov fonetiks, or re-open the kontroversi hwich haz arizen between the advokets ov diferent sistemz ov fonetik reiting. Ov kourse, ther ar diferent degreez ov ekselens in diferent sistemz ov fonetik speling; bɒt even the wɒrst ov theze sistemz iz infinitli siuperior tu the tradishonal speling.

Ei giv Mr. Pitman'z alfabet, hwich komprehendz the therti-siks broad tipikal soundz ov the Inglish langwej, and aseinz tu each a definit sein. With theze therti-siks seinz, Inglish kan be riten rashonali and red eazili; and, hwot iz most important, it haz been proved bei an eksperiens ov meni yearz, bei niumerɒs pɒblikashonz, and bei praktikal eksperiments in teaching both children and adɒlts, that sɒch a sistem az Mr. Pitman'z iz perfektli praktikal.

THE PHONETIC ALPHABET.

The phonetic letters in the first column are pronounced like the italic letters in the words that follow. The last column contains the *names* of the letters.

CONSONANTS.

Mutes.

P	p	ro*p*e	pį
B	b	ro*b*e	bį
T	t	fa*t*e	tį
D	d	fa*d*e	dį
Є	ç	e*tch*	çε
J	j	e*dg*e	jε
K	k	lee*k*	kε
G	g	lea*gu*e	gε

Continuants.

F	f	sa*f*e	ef
V	v	sa*v*e	vį
Ŧ	ŧ	wrea*th*	iŧ
Đ	đ	wrea*the*	đį
S	s	hi*ss*	es
Z	z	hi*s*	zį
Σ	ʃ	vi*ci*ous	iʃ
Ʒ	ʒ	vi*si*on	ʒį

Nasals.

M	m	see*m*	em
N	n	see*n*	en
Ŋ	ŋ	si*ng*	iŋ

Liquids.

L	l	fa*ll*	el
R	r	*r*a*r*e	ar

Coalescents.

W	w	*w*et	wε
Y	y	*y*et	yε

Aspirate.

H	h	*h*ay	εç

VOWELS.

Guttural.

A	a	*a*m	at
Ɑ	ɑ	*a*lms	ɑ
E	e	*e*ll	et
Ɛ	ε	*a*le	ε
I	i	*i*ll	it
Ɨ	į	*ee*l	į

Labial.

O	o	*o*n	ot
Ω	ω	*a*ll	ω
Ȣ	ȣ	*u*p	ȣt
Θ	ɵ	*o*pe	ɵ
U	u	f*u*ll	ut
Ɯ	ɥ	f*oo*d	ɥ

DIPHTHONGS: EI ei, IU iu, OU ωu, AI ai, OI oi,
as heard in b*y*, n*ew*, n*ow* K*ai*ser, b*oy*.

[In the next fourteen pages, five of the new letters will be employed, viz., ɑ, ɤ, ŧ, ʒ, ŋ, for the sounds represented by the italic letters in *f*a*ther*, s*o*n, b*u*t, *th*in, vi*s*ion, si*ng*.]

Nou ei ask eni intelijent reader who dɤz not ŧiŋk that everiŧiŋ niu and stranje iz, *ipso facto*, ridikiulɤs and absɤrd, hwether after a fiu dayz' praktis, he or she wud not read and reit Iŋglish, akordiŋ tu Mr. Pitman'z sistem, with perfekt eaze? Ov kourse it takes more than feiv minits tu master it, and more than feiv minits tu form an opinion ov its merits. Bɤt admitiŋ even that peopel ov a serten aje shud feind this niu alfabet trɤbelsɤm, we mɤst not forget that no reform kan be karid out without a jenerashon or two ov marterz; and hwot true reformerz hav tu ŧiŋk ov iz not themselvz, bɤt thoze who kɤm after them—thoze, in fakt, who ar nou growiŋ ɤp tu inherit hereafter, hwether they leik it or not, all the gud and all the evil hwich we chooz tu leav tu them.

It meit be sed, houever, that Mr. Pitman'z sistem, beiŋ enteirli fonetik, iz too radikal a reform, and that meni and the wɤrst irregiularitiz in Iŋglish speliŋ kud be removed without goïŋ kweit so far. The prinsipel that hɑf a loaf iz beter than no bred iz not without sɤm truŧ, and in meni kasez we nó that a polisi ov kompromeiz haz been prodɤktiv ov veri gud rezɤlts. Bɤt, on the ɤther hand, this hɑf-harted polisi haz often retarded a real and komplete reform ov ekzistiŋ abiúsez; and in the kase ov a reform ov speliŋ, ei almost dout hwether the difikɜltiz inherent in haf-meʒurz ar not az great az the difikɜltiz ov kariiŋ a komplete reform. If the wɜrld iz not redi for reform, let ɜs wait. It seemz far beter, and at all events far more onest, tu wait til it iz redi than tu kari the relɜktant wɜrld with you a litel way, and then tu feind that all the impɜlsiv forse iz spent, and the greater part ov the abiúsez establisht on fermer ground than ever.

Mr. Jones,* who reprezents the konsiliatori reformerz ov speliŋ, wud be satisfeid with a moderet skeme ov speliŋ reform, in hwich, bei obzerviŋ analoji and folowiŋ presedent in olteriŋ a komparativli small nɜmber ov wɜrdz, it wud be posibel tu simplifei orŧografi tu a konsiderabel ekstent without upleiiŋ eni niu prinsipel, or introdiúsiŋ niu leterz, and yet tu rediús the teim and labor in teachiŋ readiŋ and speliŋ bei at least wɜn-haf. It meit at all events be posibel tu setel the speliŋ ov thoze two or three ŧouzand wɜrdz hwich at prezent ar speld difẹrentli bei diferent auŧoritiz. This skeme, advokated bei Mr. Jones, iz sertenli veri klever; and if it had a ċhans ov sɜkses, ei meiself shud konsider it a great step in adváns. Mei onli dout iz hwether, in a kase leik this, a small meʒur ov reform wud be karid more eazili than a komplete reform. It iz diferent in Jerman, hwere the diseaz haz not spred so far. Here the Komíti

* Popular Education—A Revision of English Spelling a National Necessity. By E. Jones, B.A. London, 1875.

apointed bei Gɤvernment tu konsider the kwestion ov a reform ov speliŋ haz deklared in favor ov sɤm sɤch moderet prinsipelz az Mr. Jones advokates for Iŋglish. In Iŋglish, houever, the difikɤlti leiz in chanjiŋ eniƀiŋ; and if the prinsipel ov eni chanje iz wɤns admited, it wud reali be eazier, ei believ, tu begin *de novo* than tu chanje sɤmƀiŋ, and leav the rest ɤnchanjed.

Let ɤs nou see hou Mr. Pitman'z or eni similar sistem ov fonetik reitiŋ haz wɤrkt hwere it haz been put tu the test.

Mr. William White reits: "Ei speak from eksperiens. Ei hav taught poor children in Glasgow tu read the Sermon on the Mount after a kourse ov eksersеizez ekstendiŋ over no more than siks ourz."

The folowiŋ iz an ekstrakt from a leter riten sɤm teim ago bei the late Mr. William Colbourne, manajer ov the Dorset Baŋk at Stɤrminster, tu a frend ov hiz a skoolmaster. He sez:—

"Mei litel Sidney, who iz nou a fiu mɤnƀs more than four yearz old, wil read eni fonetik buk without the sleitest hezitashon; the hardest namez or the loŋgest wɤrdz in the Old or Niu Testament form no obstakel tu him. And hou loŋ do you ƀiŋk it tuk me (for ei am hiz teacher) tu impart tu him this pouer? Hwei sɤmƀiŋ les than eight ourz! You may believ it or not, az you leik, bɤt ei am konfident that not more than that amount ov teim woz spent on him, and that woz in snachez ov feiv minits at a teim, hweil tea woz getiŋ redi. Ei no you wil be inkleind tu say, 'All that iz veri wel, bɤt hwot iz the use ov readiŋ fonetik buks? he iz stil az far of, and may be farther, from readiŋ romanik buks.' Bɤt in this you ar mistaken. Take anɤther ekzampel. Hiz nekst elder brɤther, a boi ov siks yearz, haz had a fonetik ediukashon so far. Hwot iz the konsekwens? Hwei, readiŋ in the ferst staje woz so deleitful and eazi a ŧiŋ tu him that he taught himself tu read romanikali, and it wud be a difikɤlt mater tu feind wɤn boi in twenti, ov a korespondiŋ aje, that kud read haf so wel az he kan in eni buk. Agen, mei oldest boi haz riten more fonetik shorthand and loŋhand, perhaps, than eni boi ov hiz aje (eleven yearz) in the kiŋdom; and nowɤn ei daresay haz had les tu do with that absɤrditi ov absɤrditiz, the speliŋ-buk! He iz nou at a ferst-rate skool in Wiltshire, and in the haf-year presediŋ Kristmas, he karid of the preiz for orŧografi in a kontest with boiz sɤm ov them hiz seniorz bei yearz!"

Bei the adopshon ov the fonetik alfabet, the difikɤltiz that lei in the way ov forenerz lerniŋ Iŋglish, also wud be dɤn away with. The Rev. Newman Hall reits, "Ei met with a Danish jentelman the ɤther day who heili preizd the Iŋglish fonotipik Niu Testament. It had been ov great use tu him, and *enabeld him tu read [buks in the komon speliŋ] without an instrɤkter*, removiŋ the greatest obstakel in akweiriŋ Iŋglish, the monstrɤs anomaliʒ ov pronɤnsiashon." Ekzampelz leik theze go a loŋ way.

Mr. A. J. Ellis, than whom nowɤn haz labord more devotidli for a reform ov speliŋ, az a ferst step in a reform ov nashonal ediukashon, and who haz himself elaborated several most injeniɤs sistemz ov fonetik reitiŋ, givz ɤs the folowiŋ az the rezɤltz ov hiz praktikal eksperiens:

"With the fonetik sistem ov speliŋ, the Primer iz masterd within ŧree mɤnŧs at most. The children then proseed tu praktis this fonetik readiŋ for sɤm teim, til they kan read with fluensi from the jeneral luk ov the wɤrd, and not from konsideriŋ the pouerz ov its leterz. Ŧree mɤnŧs more, at most, ar rekweird for this staje.

"Hwen this pouer ov fluent readiŋ in fonetik print iz akweird, buks in the ordinari print, siuted tu their kapasitiz, ar tu be put intu the children'z handz and they ar told tu read them. Each wɤrd hwich they fail tu ges iz told them immedietli; but it iz found that children ar mostli abel tu read the ordinari print without eni fɤrther instrɤkshon. The teim nesesari for kompletiŋ this step may be taken, at the loŋgest, az two mɤnŧs, so that the hole teim ov lerniŋ tu read in the ordinari print, on the Readiŋ Reform sistem, may be rekond az feiv ourz a week for eight mɤnŧs. The hole task haz, in meni kasez, been akomplisht in les teim, even in ŧree mɤnŧs. On the ɤther hand, in wɤn skool hwere it iz uzed, eleven mɤnϑs ar okiupeid, az the master feindz it advantajɤs in ɤther respekts tu keep the piupil loŋger at fonetik readiŋ. Bɤt onli wɤn our a day iz rekweird." Mr. Ellis sɤmz ɤp az folowz :

"Kareful eksperiments in teachiŋ children ov varisɤs ajez and raŋks, and even pauperz and kriminal adɤlts, hav establisht—

"1. That piupilz may be taught tu read buks in fonetik print, slowli bɤt shureli, in from ten tu forti ourz, and wil atain konsiderabel fluensi after a fiu weeks' praktis.

"2. That hwen the piupilz hav ataind fluensi in readiŋ from fonetik print, a veri fiu ourz wil sɤfeis tu giv them the same fluensi in readiŋ ordinari print.

"3. That the hole teim nesesari for impartiŋ a nolej ov boϑ fonetik and ordinari readiŋ dɤz not ekseed eight mɤnϑs for children ov averej intelijens, between four and feiv yearz ov aje, taught in klas, at skool, not more than haf-an-our tu an our each day; and that in this teim an abiliti tu read iz akweird siuperior tu that uʒuali ataind in two or ϑree teimz the period on the old plan; hweil the pronɤnsiashon ov the piupil iz mɤch improved, hiz interest in hiz stɤdi iz kept aleiv, and a lojikal trainiŋ ov endiuriŋ valiu iz given tu hiz meind bei the habitiual analisis and sinϑesis ov spoken soundz.

"4. That thoze taught tu read in this maner akweir the art ov ordinari speliŋ more redili than thoze instrɤkted on the old meϑod."

Tu all who no Mr. A. J. Ellis, this evidens wil be be sɤfishent az tu the praktikal usefulnes ov the Fonetik Sistem ov speliŋ. Tu thoze who wish for more evidens ei rekomend a pamflet bei Mr. G. Withers, "The Iŋglish Laŋgwej Speld az Pronounst," 1874; and wɤn bei Dr. J. W. Martin, "The Gordian Not Kɤt," 1875, hwere they wil feind the konkɤrent testimoni ov praktikal teacherz in Iŋgland, Skotland, Eirland, and Amerika, all agreeiŋ that, boŧ az a praktikal and a lojikal trainiŋ, the Fonetik Sistem haz proved the greatest sɤkses.

Ther remainz, therefor, this wɤn objekshon onli, that hwotever the praktikal, and hwotever the ŧeoretikal advantejez ov the fonetik sistem may be, it wud ɤterli destroi the historikal or etimolojikal karakter ov the Iŋglish laŋgwej.

Sɤpoze it did; hwot then? The Reformashon iz sɤpozed tu hav destroid the historikal karakter ov the Iŋglish Chɤrch, and that sentimental grievans iz stil felt bei sɤm stiudents ov ekleziastikal antikwitiz. Bɤt did Iŋgland, did all the reali progresiv nashonz ov Europe, alou this sentimental grievans tu outweigh the praktikal and ŧeoretikal advantejez ov Protestant Reform? Laŋgwej iz not made for skolarz and etimolojists; and if the hole rase ov Iŋglish etimolojists wer reali tu be swept away bei the introdɤkshon ov a Speliŋ Reform, ei hope they wud be the ferst tu rejois in sakrifeiziŋ themselvz in so gud a kauz.

Bɤt iz it reali the kase that the historikal kontiniúiti ov the Iŋglish laŋgwej wud bei broken bei the adopshon ov fonetik speliŋ, and that the profeshon ov the etimolojist wud be gon for ever? Ei say No, most emfatikali, tu boŧ propozishonz. If the seiens ov laŋgwej haz proved eniŧiŋ, it haz proved that all laŋgwejez chanje akordiŋ tu law, and with konsiderabel uniformiti. If, therefor, the reitiŋ folowd, *pari passu,* on the chanjez in pronɤnsiashon, hwot iz kalld the etimolojikal konshɤsnes ov the speakerz and the readerz—ei speak, ov kourse, ov ediukated peopel onli—wud not sɤfer in the least. If we retain the feeliŋ ov an etimolojikal konekshon between *gentlemanly* and *gentlemanlike*, we shud shureli retain it hwether we reit *gentlemanly* or *gentelmanli.* If we feel that *think* and *thought*, *bring* and *brought*, *buy* and *bought*, *freight* and *fraught*, beloŋ tugether, shud we feel it les if we rote *ŧωt, brωt, bωt, frωt?* If, in speakiŋ, thoze who no Latin retain the feeliŋ that wɤrdz endiŋ in *-ation* korespond tu Latin wɤrdz in *-atio*, wud they looz the feeliŋ if they saw the same wɤrdz speld with *ɛʃon,* or even "-eʃɤn?" Do they not rekogneiz Latin *-itia* in *-ice;* or *-ilis* in *-le*, az in *-able* (Latin *abilis*)? If the skolar noz, at wɤns, that sɤch wɤrdz az *barbarous, anxious, circus, genius,* ar ov Latin orijin, wud he hezitate if the last silabel in all ov them wer uniformli riten "ɤs?" Nay, iz not the prezent speliŋ ov *barbarous* and *anxious* enteirli misleadiŋ, bei konfoundiŋ wɤrdz endiŋ in

-*osus*, svch az *famous* (*famosus*) with wvrdz endiŋ in -*us*, leik *barbarous*, *anxious*, ets.? Bekauz the Italianz reit *filosofo*, ar they les aware than the Iŋglish, who reit *philosopher*, and the French, who reit *philosophe*, that they hav before them the Latin *philosophus*, the Greek *φιλόσοφος*? If we reit *f* in *fansi*, hwei not in *phantom*? If in *frenzy* and *frantic*, hwei not in *phrenology*? A laŋgwej hwich tolerates *vial* for *phial*, need not shiver at *filosofer*. Everi eidiukated speaker nóz that svch wvrdz az *honour*, *ardour*, *colour*, *odour*, *labour*, *vigour*, *error*, *emperor*, hav past from Latin tu French, and from French tu Iŋglish. Wud he nó it les if all wer speld aleik, svch az *onor* (*onorable*), *ardor*, *vigor* (*vigorous*), *labor* (*laborious*), or even "onvr, ardvr, vigvr?" The old speliŋ ov *emperor*, *doctor*, *governor*, and *error*, woz *emperour*, *doctour*, *governour*, and *errour*. If theze kud be chanjed, hwei not the rest? Spenser haz *neibor* for *neighbor*, and it iz difikvlt tu say hwot woz gaind bei chanjiŋ -*bor* intu -*bour* in svch piurli Sakson wvrdz az *neighbor*, *harbor*. No dout if we see *laugh* riten with *gh* at the end, thoze who nó Jerman ar at wvns remeinded ov its etimolojikal konekshon with the Jerman *lachen*; bvt we shud soon nó the same bei analoji, if we found not onli "laf," bvt "kof" for *cough* (Jerman, *keuchen*), "envf" for *enough* (Jerman, *genug*), ets. In "draft," fonetik speliŋ haz nearli svplanted the so-kalld historikal speliŋ *draught*; in "dwarf" (*dwergh*, *thweorh*) and in "ruff" (*rough*), altugether.

Hwot peopel kall the etimolojikal konshʊsnes ov the speaker iz striktli a mater ov oratorikal sentiment onli, and it wud remain nearli az stróŋ az it iz nou, hwotever speliŋ be adopted. Bʊt even if it shud sʊfer here and there, we ought tu bear in meind that, eksept for oratorikal pʊrposez, that konshʊsnes, konfeind az it iz tu a veri fiu ediukated peopel, iz ov veri small importans, ʊnles it haz ferst been korekted bei a strikt etimolojikal disiplin. Without that, it often dejenerates intu hwot iz kalld "popiular etimoloji," and aktiuali tendz, in sʊm kasez, tu vishiate the korekt speliŋ ov wʊrdz.

Ei hav frekwentli dwelt on this before, in order tu show hou, hwot iz nou kalld the etimolojikal or historikal speliŋ ov wʊrdz iz, in meni kasez, ʊterli ʊnetimolojikal and ʊnhistorikal. We spel *to delight*, and thʊs indiús meni peopel tu believ that this wʊrd iz sʊmhou konekted with *light* [lux], or *light* [levis]; hwereaz the old speliŋ woz *to delyt* or *to delite* (Tyndale), reprezentiŋ the old French *deleiter*. On the ʊther hand, we feind for *quite* and *smite*, the old speliŋ *quight*, *smight*, hwich may be old and historikal, bʊt iz deseidedli ʊnetimolojikal.

Sovereign and *foreign* ar speld az if they wer konekted with *reign*, *regnum*; the true etimoloji ov the former beiŋ *superanus*, Old French, *sovrain*, Old Iŋglish, *soveraine*; hweil *foreign* iz the late Latin *foraneus;* Old French *forain;* Old Iŋglish *forein.* And hwei du we reit *to feign?* Archbishop Trench ("Iŋglish Past and Prezent," p. 238) ŧiŋks the *g* in *feign* iz elokwent tu the eí; bʊt its elokwens iz misleadiŋ. *Feign* iz not taken from Latin *fingo,* az litel az *honour* iz taken from Latin *honor.* *Feign* kʊmz from the Old French *faindre;* it woz in Old Iŋglish *faynen* and *feynen,* and it woz therefor a mere etimolojikal feint tu insert the *g* ov the Latin *fingo,* and the French *feignant.* The Old Iŋglish *shammfasst* (Orm.), formd leik *stedefasst* (stedfast), iz nou speld *shamefaced,* az if it had sʊmŧiŋ tu do with a blʊshiŋ fase. *Aghast,* insted ov Old Iŋglish *agast,* iz sʊpozed tu luk more freitful bekauz it remeindz ʊs ov *ghost.* The French *lanterne* woz riten *lant-horn,* az if it had been so kalld from the transparent sheets ov horn that enklozed the leit. The *s* in *island* owez its orijin tu a mistaken belief that the wʊrd iz konekted with *isle* (*insula*), hwereaz it iz the Aŋglo-Sakson *eáland* (Jerman *eiland*), that iz, water-land. The speliŋ *iland* woz stil kʊrent in Shakspere'z teim. In *aisle,* too, the *s* iz ʊnetimolojikal, though it iz historikal, az haviŋ been taken over from the Old French *aisle.*

This tendensi tu olter the speliŋ in order tu impart tu a wʊrd, at all hazardz, an etimolojikal karakter, beginz even in Latin, hwere *postumus,* a siuperlativ ov *post,* woz sʊmteimz riten *posthumus,* az if, hwen apleid tu a late-born sʊn, it woz dereivd from *humus.*

In Iŋglish, this fols speliŋ iz retaind in *posthumous*. *Cena* woz speld bei peopel who wonted tu show their nolej ov Greek *cœna*, az if konekted with *κοινή*, hwich it iz not.

Bɤt nou let ɤs luk more karefuli intu the far more important statement, that the Iŋglish laŋgwej, if riten fonetikali, wud reali looz its historikal and etimolojikal karakter. The ferst kwestion iz, in hwot sens kan the prezent speliŋ ov Iŋglish be kalld historikal? We hav onli tu go bak a veri short way in order tu see the modern ɤpstart karakter ov hwot iz kalld historikal speliŋ. We nou reit *pleasure*, *measure*, and *feather*, bɤt not veri loŋ ago, in Spenser'z teim, theze wɤrdz wer speld *plesure*, *mesure*, *fether*. Tyndale rote *frute;* the *i* in *fruit* iz a mere restorashon ov the French speliŋ. For *debt*, on the kontrari, we feind, bɤt ŧree or four hɤndred yearz ago, *dett*. This iz more historikal therefor than *debt*, bekauz in French, from hwich the wɤrd woz borowd, the *b* had disapeard, and it woz a piurli etimolojikal fansi tu restore it. The *b* woz leikweiz re-introdiúst in *doubt*, bɤt the *p* woz not restored in *tu kount* (French *compter*, Latin *computare*), hwere *p* had at least the same reit az *b* in *doute*. Thɤs *receipt* reziúmz the Latin *p*, bɤt *deceit* dɤz without it. Tu *deign* keeps the *g*, tu *disdain* dɤz without it. Ther iz anɤther *b* hwich haz a serten historikal air in sɤm Iŋglish wɤrdz, bɤt hwich woz orijinali piurli fonetik, and iz nou simpli siupérfluɤs. The old wɤrd for *member* woz *lim.* In sɤch kompoundz az *lim-lama,* lim(b)-lame; *lim-leas,* lim(b)-less; it woz imposibel tu avoid the interkalashon ov a *b* in pronɤnsiashon. In this maner the *b* krept in, and we hav nou tu teach that in *limb, crumb* (crume), *thumb* (thuma), the *b* mɤst be riten, bɤt not pronoúnst. Agen, *tung* (Jerman *zunge*), *yung* (Jerman *jung*), az speld bei Spenser, hav a far more historikal aspekt than *tongue* and *young.*

If we wisht tu reit historikali, we ought tu reit *salm* insted ov *psalm,* for the inishal *p,* beïŋ lost in pronɤnsiashon, woz dropt in reitiŋ at a veri erli teim (Aŋglo-Sakson *sealm*), and woz re-introdiúst simpli tu pleaz sɤm ekleziastikal etimolojists; also *nevew* (French *neveu*) insted ov *nephew,* hwich iz both ɤnetimolojikal and ɤnfonetik.

In hwot sens kan it be kalld historikal speliŋ if the old pluralz ov *mouse* and *louse,* hwich wer *mys* and *lys,* ar nou speld *mice* and *lice?* The plural ov *goose* iz not speld *geece* bɤt *geese,* yet everibodi nóz hou tu pronoúns it. The same mistaken atempt at an okazhonal fonetik speliŋ haz separated *dice* from *die,* and *pence* from *pens,* thát iz, *penyes;* hweil in *nurse,* hwere the speliŋ *nurce* wud hav been useful az remeindiŋ ɤs ov its true etimon *nourrice,* the *c* haz been replast bei *s.*

Ther ar, in fakt, meni speliŋz hwich wud be at the same teim more historikal and more fonetik. Hwei reit *little,* hwen nowɤn pronoúnsez *little,* and hwen the old speliŋ woz *lytel*? Hwei *girdle*, hwen the old speliŋ woz *girdel*? The same rule apleiz tu nearli all wɤrdz endiŋ in *le*, sɤch az *sickle*, *ladle*, *apple*, ets., hwere the etimoloji iz kompleteli obskiúrd bei the prezent orþografi. Hwei *scent*, bɤt *dissent*, hwen even Milton stil rote *sent*? Hwei *ache*, insted ov the Shaksperian *ake*? Hwei *cat*, bɤt *kitten*; hwei *cow*, bɤt *kine*? Hwei *accede*, *precede*, *secede*, bɤt *exceed*, *proceed*, *succeed*? Hwei, indeed, eksept tu waste the preshɤs teim ov children?

And if it iz difikɤlt tu say hwot konstitiuts historikal speliŋ, it iz ekwali perpleksiŋ tu defein the real meaniŋ ov etimolojikal speliŋ. For hwere ar we tu stop? It wud be konsiderd veri ɤnetimolojikal wer we tu reit *nee* insted ov *knee*, *now* insted ov *know*, *night* insted ov *knight*; yet nowɤn komplainz about the los ov the inishal *h*, the reprezentativ ov an orijinal *k*, in *loaf*, A. S. hlâf (cf. κλίβανος), in *ring* (A. S. *hring*); in *lade*, *ladder*, *neck*, ets.

If we ar tu reit etimolojikali, then hwei not retɤrn tu *loverd*, or *hlaford*, insted ov *lord*? tu *nosethrill*, or *nosethirle* insted ov *nostril*; tu *swister* insted ov *sister*; hwich wud not be more trɤbelsɤm than *sword*. *Wifmann* shureli wud be beter than *woman*; *meadwife* beter than *midwife*; *godspel* beter than *gospel*, *ortyard* beter than *orchard*, *puisne* beter than *puny*. Frekwentli the prezent rekogneizd speliŋ luks etimolojikal, bɤt iz ɤterli ɤnetimolojikal. *Righteous* luks leik an ajektiv in *-eous*, sɤch az *plenteous*, bɤt it iz reali a Sakson wɤrd, *rightwis*, thát iz *rightwise*, formd leik *otherwise*, ets.

Could iz riten with an *l* in analoji tu *would*, bɤt hweil the *l* iz jɤstifeid in *would* from *will*, and *should* from *shall* we feind the Old Iŋglish imperfekt ov *can* riten *cuthe*, then *couthe*, *coude*. The *l*, therefor, iz neither fonetik nor etimolojikal. Nɤ-ŧiŋ, agen, kan be more misleadiŋ tu an etimolojist than the prezent speliŋ ov *whole* and *hale*. Both kɤm from the same sourse, the Goŧik *hail-s*, Sanskrit *kalya-s*, meaniŋ orijinali, *fit*, *redi;* then *sound*, *complete*, *whole*. In Aŋglo-Sakson we hav *hæl*, hole; and *hal*, helŧi, without eni trase ov a *w*, either before or after. The Old Iŋglish *halsum*, holesɤm, iz the Jerman *hailsam*. *Whole*, therefor, iz a mere mis-speliŋ the *w* haviŋ probabli been aded in analoji tu *who*, *which*, ets. From a piurli etimolojikal point ov viu, the *w* iz roŋli left out before *h* in *hou;* for az Aŋglo-Sakson *hwy* bekame *why*, Aŋglo-Sakson *hwa* shud hav bekɤm *whow*.

If we reali atempted tu reit etimolojikali, we shud hav tu reit *bridegroom* without the *r*, bekauz *groom* iz a mere korɤpshon ov *guma*, man, Aŋglo-Sakson *bryd-guma*. We shud hav tu reit *burse* insted ov *purse*, az in *disburse*. In fakt, it iz difikɤlt tu say hwere we shud stop. Hwei do we not reit *metal* insted ov *mettle*, *worthship* insted ov *worship*, *chirurgeon* insted ov *surgeon*, *furhlong* (thát iz, fɤrow loŋ) insted ov *furlong*, *feordhing* (thát iz fourθ part) insted ov *farthing*? If we reit piuni *puisne*, we meit az wel reit *post-natus*. We meit spel koi, *quietus;* pert, *apertus;* priest, *presbyter;* master, *magister;* sekston, *sacristan;* alms, *eleemosyne*, ets. If enibodi wil tel me at hwot date etimolojikal speliŋ iz tu begin, hwether at 1,500 A. D., or at 1,000 A. D., or 500 A. D., ei am wiliŋ tu diskɤs the kwestion. Til then, ei beg leav tu say that etimolojikal speliŋ wud play greater havok in Iŋglish than fonetik speliŋ, even if we wer tu draw a lein not more than feiv hɤndred yearz ago.

The two stroŋgest argiuments, therefor, agenst fonetik speliŋ, nameli, that it wud destroi the historikal and etimolojikal karakter ov the Iŋglish laŋgwej, ar, after all, bɤt veri parshali true. Here and there, no dout, the etimoloji and histori ov an Iŋglish wɤrd meit be obskiúrd bei fonetik speliŋ; az if, for instans, we rote "Yɥσp" insted ov *Europe*. Bɤt even then analoji wud help ɤs, and teach thoze who nó Greek, ov whom ther ar not meni, that "Yɥr" in sɤch wɤrdz az *Europe*, *Eurydice*, reprezented the Greek εὐρύς. The real anser, houever, iz, that nowɤn kud onestli kall the prezent sistem ov speliŋ either historikal or etimolojikal; and, ei believ, that, taken az a hole, the los okaʒond bei konsistent fonetik speliŋ wud not be greater than the gain.

Anɤther objekshon ɤrjd agenst fonetik speliŋ, nameli, that with it it wud be imposibel tu distiŋgwish homonimz, mɤst be met in the same way. No dout it iz a serten advantej if in reitiŋ we kan distiŋgwish *right*, *rite*, *write*, and *wright*. Bɤt if, in the hɤri ov konversashon, ther iz hardli ever a dout hwich wɤrd iz ment, shureli ther wud be mɤch les danjer in the slow proses ov readiŋ a kontiniuɤs sentens. If variɤs speliŋz ov the same wɤrd ar nesesari tu point out diferent meaniŋz, we shud rekweir eight speliŋz for *box*, tu signifei a chest, a Kristmas gift, a hɤntiŋ seat, a tree, a slap, tu sail round, seats in a ŧeater, and the frɤnt seat on a koach; and this prinsipel wud hav tu be apleid tu abɤv 400 wɤrdz. Who wud ɤndertake tu proveid all theze variashonz ov the prezent uniform speliŋ ov theze wɤrdz? And we mɤst not forget that, after all, in readiŋ a paje we ar seldom in dout hwether *sole* meanz a fish, or the *sole* ov a fut, or iz uzed az an ajektiv. If ther iz at eni teim eni real difikɤlti, laŋgwej proveidz its own remedi. It either drops sɤch wɤrdz az *rite* and *sole*, replasiŋ them bei *seremony* and *only*, or it uzez a perifrastik ekspreshon, sɤch az the sole ov the fut, or the sole and onli ground, ets.

[Five other new letters, representing the long vowels, will now be introduced, namely

ε,	ʝ,	ɷ,	ɵ,	ɥ

for the sounds heard in

th*ey*,	f*ie*ld,	s*aw*,	n*o*,	d*o*,
m*a*te,	s*ee*,	c*a*ll,	c*o*re,	tr*ue*,
m*a*re,	pol*i*ce,	*ou*ght,	c*oa*l,	p*oo*r.]

Thɤs far ei hav treid tu anser the rʝali important

argiuments hwich hav bįn brɷt forward agenst fonetik speliŋ. Ei hav dɜn so with speshal referens tų the pouerful remonstransez ov Archbishop Trench, and hiz most ɛbel plįdiŋ in fɛvor ov the establisht sistem ov orŧografi. Az a mįr skolar, ei fuli shɛr hiz fįliŋz, and ei sinsįrli admeir hiz elokwent advokasi. Ei difer from him bekɷz ei dų not ŧink, az hį dɜz, that the los entɛld bei fonetik speliŋ wud bį so grɛt az wį imajin; or that it wud bį ɷl on wɜn seid. Beseidz, ɜnles hį kan sho hou a reform ov speliŋ iz not onli for the prezent tu bį avoided, bɜt ɷltugether tu bį renderd ɜnnesesari, ei konsider that the sųner it iz tɛken in hand the beter. It sįmz tu mį that the Archbishop luks on the introdɜkshon ov fonetik speliŋ az a mįr krochet ov a fiu skolarz, or az an atempt on the part ov sɜm haf-ediukɛted personz, wishiŋ tu avoid the trɜbel ov lerniŋ hou tu spel korektli. If that wer so, ei kweit agrį with him that pɜblik opinion wud never asiúm sɜfishent fors for kariiŋ ther skįm. Bɜt ther iz a motiv pouer beheind thįz fonetik reformerz hwich the Archbishop haz hardli tɛken intu akount. Ei mįn the mizeri endiúrd bei milionz ov children at skųl, hų meit lern in wɜn yįr, and with rįal advantej tu themselvz, hwot thɛ nou rekweir for or feiv yįrz tu lern, and seldom sɜksįd in lerniŋ after ɷl. If the evidens ov sɜch men az Mr. Ellis iz tu bį depended on, and ei belįv hį iz wiliŋ tu sɜbmit tu eni test, then shųrli the los ov sɜm historikal and etimolojikal *souvenirs* wud be litel agenst the hapines ov milionz ov children, and the stil heier hapines ov milionz ov Iŋglishmen and Iŋglisewimen, grɵiŋ ɤp az the ɛrz tu ꝏl the welƀ and streŋƀ ov Iŋglish literatiur, or ɤnɛbel tu rįd įven thɛr Beibel. Hįr it iz hwɛr ei ventiur tu difer from the Archbishop, not az bįiŋ saŋgwin az tu eni immįdiet sɤkses, bɤt simpli az fįliŋ it a diuti tu help in a kꝏz hwich at prezent iz mɵst ɤnpopiular. The įvil dɛ mɛ bį put of for a loŋ teim, partikiularli if the wɛt ov sɤch men az Archbishop Trench iz ƀrɵn intu the ɤther skɛl. Bɤt ɤnles làŋgwej sįsez tu bį laŋgwej, and reitiŋ sįsez tu bį reitiŋ, the dɛ wil shɥrli kɤm hwen pįs wil hav tu bį mɛd betwįn the tɥ́. Jermani haz apointed a Gɤvernment Komishon tu konsider hwot iz tu bį dɤn with Jerman speliŋ In Amerika, tɥ, sɤm lįdiŋ stɛtsmen sįm inkleind tu tɛk ɤp the reform ov speliŋ on nashonal groundz. Iz ther nɵ stɛtsman in Iŋgland sɤfishentli prɥf agenst ridikiul tu kꝏl the atenshon ov Parliment tu hwot iz a grɵiŋ misfortiun?

Mɤch, houever, az ei difer from the Archbishop on thįz groundz, ei kanot bɤt deprekɛt the tɵn in hwich hiz pouerful opozishon ház bįn met bei meni ov the ɤphɵlderz ov fɵnetik speliŋ. Nɛ, ei mɤst gɵ stil fɤrther, and fraŋkli konfés that tu wɤn ov hiz argiuments ei feind it difikɤlt, at prezent, tu giv a satisfaktori anser.

"It iz a mįr asɤmpshon," the Archbishop remarks, "that ꝏl men pronoúns ꝏl wɤrdz aleik; or that hwenever thɛ kɜm tu spel a wɜrd thɛ wil ekzaktli agrį az tu hwot the outlein ov its sound iz. Nou wį ar shɥr men wil not dɥ this, from the fakt that, befɵr ther woz eni fikst and seteld orϑografi in our laŋgwej, hwen, thɛrfor, everibodi woz mɵr or les a a fɵnografer, sįkiŋ tu reit doun the wɜrd az it sounded tu *him*,—for hį had nɵ ɜther lꝏ tu geid him,—the vɛriɛshonz ov speliŋ ar infinit. Tɛk, for instans, the wɜrd *sudden*, hwich dɜz not sįm tu promis eni grɛt skɵp for vareieti. Ei hav meiself met with this wɜrd speld in nɵ les than fɵ́rtįn wɛz amɜŋ our erli reiterz. Agen, in hou meni wɛz woz Raleigh'z nɛm speld, or Shakspere'z? The sɛm iz evident from the speliŋ ov ɜnediukated personz in our ɵn dɛ. Thɛ hav nɵ ɜther rɥl bɜt the sound tu geid them. Hou iz it that thɛ dɥ not ꝏl spel aleik?" *Iŋglish, Past and Prezent*, p. 203.

Leik mɵst men hɥ plįd with thɛr hart az wel az with thɛr hed, the Archbishop haz hįr ɵverlukt wɜn obviɜs anser tu hiz kwestion. Thɛ dɥ not spel aleik bekꝏz thɛ hav bįn brꝏt ɜp with a sistem ov speliŋ in hwich the sɛm sound kan bį reprezented in ten diferent wɛz, and in hwich hardli eni wɜn leter iz restrikted tu wɜn fɵnetik pouer onli. If children wer brꝏt ɜp with an alfabet in hwich įch leter had bɜt wɜn sound, and in hwich the sɛm sound woz ꝏlwɛz reprezented bei the sɛm sein—and this iz the veri esens ov fɵnetik reitiŋ—then it wud bį simpli imposibel that thɛ shud drįm ov reitiŋ *sudden* in fɵr-tįn, or *Woburn* in 140, diferent wɛz.

Bɤt for ɷl thát ther iz sɤm trɑθ in the Arch-bishop's remark; and if wį kompɛr the diferent wɛz in hwich the advokets ov fɵnetik speliŋ—men leik Pitman, Bell, Ellis, Withers, Jones—reit the sɛm wɤrdz, įven hwen yɑziŋ the sɛm fɵnetik alfabet, wį shal sį that the difikɤlti pointed out bei the Arch-bishop iz a rįal wɤn. Everiwɤn nɵz hou diferentli the sɛm wɤrdz ɷlwɛz hav bįn and stil ar pronoúnst in diferent parts ov Iŋgland. And it iz not ɵnli in tounz and kountiz that thįz pekiuliaritiz prevɛl; ther ar serten wɤrdz hwich wɤn famili pronoúnsez difer-entli from anɤther; and ther ar beseidz the stɤdid and ɤnstɤdid pekiuliaritiz ov individiual spįkerz. Tu konvíns pįpel that wɤn pronɤnsiɛshon iz reit and the ɤther roŋ, sįmz ɤterli hɵples. Ei hav herd a heili kɤltivɛted man defendiŋ hiz dropiŋ the *h* at the be-giniŋ ov serten wɤrdz, bei the ɤnanserabel argiu-ment that in the plɛs hwɛr hį woz brɷt ɤp, nɵwɤn pronoúnst thįz inishal *h*z. Hwot Skochman wud admit that hiz pronɤnsiɛshon woz fɷlti? Hwot Eirishman wud sɤbmit tu lɷz ov speliŋ past in Lɤn-don? And hwot renderz argiument on eni neisetiz ov pronɤnsiɛshon stil mɵr difikɤlt iz, that bɵθ the įr and the tɤŋ ar mɵst trecherɤs witnesez. Ei hav herd Amerikanz mɛntɛn in gud ernest that ther woz mɤch les of nɛzal twaŋ in Amerika than in Iŋgland. Pįpel ar not awɛr hou thɛ pronoúns, and hou diferentli thɛ pronoúns wʊn and the sɛm wʊrd. Az a forener ei hav had ampel oportiunitiz for obzervɛshon on this point. Sʊm frendz wud tel mį, for instans, that *world* woz pronoúnst leik *whirl'd*, *father* leik *farther*, *nor* (befor konsonants) leik *gnaw*, *bud* leik *bird*, *burst* leik *bust*, *for* leik *fur*, *birth* leik *berth;* that the vouelz had the sɛm sound in *where* and *were*, in *not* and *war*, in *God* and *gaudy;* hweil ʊtherz ashųrd mį that nowʊn bʊt a forener kud ŧiŋk so. And the wʊrst iz that įven the sɛm person dʊz not œlwɛz pronoúns the sɛm wʊrd in ekzaktli the sɛm maner. Konstantli, hwen ei askt a frend tu repįt a wʊrd hwich hį had jʊst pronoúnst, hį wud pronoúns it agen, bʊt with a sleit diferens. The mįr fakt ov hiz treiiŋ tu pronoúns wel wud give tu hiz pronʊnsiɛshon a konshʊs and emfatik karakter. The prepozishon *of* iz pronoúnst bei most pįpel *ov*, bʊt if kros-ekzamind, meni wil sɛ that thɛ pronoúns *ov*, bʊt the *o* not ekzaktli leik *off*.

The konfiuʒon bekʊmz grɛtest hwen it iz atempted tu eidentifei the pronʊnsiɛshon, sɛ ov a vouel in Jerman with a vouel in Iŋglish. No tų Iŋglishmen and no tų Jermanz sįmd tu bį ɛbel tu agrį on hwot thɛ herd with thɛr įrz, or hwot thɛ sed with thɛr tʊŋz; and the rezʊlt in the end iz that no vouel in Jerman woz rįali the sɛm az eni ʊther vouel in Iŋglish. Tu tɛk wʊn or tų instansez, from Mr. Ellis'z kį tu Palioteip (Palœtype), ei kan hįr no diferens betwįn the ą in Italian *mąno*, Iŋglish *father*, and Jerman *mahnen*, ɤnles ei restrikt mei obzervɛshonz tu the ɤterans ov serten individiualz; hwɛraz ei dʮ hįr a veri deseided, and jenerali adopted, diferens betwįn the vouelz in Jerman *böcke* and French *jeune*. Mr. Ellis, tɤchiŋ on the sɛm ꞓifikɤlti, remarks, "Mr. Bell's pronɤnṡiɛshon, in meni instansez, diferz from thát hwich ei am akɤstomd tu giv, espeshali in foren wɤrdz. Bɵŧ ov ɤs mɛ bį roŋ." Mr. Sweet remarks, p. 10, "Mr. Ellis insists stroŋli on the monofŧoŋgal karakter ov hiz ɵn *eez* and *ooz*. Ei hįr hiz *ee* and *oo* az distiŋkt difŧoŋz, not ɵnli in hiz Iŋglish pronɤnsiɛshon, bɤt ꝏlsɵ in hiz pronɤnsiɛshon ov French, Jerman, and Latin." If fɵnetik reitiŋ ment this miniút fɵtografi ov spɵken soundz, in hwich Mes. Bell and Ellis eksél; if eni atempt had ever bįn mɛd tu emploi this hɛr-splitiŋ mashįneri for a praktikal reform ov Iŋglish speliŋ, the objekshonz rɛzd bei Archbishop Trench wud bį kweit ɤnanserabel. Ther wud bį fifti diferent wɛz ov speliŋ Iŋglish, and the konfiuȝon wud bį grɛter than it iz nou. Not įven Mr. Bell'z ŧerti-siks kategoriz ov vouel sound wud bį sɤfishent tu render everi pekiuliariti ov vouel kwoliti, pich and kwontiti, with perfekt akiurasi. (Sį H. Sweet, "Histori ov Iŋglish Soundz," pp. 58, 68.) Bɤt this woz never intended, and hweil konsįdiŋ mɤch tu the Archbishop's argiuments, ei mɤst not konsįd tʮ mɤch.

Hwot ei leik in Mr. Pitman'z sistem ov speliŋ iz ekzaktli hwot ei nó haz bįn found fꝏlt with bei ɤtherz nɛmli that hį dɤz not atempt tu refein tɥ mɤch, and tu ekspres in reitiŋ thoz endles shɛdz ov pronɤnsiɛshon, hwich mɛ bį ov the grɛtest interest tu the stiudent ov akoustiks, or ov fonetiks, az apleid tu the stɤdi ov liviŋ deialekts, bɤt hwich, for praktikal az well az for seientifik filolojikal pɤrposez, mɤst bį enteirli ignord. Reitiŋ woz never intended tu fotograf spoken laŋgwejez: it woz ment tu indikɛt, not tu pɛnt soundz. If Voltaire sez, "L'écriture c'est la peinture de la voix," hį iz reit; bɤt hwen hį goz on tu sɛ, "plus elle est ressemblante, meilleur elle est," ei am not serten that, az in a piktiur ov a landskɛp, so in a piktiur ov the vois, prį-Rafɛleit miniútnes mɛ not destroi the veri objekt ov the piktiur. Laŋgwej dįlz in brɷd kɤlorz, and reitiŋ ɷt tu folo the ekzampel ov laŋgwej, hwich tho it alouz an endles vareiti ov pronɤnsiɛshon, restrikts itself for its on pɤrpos, for the pɤrpos ov ekspresiŋ ŧɷt in ɷl its modifikɛshonz, tu a veri limited nɤmber ov tipikal vouelz and konsonants. Out ov the larj nɤmber ov soundz, for instans, hwich hav bįn katalogd from the vɛriɤs Iŋglish deialekts, thoz onli kan bį rekogneizd az konstitiuent elements ov the laŋgwej hwich in, and bei, thɛr diferens from įch ɤther, konvɛ a diferens ov mįniŋ. Ov sɤch pregnant and ŧɷt-konvɛiŋ vouelz, Iŋglish pozésez no mor than twelv. Hwotever the meinor shɛdz ov vouel soundz in Iŋglish deialekts mɛ bį, thɛ dɥ not enrich the laŋgwej, az sɤch, thát iz, thɛ dɥ not enɛbel the spįker tu konvɛ mor miniút shɛdz ov ŧꝏt than the twelv tipikal siŋgel vouelz. Beseidz, ther jenerali iz hwot the French meit kꝏl a fɵnetik solidariti in įch deialekt. If wɤn vouel chɛnjez, the ɤtherz ar apt tu folɵ, and the mɛn objekt ov laŋgwej remɛnz the sɛm ŧrɥout, nɛmli, tu prevent wɤn wɤrd from rɤniŋ intu anɤther, and yet tu abstɛn from tɥ miniút fɵnetik distiŋkshonz, hwich an ordinari įr meit feind it difikɤlt tu grasp. This prinsipel ov fɵnetik solidariti iz ov grɛt importans, not onli in eksplɛniŋ the gradiual chɛnjez ov vouelz, bɤt ꝏlsɵ sɤch jeneral chɛnjez ov konsonants az wį sį, for instans, in the Jerman *Lautverschiebung*. Az sɥn az wɤn plɛs iz left vɛkant, ther iz preshur tu fil it, or sɵ mɤch ov it az iz left vɛkant, bɤt nɵ mɵr.

Ther ar, in fakt, tɥ́ branchez, or at ꝏl events, tɥ́ kweit distiŋkt praktikal aplikɛshonz ov the seiens ov Fɵnetiks, hwich for wont ov beter nɛmz, ei designɛt az *filolojikal* and *deialektikal.* Ther iz hwot mɛ bį kꝏld a filolojikal stɤdi ov Fɵnetiks, hwich iz an esenshal part ov the Seiens ov Laŋgwej, and haz for its objekt tu giv a klįr eidįa ov the alfabet, not az riten, bɤt az spɵken. It trįts ov the matįrialz out ov hwich, the instruments with hwich, and the proses bei hwich, vouelz and konsonants ar formd; and after eksplɛniŋ hou serten leterz agrį, and difer, in thɛr matįrial, in the instruments with hwich, and the proses bei hwich thɛ ar prodiúst, it enɛbelz ɤs tu ɤnderstand the kꝏzez and rezɤlts ov hwot iz kꝏld

Fɵnetik Chɛnj. In meni respekts the mɵst instrɤktiv trįtment ov the jeneral ŧįori ov Fɵnetiks iz tu bį found in the Prâtisâkhyas; partikiularli in the ɵldest (400 B. K.), thát atacht tu the Rig Vɛda.* Thɵ the nɤmber ov posibel soundz mɛ sįm infinit the nɤmber ov rįal soundz yɑzd in Sanskrit or eni ɤther given laŋgwej for the pɤrpos ov ekspresiŋ diferent shɛdz ov mįniŋ, iz veri limited. It iz with thįz brꝏd kategoriz ov sound alɵn that the Prâtisâkhyas dįl; and it iz for a proper ɤnderstandiŋ ov thįz the Seiens ov Laŋgwej haz tu inklɑd within its sfįr a kɛrful stɤdi ov Fɵnetiks.

The deialektikal stɤdi ov Fɵnetiks haz larjer objekts. It wishez tu ekzꝏst ꝏl posibel soundz hwich kan bį prodiúst bei the vɵkal organz, litel konsɛrnd az tu hwether thįz soundz okɤ́r in eni rįal laŋgwej or not. It iz partikiularli yɑsful for the pɤrpos ov pɛntiŋ, with the ɤtmɵst akiurasi, the aktiual pronɤnsiɛshon ov individiualz, and ov fiksiŋ the fɛntest shɛdz ov deialektik vareieti. The mɵst marvelɤs achįvment in this branch ov apleid fɵnetiks mɛ bį sįn in Mr. Bell'z "Vizibel Spįch."

Thįz tɑ́ branchez ov fɵnetik seiens, houever, shud bį kept kɛrfuli distiŋkt. Az the foundɛshon ov a praktikal alfabet, leikweiz az the ɵnli sɛf foundɛshon for the Seiens ov Laŋgwej, wį wont filolojikal or ŧįoretik Fɵnetiks. Wį wont an ɤnderstandiŋ ov

* "Rig-Veda-Prâtisâkhya, Das älteste Lehrbuch der Vedischen Phonetik, Sanskrit Text, mit Übersetzung und Anmerkungen, herausgegeben," von F. Max Müller, Leipzig, 1869.

thɵz jeneral prinsipelz and thɵz brꝏd kategoriz ov sound hwich ar trįted in the Prâtiŝâkhyas; wį dɑ not wont eni ov the miniút deialektikal distiŋkshonz hwich hav nɵ gramatikal pɜrpos, and ar thɛrfor outseid the pɛl ov gramatikal seiens. Tɑ miniút distiŋkshon prodiɑsez konfiuʒon, and hwɛr it kan bį avoided, without a sakrifeiz ov akiurasi, it ꝏt tu bį avoided. Hwɛr vɛgnes ekzists in rįaliti, and hwɛr nɛtiur alouz a brꝏd marjin on either seid, it wud bį roŋ tu ignɵr thát latitiud. Akiurasi itself wud hįr bekɜm inakiurasi.

Bɜt hwen wį wont tu ekzꝏst ꝏl posibel shɛdz ov sound, hwen wį wont tu fɵtograf the pekiuliaritiz ov serten deialekts, or meʒur the dįviɛshonz in the pronɜnsiɛshon ov individiualz bei the mɵst miniút degrįz, wį then mɜst avɛl ourselvz ov thát ekskwizit artistik mashįneri konstrɜkted bei Mr. Bell, and handeld with sɵ mɜch skil bei Mr. A. J. Ellis, thɵ fiu ɵnli wil bį ɛbel tu yɑz it with rįal sɜkses.

Sɜm pįpel sįm tu imajin that the pouer ov distiŋgwishiŋ miniút diferensez ov soundz iz a natiural gift, and kanot bį akweird. It mɛ bį sɵ in kweit eksepshonal kɛsez, bɜt ei nɵ az a fakt that a cheild that had, az pįpel sɛ, nɵ įr for miuzik, and kud not siŋ "God sɛv the Kwįn," gradiuali akweird the pouer ov distiŋgwishiŋ the ordinari nɵts, and ov siŋiŋ a tiun. Spįkiŋ from mei ɵn ekspįriens ei shud sɛ that a gud įr kɜmz bei inheritans, for, az loŋ az ei kan remember, a fols nɵt, or, az wį yɑst tu kꝏl it, an impiur (*unrein*) nɵt, woz tu mį fizikali pɛnful.

Bɤt this apleiz tu miuzik ɵnli, and it iz bei nɵ mįnz jenerali trų, that pįpel hų hav a gud miuzikal įr, hav ꝏlsɵ a gud įr for laŋgwej. Ei hav nɵn pįpel kweit ɤnmiuzikal, pozést ov a veri gud įr for laŋgwej, and *vice versâ.* The tų́ natiural gifts, thɛrfor, if natiural gifts thɛ ar, ov distiŋgwishiŋ miniút degrįz ov pich and kwoliti ov sound dų not sįm tu bį the sɛm. The rįal difikɤlti, houever, hwich mɛks itself felt in diskɤ́siŋ miniút shɛdz ov sound, areizez from the insɤfishensi ov our nomenklatiur, from the ꝏlmɵst irrezistibel influens ov imajinɛshon, and in the end, from the wont ov a fɵnometer. A gud miuzishan kan distiŋgwish betwįn *C sharp* and *D flat,* a gud fɵnetishan betwįn a "lɵ-bak-nar ɵ" and a "lɵ-mikst-narɵ" vouel. Bɤt thɛ kanot ꝏlwɛz translɛt thɛr sentiments intu definit laŋgwej, and if thɛ trei bei aktiual eksperiment tu imitɛt thįz tų́ soundz or vouelz, the imperfekshonz ov the įr and tɤŋ, bɵƀ in the spįker and the lisener, frįkwentli render ꝏl atempts at a miutiual ɤnderstandiŋ imposibel. Wį shal never areiv at seientifik presiʒon til wį hav a fɵnometer for kwoliti ov sound, nor dų ei sį hwei sɤch an instrument shud bį imposibel. Ei wel remember Wheatstone teliŋ mį, that hį wud ɤndertɛk tu rįprodiús bei mįnz ov an instrument everi shɛd ov vouel in eni laŋgwɛj ov the wɤrld, and ei shud ƀiŋk that Willis'z and Helmholtz'z eksperiments wud sɜplei the elements from hwich sɜch a fənometer meit bį konstitiuted. Az sųn az wį kan meʒur, defein, and rįprodiús, at pleʒur, hwot at prezent wį kan ənli deskreib in aproksimɛt termz, the seiens ov fənetiks wil bekɜm məst frųtful, and asiúm its lejitimet plɛs az a *sine quâ non* tu the stiudent ov laŋgwej.

Ei hav sɜmteimz bįn blɛmd for haviŋ insisted on Fənetiks bįiŋ rekogneizd az the foundɛshon ov the Seiens ov Laŋgwej. Prof. Benfey and ɜther skolarz protested agenst the chapter ei hav devəted tu Fənetiks in the Sekond Sįrįz ov mei "Lektiurz," az an ɜnnesesari inovɛshon, and thəz prətests hav bekɜm stil stroŋger ov lɛt. Bɜt hįr, tų, wį mɜst distiŋgwish betwįn tų ŧiŋz. Filolojikal or jeneral Fənetiks, ar, ei həld, az stroŋli az ever, an integral part ov the Seiens ov Laŋgwej; deialektik Fənetiks mɛ bį yųsful hįr and thɛr, bɜt thɛ shud bį kept within thɛr proper sfįr; ɜtherweiz, ei admit az redili az eniwɜn els, thɛ obskiúr rather than revįl the brœd and masiv kɜlorz ov sound hwich laŋgwej yųzez for its ordinari wɜrk.

If wį reflekt a litel, wį shal sį that the filolojikal konsepshon ov a vouel iz sɜmŧiŋ tətali diferent from its piurli akoustik or deialektik konsepshon. The former iz chįfli konsernd with the sfįr ov posibel vɛrieshon, and the later with the piurli fenomenal individiualiti ov įch vouel. Tu the filolojist, the ŧrį vouelz in *septimus*, for instans, hwotever thɛr ekzakt pronɜnsiɛshonz mɛ hav bįn at diferent teimz, and in diferent provinsez ov the Roman Empeir, ar potenshali wɜn and the sɛm. Wį luk on *septimus* and *ἕβδομος* az on Sanskrit *saptamas*, and onli bei noiŋ that *e*, *i*, and *u* in *septimus* ar ɶl reprezentativz ov a short *a*, or that *optimus* standz for the mor ɛnshent *optumus* and *optomos*, dų wį tɛk in at wɜn glans the hol histori and posibel vɛriɛshon ov thįz vouelz in diferent laŋgwejez and deialekts. Įven hwɛr a vouel disapįrz komplįtli, az in *gigno* for *gigeno*, in *πίπτω* for *πιπετω*, the mental ei ov the filolojist disérnz and wɛz hwot no įr kan hįr. And hweil in thįz kɛsez the etimolojist, disregardiŋ the klįrest vareieti ov pronɜnsiɛshon, trįts sɜch vouelz az *a*, *e*, *i*, *o*, *u* az wɜn and the sɛm, in ɜtherz hwɛr tų́ vouelz sįm tu hav ekzaktli the sɛm sound tu the deialektishan, the filolojist on hiz part persįvz diferensez ov the grɛtest importans. The *i* in *fides* and *cliens* mɛ hav the sɛm sound az the *i* in *gigno* or *septimus*, the *u* ov *luo* mɛ not difer from the *u* in *optumus* or *lubens*, bɜt thɛr intrinsik valiu, thɛr kɛpabilitiz ov groŧ and deké, ar totali diferent in įch. Wį shal never bį ɛbel tu spįk with eniŧiŋ leik rįal seientifik akiurasi ov the pronɜnsiɛshon ov ɛnshent laŋgwejez, bɜt įven if wį luk tu thɛr riten apįrans onli, wį sį agén and agén hou vouelz, riten aleik, ar historikalį totali distiŋkt. Grimm introdiúst the distiŋkshon betwįn *ái* and *aí*, betwįn *áu* and *aú*, not bekɶz it iz bei eni mįnz serten that the pronɜnsiɛshon ov thj̨z difƫoŋz vεrid, bɜt bekꝏz hj̨ wisht tu indikεt that the antesj̨dents ov *ái* and *áu* wer diferent from thɵz ov *aí* and *aú*. In Goƫik *faíhu*, (Sk. pa*s*u, pecu), *aí* iz *a* shortend tu *i*, and brɵken befɵr *h* tu *ái;* in Goƫik *váit* (Sk. veda, οἶδα), *ai*, iz radikal *i* streŋƫend tu *ái*. In Goƫik *daúhtar* (Sk. duhitar θυγάτηρ), *aú* iz radikal *u* brɵken tu *aú ;* in *aúhna* ɜven (Sk. a*s*na, ἰπνό=ἰχνο=ἀχνο), the *au* iz *a*, darkend tu *u*, and brɵken tu *áu;* hweil in Goƫik *báug* (πέφευγα), *áu* iz orijinal *u* streŋƫend tu *áu*. Hwen wj̨ hj̨r *ê* and *ô* in Goƫik wj̨ sj̨ *â*, jɜst az wj̨ sj̨ Dorik *ā* beheind Eionik *η*. Hwen wj̨ hj̨r *c* in *canis*, wj̨ sj̨ Sanskrit *s ;* hwen wj̨ hj̨r *c* in *cruor*, wj̨ sj̨ Sanskrit *k*. Hwen wj̨ hj̨r γ in γένος, wj̨ sj̨ Ⱥrian *g ;* hwen wj̨ hj̨r γ in φλέγω, wj̨ sj̨ Ⱥrian *z*.

Thj̨z fiu ilɜstrεshonz wil eksplεn, ei hɵp the esenshal diferens in the aplikεshon ov fɵnetiks tu filoloji and deialektoloji, and wil shɵ that in the former our brɜsh mɜst ov nesesiti be brꝏd, hweil in the later it mɜst bj̨ fein. It iz bei miksiŋ ɜp tú separεt leinz ov reserch, j̨ch heili important in itself, that sɵ mɜch konfiuʒon haz ov lεt bj̨n okεʒond. The valiu ov piurli fɵnetik obzervεshonz shud on nɵ akount bj̨ ɜnderrεted; bɜt it iz nesesari, for thát veri rj̨zon, that deialektikal az wel az filolojikal fɵnetiks shud bj̨ konfeind tu thεr proper sfj̨r. The filolojist haz mɜch tu lern from the fɵnetishan, bɜt hj̨ shud never forget that hj̨r, az elshwεr, hwot iz brꝏd and tipikal iz az important and az seientifikali akiuret az hwot iz miniút and speshal.

Hwot iz brɷd and tipikal iz often mɵr akiuret įven than hwot iz miniút and speshal. It meit bį posibel, for instans, bei a fɵtografik proses, tu reprezent the ekzakt pozishon ov the tɜŋ and the inseid wɷlz ov the mouƀ hweil wį pronoúns the Italian vouel į. Bɜt it wud bį the grɛtest mistɛk tu sɜpɵz that this imej givz ɜs the ɵnli wɛ in hwich thát vouel iz, and kan bį, pronoúnst. Thɵ įch individiual mɛ hav hiz ɵn wɛ ov plɛsiŋ the tɜŋ in pronoúnsiŋ į, wį hav ɵnli tu trei the eksperiment in order tu konvins ourselvz that, with sɜm efort, wį mɛ vɛri that pozishon in meni wɛz and yet prodiús the sound ov į. Hwen, thɛrfor, in mei "Lektiurz on the Seiens ov Laŋgwej," ei gɛv piktiurz ov the pozishonz ov the vɵkal organz rekweird for pronounsiŋ the tipikal leterz ov the alfabet, ei tuk grɛt kɛr tu mɛk them tipikal, thát iz, tu lįv them rɜf skechez rather than miniút fɵtografs. Ei kanot beter ekspres hwot ei fįl on this point than bei kwɵtiŋ the wɜrdz ov Hæckel:—

"For didaktik pɜrposez, simpel skįmatik figiurz ar far mɵr yʋsful than piktiurz prezerviŋ the grɛtest fɛƀfulnes tu nɛtiur and karid out with the grɛtest akiurasi." ("Ziele und Wege," p. 37.)

[The following three letters, now introduced, will complete the Phonetic Alphabet—

đ ç, ʃ,

for the sounds heard in—*th*en, *ch*eap, *sh*e.]

Tu retɜrn, after ꝺis digreʃon, tu Mr. Pitman'z alfabet, ei repįt ꝺat it rekomendz itself tu mei meind bei hwot ɜꝺerz kꝏl its inakiurasi. It ʃoz its rįal and praktikal wizdom bei not atemptiŋ tu fiks eni distiŋkʃonz hwiç ar not absolutli nesesari. If, for instans, wį tεk ꝺe gɜtɜral teniuis, wį feind that Iŋgliʃ rekogneizez wɜn *k* onli, ꝏlꝺo its pronɜnsiεʃon vεriz konsiderabli. It iz sɜmteimz pronoúnst so az tu prodiús ꝏlmost a ʃarp krak; sɜmteimz it haz a dįp, holo sound; and sɜmteimz a soft, lεzi, *mouillé* karakter. It vεriz konsiderabli akordiŋ tu ꝺe vouelz hwiç folo it, az enibodi mε hįr, nε fįl, if hį pronoúnsez in sɜkseʃon, *kot, kul, kar, kat, kit.* Bɜt az Iŋgliʃ dɜz not yuz ꝺįz diferent *k*z for the pɜrpos ov distiŋgwiʃiŋ wɜrdz or gramatikal formz, wɜn brꝏd kategori onli ov voisles gɜtɜral çeks haz tu bį admited in reitiŋ Iŋgliʃ. In ꝺe Semitik laŋgwejez ꝺe kεs iz diferent; not onli ar *kaf* and *kof* diferent in sound, bɜt ꝺis diferens iz yuzd tu distiŋgwiʃ diferent mįniŋz.

Or if wį tεk ꝺe vouel *a* in its orijinal, piur pronɜnsiεʃon, leik Italian *a*, wį kan įzili persįv ꝺat it haz diferent kɜlorz in diferent kountiz ov Iŋgland. Yet in reitiŋ it mε bį trįted az wɜn, bekꝏz it haz bɜt wɜn and ꝺe sεm gramatikal intenʃon, and dɜz not konvέ a niu mįniŋ til it eksįdz its weidest limits. Gud spįkerz in Iŋgland pronoúns ꝺe *a* in *last* leik ꝺe piur Italian *a;* wiꝺ ɜꝺerz it bekɜmz brꝏd, wiꝺ ɜꝺerz ŧin. Bɜt ꝺo it mε ꝺɜs osilεt konsiderabli, it mɜst not enkrɵç on đe provins ov *e*, hwiç wud çɛnj its mịniŋ tu *lest;* nor on đe provins ov *o*, hwiç wud çenj it tu *lost;* nor on đe provins ov *u*, hwiç wud çenj it tu *lust.*

Đe difikɜlti, đɛrfor, hwiç Arçbiʃop Trench haz pointed out iz rịali restrikted tu đɵz kɛsez hwɛr đe pronɜnsiɛʃon ov vouelz—for it iz wiđ vouelz çịfli đat wị ar trɜbeld—vɛriz sɵ mɜç az tu ɵverstep đe brœdest limits ov wɜn ov đe rekogneizd kategoriz ov sound, and tu enkrɵç on anɜđer. If wị tɛk đe wɜrd *fast,* hwiç iz pronoúnst veri diferentli ịven bei ediukɛted pịpel, đer wud bị nɵ nesesiti for indikɛtiŋ in reitiŋ đe diferent ʃɛdz ov pronɜnsiɛʃon hwiç lei betwịn đe sound ov đe ʃort Italian *a* and đe loŋ *a* herd in *father*. Bɜt hwen đe *a* in *fast* iz pronoúnst leik đe *a* in *fat,* đen đe nesesiti ov a niu grafik ekspɵnent wud areiz, and Arçbiʃop Trench wud bị reit in twitiŋ fɵnetik refórmerz wiđ saŋkʃoniŋ tụ́ speliŋz for đe sɛm wɜrd.

Ei kud menʃon đe nɛmz ov ŧrị biʃops, wɜn ov hụm pronoúnst đe vouel in *God* leik *Gœd,* anɜđer leik *rod,* a ŧerd leik *gad.* Đe last pronɜnsiɛʃon wud probabli bị kondemd bei everibodi, bɜt đe ɜđer tụ́ wud remɛn saŋkʃond bei đe heiest œŧoriti, and đerfor retɛnd in fɵnetik reitiŋ.

Sɵ far, đen, ei admit đat Arçbiʃop Trench haz pointed out a rịal difikɜlti inhịrent in fɵnetik reitiŋ; bɜt hwot iz đát wɜn difikɜlti komperd wiđ đe difikɤltiz ov đe prezent sistem ov Iŋgliʃ speliŋ? It wud not bį onest tu trei tu evɛd hiz çarj, bei sɛiŋ đat đer iz bɤt wɤn pronɤnsiɛʃon rekogneizd bei đe yųzej ov ediukɛted pįpel. Đát iz not sɵ, and đɵz hų nɵ best đe beiolǫji ov laŋgwej, nɵ đat it kanɔt bį sɵ. Đe veri leif ov laŋgwej konsists in a konstant frikʃon betwįn đe sentripetal fɵrs ov kɤs-tom and đe sentrifiugal fɵrs ov individiual frįdom. Agenst đát difikɤlti đɛrfor, đer iz nɵ remedi. Ɵnli hįr agen đe Arçbiʃop sįmz tu hav ɵverlukt đe fakt đat đe difikɤlti beloŋz tu đe prezent sistem ov spel-iŋ nįrli az mɤç az tu đe fɵnetik sistem. Đer iz bɤt wɤn rekogneizd wɛ ov speliŋ, bɤt everibodi pro-noúnsez akordiŋ tu hiz ɵn idiosinkrasiz. It wud bį đe sɛm wiđ fɵnetik speliŋ. Wɤn pronɤnsiɛʃon, đe best rekogneizd, wud hav tu bį adopted az a standard in fɵnetik reitiŋ, lįviŋ tu everi Ingliʃman hiz frįdom tu pronoúns az sįmeŧ gud tu him. Wį ʃud lųz nɤ-ŧiŋ ov hwot wį nou pozés, and ɷl đe advantejez ov fɵnetik reitiŋ wud remɛn ɤnimpɛrd. Đe rįal stɛt ov đe kɛs iz, đɛrfor, đis—Nɵwɤn defendz đe prezent sistem ov speliŋ; everiwɤn admits đe sįriɤs injuri hwiç it inflikts on naʃonal ediukɛʃon. Everibodi admits đe praktikal advantejez ov fɵnetik speliŋ, bɤt after đát, ɷl eksklɛm đat a reform ov speliŋ, hweđer parʃal or komplįt, iz imposibel. Hweđer it iz imposibel or not, ei gladli lįv tu men ov đe wɤrld tu deseid. Az a skolar, az a stiudent ov đe histori ov laŋgwej, ei simpli mɛntɛn đat in everi riten laŋgwej a reform ov speliŋ iz, sųner or lɛter, inevitabel. Nɵ dout đe įvil dɛ mɛ bį put of. Ei hav litel dout đat it wil bį put of for meni jenerɛʃonz, and đat a rįal reform wil probabli not bį karid ɵksept konkɜrentli wiđ a veiolent sɵʃal konvɜlʃon. Ɵnli let đe kwestion bį argiud fɛrli. Let fakts hav sɜm wɛt, and let it not bį sɜpɵzd bei men ov đe wɜrld đat đɵz hų defend đe prinsipelz ov đe *Fɵnetik Niuz* ar ɵnli tįtɵtalerz and vejetɛrianz, hų hav never lernd hou tu spel.

If ei hav spɵken stroŋli in sɜport ov Mr. Pitman'z sistem, it iz not bekꝏz on ꝏl points ei konsider it siupįrior tu đe sistemz prepɛrd bei ɜđer reformerz, hų ar dɛli inkrįsiŋ in nɜmber, bɜt çįfli bekꝏz it haz bįn tested sɵ larjli, and haz stud đe test wel. Mr. Pitman'z *Fɵnetik Jɜrnal* haz nou [1880] bįn pɜbliʃt ŧerti-ɛt yįrz, and if it iz nɵn đat it iz pɜbliʃt wįkli in 12,000 kopiz, įç kopi reprezentiŋ at lįst fɵr or feiv rįderz, it mɛ not sįm sɵ veri fųliʃ, after ꝏl, if wį imajin đat đer iz sɜm veital pouer in đát insignifikant jerm.

V.

ON SANSKRIT TEXTS DISCOVERED IN JAPAN.

READ AT THE MEETING OF THE ROYAL ASIATIC SOCIETY, FEBRUARY 16, 1880.

It is probably in the recollection of some of the senior members of this Society how wide and deep an interest was excited in the year 1853 by the publication of Stanislas Julien's translation of the "Life and Travels of Hiouen-thsang." The account given by an eye-witness of the religious, social, political, and literary state of India at the beginning of the seventh century of our era was like a rocket, carrying a rope to a whole crew of struggling scholars, on the point of being drowned in the sea of Indian chronology; and the rope was eagerly grasped by all, whether their special object was the history of Indian religion, or the history of Indian literature, architecture, or politics. While many books on Indian literature, published five-and-twenty years ago, are now put aside and forgotten, Julien's three volumes of Hiouen-thsang still maintain a fresh interest, and supply new subjects for discussion, as may be seen even in the last number of the Journal of your Society.

I had the honor and pleasure of working with Stanislas Julien, when he was compiling those large lists of Sanskrit and Chinese words which formed the foundation of his translation of Hiouen-thsang, and enabled him in his classical work, the "Méthode pour déchiffrer et transcrire les noms Sanskrits" (1861), to solve a riddle which had puzzled Oriental scholars for a long time — viz., how it happened that the original Sanskrit names had been so completely disguised and rendered almost unrecognizable in the Chinese translations of Sanskrit texts, and how they could be restored to their original form.

I had likewise the honor and pleasure of working with your late President, Professor H. H. Wilson, when, after reading Julien's works, he conceived the idea that some of the original Sanskrit texts of which the Chinese translations had been recovered might still be found in the monasteries of China. His influential position as President of your Society, and his personal relations with Sir John Bowring, then English Resident in China, enabled him to set in motion a powerful machinery for attaining his object; and if you look back some five-and-twenty years, you will find in your Journal a full account of the correspondence that passed between Professor Wilson, Sir J. Bowring, and Dr. Edkins, on the search after Sanskrit MSS. in the temples or monasteries of China.

On February 15, 1854, Professor Wilson writes from Oxford to Sir John Bowring: —

"I send you herewith a list of the Sanskrit works carried to China by Hwen Tsang in the middle of the seventh century, and in great part translated by him, or under his supervision, into Chinese. If any of them, *especially the originals*, should be still in existence, you would do good service to Sanskrit literature and to the history of Buddhism by procuring copies."

Chinese Translators of Sanskrit Texts.

It is a well-known fact that, even long before the time of Hiouen-thsang — that is, long before the seventh century of our era — large numbers of Sanskrit MSS. had been exported to China. These literary exportations began as early as the first century A. D. When we read for the first time of commissioners being sent to India by Ming-ti, the Emperor of China, the second sovereign of the Eastern Han dynasty, about 62 or 65 A. D., we are told that they returned to China with a white horse, carrying books and images.[1] And the account proceeds to state that "these books still remain, and are reverenced and worshipped."

From that time, when Buddhism was first officially recognized in China,[2] there is an almost unbroken succession of importers and translators of Buddhist, in some cases of Brahmanic texts also, till we come to the two famous expeditions, the one undertaken by Fa-hian in 400–415, the other by Hiouen-thsang, 629–645 A. D. Fa-hian's Travels were translated into French by Abel Rémusat (1836), into English by Mr. Beal (1869). Hiouen-thsang's Travels are well known through Stanislas Julien's admirable translation. Of Hiouen-thsang we are told that he brought back from India no less than 520 fasciculi, or 657 separate works, which had to be carried by twenty-two horses.[3] He translated, or had translated, 740 works, forming 1,335 fasciculi.

1 Beal, *Travels of Buddhist Pilgrims*, Introd. p. xxi.; *Chinese Repository*, vol. x. No. 3, March, 1841.

2 See an account of the Introduction of Buddhism into China, in *Journal Asiatique*, 1856, August, p. 105. *Recherches sur l'origine des ordres religieux dans l'empire chinois*, par Bazin.

3 Stan. Julien, *Pèlerins Bouddhistes*, vol. i. p. 296.

I say nothing of earlier traces of Buddhism which are supposed to occur in Chinese books. Whatever they may amount to, we look in vain in them for evidence of any Chinese translations of Buddhist books before the time of the Emperor Ming-ti; and what concerns us at present is, not the existence or the spreading of Buddhism towards the north and east long before the beginning of the Christian era, but the existence of Buddhist books, so far as it can be proved at that time by the existence of Chinese translations the date of which can be fixed with sufficient certainty.

In the following remarks on the history of these translations I have had the great advantage of being able to use the Annals of the Sui Dynasty (589–618), kindly translated for me by Professor Legge. In China the history of each dynasty was written under the succeeding dynasty from documents which may be supposed to be contemporaneous with the events they relate. The account given in the Sui Chronicles of the introduction of Buddhism and Buddhist works into China is said to be the best general account to be found in early Chinese literature, and the facts here stated may be looked upon as far more trustworthy than the notices hitherto relied upon, and collected from Chinese writers of different dates and different localities. I have also had the assistance of Mr. Bunyiu Nanjio, who compared the names of the translators mentioned in the Sui Annals with the names as given in the K'ai-yuen-shih-kiao-mu-lu (Catalogue of the Buddhist books compiled in the period K'ai-yuen [A. D. 713–741]); and though there still remain some doubtful points, we may rest assured that the dates assigned to the principal Chinese translators and their works can be depended on as historically trustworthy.

With regard to the period anterior to Ming-ti, the Sui Chronicles tell us that after an investigation of the records, it was known that Buddhism had not been brought to China previously to the Han dynasty (began 206 B. C.), though some say that it had long been spread abroad, but had disappeared again in the time of the *Kh*in[1] (221–206 B. C.). Afterwards, however, when *K*ang-*kh*ien was sent on a mission to the regions of the West (about 130 B. C.), he is supposed to have become acquainted with the religion of Buddha. He was made prisoner by the Hiungnu (Huns),[2] and, being kept by them for ten years, he may well have acquired during his captivity some knowledge of Buddhism, which at a very early time had spread from Cabul[3] towards the north and the east.

In the time of the Emperor Âi (B. C. 6–2) we read that *Kh*in-*k*ing caused I-tsun to teach the Buddhist Sûtras orally, but that the people gave no credence to them. All this seems to rest on semi-historical evidence only.

The first official recognition of Buddhism in China dates from the reign of the Emperor Ming-ti, and the following account, though not altogether free from a

1 Dr. Edkins in his Notices of Buddhism in China (which unfortunately are not paged) says that Indians arrived at the capital of China in Shensi in 217 B. C. to propagate their religion.

2 Dr. Edkins, *l. c.*, states that *K*ang-*kh*ien, on his return from the country of the Getæ, informed the Emperor Wu-ti that he had seen articles of traffic from Shindo. The commentator adds that the name is pronounced Kando and Tindo, and that it is the country of the barbarians called Buddha (*sic*).

3 Kabul or Ko-fu is, in the Eastern Han annals, called a state of the Yüeh-*k*i.

legendary coloring, is generally accepted as authentic by Chinese scholars: "The Emperor Ming-ti, of the After Han dynasty (58–75 A. D.), dreamt that a man of metal (or golden color) was flying and walking in a courtyard of the palace. When he told his dream in the Court, Fu-î said that the figure was that of Buddha. On this the Emperor sent the gentleman-usher Tsâi-yin and *Kh*in-*k*ing (who must then have been growing old) both to the country of the great Yueh-*k*i[1] and to India, in order to seek for such an image."

An earlier account of the same event is to be found in the Annals of the After (or Eastern) Han dynasty (25–120 A. D.). These annals were compiled by Fan-yeh, who was afterwards condemned to death as a rebel (445 A. D.). Here we read[2] (vol. 88, fol. 8 a *seq.*): "There is a tradition that the Emperor Ming-ti (58–75 A. D.) dreamt that there was a giant-like man of golden color,[3] whose head was refulgent. The Emperor wanted his retainers to interpret it. Then some said, 'There is a god (or spirit) in the West who is called Fo, whose height is sixteen feet, and of golden color.' Having heard this, the Emperor at once sent messengers to Tien-*k*u (*i. e.* India), to inquire after the doctrine of Buddha. Subsequently, copies of the image of Buddha were drawn in the middle country (*i. e.* China)."

The emissaries whom the Emperor Ming-ti had sent to India obtained a Buddhist Sûtra in forty-two sections, and an image of Buddha, with which and the Shâmans Kâsyapa Mâtaṅga and *K*û-fa-lan, they

1 Generally identified with the Getæ, but without sufficient proof.

2 Translated by Mr. Bunyiu Nanjio.

3 The golden color or suvar*n*avar*n*atâ is one of the thirty-two marks of a Buddha, recognized both in the Southern and Northern schools (Burnouf, *Lotus*, 579).

returned to the East. When Tsâi-yin approached (the capital), he caused the book to be borne on a white horse, and on this account the monastery of the White Horse was built on the west of the Yung gate of the city of Lo to lodge it. The classic was tied up and placed in the stone house of the Lan tower, and, moreover, pictures of the image were drawn and kept in the *Kh*ing-yüan tower, and at the top of the Hsien-*k*ieh hill.

Here we seem to be on *terra firma*, for some of the literary works by Kâ*s*yapa Mâtaṅga and *K*û-fa-lan are still in existence. Kâ*s*yapa Mâtaṅga (or, it may be, Kâ*s*ya Mâtaṅga[1]) is clearly a Sanskrit name. Mâtaṅga, though the name of a *K*andâla or low-caste man, might well be borne by a Buddhist priest.[2] The name of *K*û-fa-lan, however, is more difficult. Chinese scholars declare that it can only be a Chinese name,[3] yet if *K*û-fa-lan came from India with *K*â*s*yapa, we should expect that he too bore a Sanskrit name. In that case, *K*û might be taken as the last character of Tien-*k*û, India, which character is prefixed to the names of other Indian priests living in China. His name would be Fâ-lan, *i. e.* Dharma + x, whatever lan may signify, perhaps padma, lotus.[4]

[1] This name is written in various ways, Ka-shio-ma-tô-giya, Ka-shio-ma-tô, Shio-ma-tô, Ka-tô, Ma-tô. In the Fan-i-ming-i-tsi (vol. iii. fol. 4 a), it is said "that K. was a native of Central India, and a Brâhman by caste. Having been invited by the Chinese envoy, Tsâi-yin, he came to China, saw the Emperor, and died in Lo-yang, the capital." Of *K*û-fa-lan it is said (*l. c.* vol. iii. fol. 4) that he was a native of Central India, well versed in Vinaya. When invited to go to China, the King would not let him depart. He left secretly, and arrived in China after Kâ*s*yapa. They translated the Sûtra in forty-two sections together. After Kâ*s*yapa died, *K*û-fa-lan translated five Sûtras.

[2] See Vasala-sutta (in Nipâta-sutta), *v.* 22.

[3] Fa is the Buddhist equivalent for friar.

[4] Mr. B. Nanjio informs me that both in China and Japan Buddhist priests adopt either *K*û, the last character of Tien-*k*û, India, or Shih, the first character of Shih-kia — *i. e.* *S*âkya — as their surname.

M. Feer,[1] calls him Gobhara*n*a, without, however, giving his authority for such a name. The Sutra of the forty-two sections exists in Chinese, but neither in Sanskrit nor in Pâli, and many difficulties would be removed if we admitted, with M. Feer, that this so-called Sûtra of the forty-two sections was really the work of Kâ*s*yapa and *K*û-fa-lan, who considered such an epitome of Buddhist doctrines, based chiefly on original texts, useful for their new converts in China.

It is curious that the Sui Annals speak here of no other literary work due to Kâ*s*yapa and *K*û-fa-lan, though they afterwards mention the Shih-*k*u *S*ûtra by *K*û-fa-lan as a work almost unintelligible. In the Fan-i-ming-i-tsi (vol. iii. fol. 4 b), mention is made of five Sûtras, translated by *K*û-fa-lan alone, after Kâ*s*yapa's death. In the K'ai-yuen-shih-kiao-mu-lu catalogue of the Buddhist books, compiled in the period K'ai-yuen (713–741 A. D.), vol. i. fol. 6, four Sûtras only are ascribed to *K*û-fa-lan : —

1. The Da*s*abhûmi, called the Sûtra on the destruction of the causes of perplexity in the ten stations ; 70 A. D. This is the Shi-*k*û Sûtra.

2. The Sûtra of the treasure of the sea of the law (Dharma-samudra-kosha ?).

3. The Sûtra of the original conduct of Buddha (Fo-pen-hing-king) ; 68 A. D. (taken by Julien for a translation of the Lalita-vistara).

4. The Sûtra of the original birth of Buddha (*G*âtaka).

The compiler of the catalogue adds that these translations have long been lost.

[1] L. Feer, *Sutra en 42 articles*, p. xxvii. *Le Dhammapada par F. Hû, suivi du Sutra en 42 articles*, par Léon Feer, 1878, p. xxiv.

The next patron of Buddhism was Ying, the King of *Kh*û, at the time of the Emperor *K*ang, his father (76–88). Many Shâmans, it is said, came to China then from the Western regions, bringing Buddhist Sûtras. Some of these translations, however, proved unintelligible.

During the reign of the Emperor Hwan (147–167), An-shi-kao (usually called An-shing), a Shâman of An-hsi,[1] brought classical books to Lo, and translated them. This is evidently the same translator of whom Mr. Beal ("J. R. A. S." 1856, pp. 327, 332) speaks as a native of Eastern Persia or Parthia, and whose name Mr. Wylie wished to identify with Arsak. As An-shi-kao is reported to have been a royal prince, who made himself a mendicant and travelled as far as China, Mr. Wylie supposes that he was the son of one of the Arsacidæ, Kings of Persia. Mr. Beal on the contrary, takes the name to be a corruption of A*s*vaka or Assaka — *i. e.* Ἱππάσιοι.[2]

Under the Emperor Ling, 168–189 A. D., *K*i-*kh*an (or *K*i-tsin), a Shâman from the Yueh-*k*i (called *K*i-lau-kia-*k*uai by Beal), *K*û-fo-soh (Ta-fo-sa), an Indian Shâman, and others, worked together to produce a translation of the Nirvâ*n*a-sûtra, in two sections. The K'ai-yuen-lu ascribes twenty-three works to *K*i-*kh*an, and two Sûtras to *K*û-fo-soh.

Towards the end of the Han dynasty, *K*u-yung, the grand guardian, was a follower of Buddha.

In the time of the Three Kingdoms (220–264)

1 In Beal's *Catalogue* this name is spelt An-shi-ko, An-shi-kao, and Ngan-shai-ko.

2 His translations occur in Beal's *Catalogue*, pp. 31, 35, 37, 38, 40 (*bis*), 41 (*bis*), 42 (*bis*), 43, 45, 46, 47, 49, 50, 51 (*ter*), 52 (*bis*), 54, 70, 88, 95 (*bis*). In the K'ai-yuen-lu it is stated that he translated 99 works in 115 fascicles.

Khang-sang-hui, a Shâman of the Western regions, came to Wû[1] with Sûtras and translated them. Sun-*kh*üan, the sovereign, believed in Buddhism. About the same time Khang-sang-khai translated the longer text of the Sukhavatîvyûha.

In Wei,[2] during the period Hwang-*kh*u (220–226) the Chinese first observed the Buddhist precepts, shaved their heads, and became Sang — *i. e.* monks.

Even before this, a Shâman of the Western regions had come here and translated the Hsiâo-pin Sûtra — *i. e.* the Sûtra of Smaller Matters (Khuddakanikâya ?) — but the head and tail of it were contradictory, so that it could not be understood.

In the period Kan-lû (256–259), *K*û-shi-hsing (Chu-shuh-lan, in Beal's "Catalogue") went to the West as far as Khoten, and obtained a Sûtra in ninety sections, with which he came back to Yéh, in the Tsin period of Yüen-khang (291–299), and translated it (with Dharmaraksha) under the title of "Light-emitting Pra*g*nâ-pâramitâ Sûtra."[3]

In the period Thai-shi (265–274), under the Western Tsin (265–316), Kû-fâ-hu[4] (Dharmaraksha), a Shâman of the Yüeh-*k*i, travelled through the various kingdoms of the West, and brought a large collection of books home to Lo, where he translated them. It is stated in the Catalogue of the Great *K*au, an inter-

1 Wû, comprising *K*eh-kiang and other parts, with its capital in what is now Sû-*k*au, was the southern one of the Three Kingdoms. Sun-*kh*üan was its first sovereign.

2 The northern of the Three Kingdoms, with its capital latterly in Lo-yang.

3 See Beal, *Catalogue*, p. 5.

4 This name, *K*û-fâ-hu, is generally re-translated as Dharmaraksha. *K*û is the second character in Tien-*k*û, the name of India, and this character was used as their surname by many Indian priests while living in China. In that case their Sanskrit names were mostly translated into two Chinese characters: as Fâ (law=dharma), hu (protection=raksha). — B. N.

lude in the dynasty of Thang (690–705 A. D.), that in the seventh year of the period Thai-khang (286) he translated *K*ing-fa-hwa — *i. e.* the Saddharma-pu*n*-*d*arîka (Beal, "Catalogue," p. 14).[1]

About 300 A. D. *K*i-kung-ming translated the Wei-ma (Vimala-kîrtti) and Fa-hwa (Saddharma-pu*nd*arîka).[2]

In 335 the prince of the *Kh*au kingdom (during the Tsin dynasty) permitted his subjects to become Shâmans, influenced chiefly by Buddhasi*m*ha.[3]

In the time of the rebel Shih-leh, 330–333, during the Tsin dynasty, a Shâman Wei-tao-an, or Tao-an, of *Kh*ang-shan, studied Buddhist literature under Buddhasi*m*ha. He produced a more correct translation of the Vimala-kîrtti-sûtra (and Saddharma-pu*n*-*d*arîka), and taught it widely; but as he was not an original translator, his name is not mentioned in the K'ai-yuen-lu. On account of political troubles, Tâo-an led his disciples southward, to Hsin-ye, and dispatched them to different quarters — Fâ-shang to Yang-*k*âu, Fâ-hwa to Shû — while he himself, with Wei-yüan, went to Hsiang-yang and *Kh*ang-an. Here Fu-*kh*ien, the sovereign of the Fûs, who about 350 had got possession of *Kh*ang-an, resisting the authority of the Tsin, and establishing the dynasty of the Former *Kh*in, received him with distinction. It was at the wish of Tâo-an that Fu-*kh*ien invited Kumâra*g*îva to *Kh*ang-an; but when, after a long delay, Kumâra*g*îva arrived there, in the second year of the

1 According to Mr. Beal (Fahian, p. xxiii.), this *K*û-fâ-hu, with the help of other Shâmans, translated no less than 165 texts, and among them the Lalita-vistara (Pou-yao-king), the Nirvâ*n*a Sûtra, and the Suvar*n*a-prabhâsa-Sûtra (265–308). The K'ai-yuen-lu assigns to him 275 works, in 354 fascicles.

2 Edkins, *l. c.* Beal, *Catalogue*, p. 17; 14.

3 Edkins, *l. c.*

period Hung-shi (400 A. D.), under Yâo-hsing, who, in 394, had succeeded Yâo-*kh*ang,[1] the founder of the After *Kh*in dynasty, Tâo-an had been dead already twenty years. His corrected translations, however, were approved by Kumâra*g*îva.

This Kumâra*g*îva marks a new period of great activity in the translation of Buddhist texts. He is said to have come from Ku-tsi, in Tibet, where the Emperor Yâo-hsing (397–415) sent for him. Among his translations are mentioned the Wei-ma or Vimala-kîrtti-sûtra (Beal's "Catalogue," p. 17); the Saddharma-pu*nd*arîka (Beal's "Catalogue," p. 15); the Satyasiddha-vyâkara*n*a sâstra (Beal's "Catalogue," p. 80). He was a contemporary of the great traveller, Fa-hian, who went from *Kh*ang-an to India, travelled through more than thirty states, and came back to Nanking in 414, to find the Emperor Yâo-hsing overturned by the Eastern Tsin dynasty. He was accompanied by the Indian contemplationist, Buddhabhadra.[2] Buddhabhadra translated the Fa-yan-king, the Buddhâvata*m*saka-vaipulya-sûtra (Beal's "Catalogue," p. 9), and he and Fa-hian together, the Mo-ho-sang-*k*i-liu — *i. e.* the Vinaya of the Mahâsaṅghika school (Beal, "Catalogue," p. 68).

Another Shâman who travelled to India about the same time was *K*i-mang, of Hsin-fang, a district city

[1] The Yâos subdued the Fûs, and ruled as the dynasty of the After *Kh*in.

[2] See p. 208. He is sometimes called Balasan, or, according to Edkins, Palat'sanga, Baddala, or Dabadara. In the Fan-i-ming-i-tsi (vol. iii. fol. 6) the following account of Buddhabhadra is given: "Buddhabhadra met Kumâra*g*îva in China, and whenever the latter found any doubts, the former was always asked for an explanation. In the fourteenth year of Î-hsi (418 A. D.) Buddhabhadra translated the Fa-yan-king in sixty volumes." This Sûtra is the Ta-fang-kwang-fo-fa-yan-king, Buddhâvata*m*saka-vaipulya-sûtra (Beal's *Catalogue*, p. 9). This translation was brought to Japan in 736.

of Kâo-*kh*ang. In 419, in the period Yüan-hsi, he went as far as Pâ*t*ali-putra, where he obtained the Nirva*n*a-sûtra, and the Saṅghika, a book of discipline.[1] After his return to Kâo-*kh*ang he translated the Nirvâ*n*a-sûtra in twenty sections.

Afterwards the Indian Shâman Dharmaraksha II.[2] brought other copies of the foreign MSS. to the West of the Ho. And Tsü-*kh*ü Mung-sun, the king of North Liang, sent messengers to Kâo-*kh*ang for the copy which *K*i-mang had brought, wishing to compare the two.[3]

When *K*i-mang's copy arrived,[4] a translation was made of it in thirty sections. Dharmaraksha II. translated the Suvar*n*a-prabhâsa and the Nirvâ*n*a-sûtra, 416–423 A. D. The K'ai-yuen-lu ascribes nineteen works to Dharmalatsin in 131 fascicles.

Buddhism from that time spread very rapidly in China, and the translations became too numerous to be all mentioned.

The Mahâyâna school was represented at that time chiefly by the following translations: —

1 The Sang-*k*i-liu, rules of priesthood; *i. e.* the Vinaya of the Mahâsaṅghika school.

2 I call him Dharmaraksha II., in order to prevent a confusion which has been produced by identifying two Shâmans who lived at a distance of nearly 200 years — the one 250 A. D., the other 420 A. D. The first is called *K*û-fâ-hu, which can be rendered Dharmaraksha; the second is called Fâ-făng (law-prosperity), but, if transliterated, he is best known by the names T'on-mo-la-tsin, T'an-mo-tsin, or Dharmalatsin. He was a native of Central India, and arrived in China in the first year of the period Hiouen-shi of the Tsü-*kh*ü family of the Northern Liang, 414 A. D. He was the contemporary of *K*i-mang, whom Mr. Beal places about 250 A. D., in order to make him a contemporary of Dharmaraksha I.

3 Mung-sun died 432, and was succeeded by his heir, who lost his kingdom in 439. Yâo-*kh*ang's kingdom, however, was destroyed by the Eastern Tsin, at the time of his second successor, 417, not by Mung-sun.

4 It is said in the tenth year of the period Hung-shi of Yâo-*kh*ang (better hsing), the copy arrived at *Kh*ang-an. But this cannot be, if *K*i-mang went to India in 419. There must be something wrong in these dates.

The Vimalakîrtti-sûtra (Beal, "Catalogue," p. 17.) The Saddharmapu*nd*arîka-sûtra (Beal, "Catalogue," p. 15) The Satyasiddhavyâkara*n*a-*s*âstra (Beal, "Catalogue," p. 80)	Translated by Kumâra*g*îva.
The Suvar*n*aprabhâsa-sûtra (Beal, "Catalogue," p. 15) The Nirvâ*n*a-sûtra (Beal, "Catalogue," p. 12)	Translated by Dharmalatsin, or Dharmaraksha II.

The Hînayâna school was represented by—

The Sarvâstivâda-vinaya by Kumâra*g*îva (Beal, "Catalogue," pp. 67, 68).

The Dîrghâgama-sûtra, by Buddhaya*s*as, 410 A. D. (Beal, "Catalogue," p. 36).

The Vinaya of the four Parts, by Buddhaya*s*as.[1]

The Ekottarâgama-sûtra (Aṅguttara), translated by Dharmanandin, of Tukhâra (Fa-hsi).

The Abhidharma disquisitions, by Dharmaya*s*as,[2] of Kophene.

During the period of Lung-an (397–401) the Ekottarâgama (Anguttara) and Madhyamâgama-sûtras[3] were translated by Saṅghadeva of Kophene. This is probably the Ma*ggh*ima Nikâya, translated by Gotama Saṅghadeva, under the Eastern Tsin dynasty, 317–419.

In the period Î-hsi (405–418) the Shâman *K*i-fâ-ling brought from Khoten to Nanking, the southern capital, the Hwâ-yen Sûtra in 36,000 gâthâs, and translated it. This may be the Buddhâvata*m*saka-sûtra, called the Ta-fang-kwang-fo-fa-yan-king (Beal's "Catalogue," pp. 9, 10). This translator is not mentioned in the K'ai-yuen-lu.

1 The four Nikâyas or Âgamas; *cf.* Vinayapi*t*aka, vol. i. p. xl.

2 *S*âriputrâbhidharma-*s*âstra; *cf.* Beal, *Catalogue*, p. 80.

3 Beal, *Catalogue*, p. 36.

In 420 the Tsin dynasty came to an end.

The Emperor Thai-wu (424–452), of the N. Wei dynasty, persecuted the Buddhists, 446; but from the year 452 they were tolerated. This dynasty lasted from 386 to 535, when it was divided into two.

In 458 there was a conspiracy under Buddhist influences, and more stringent laws were enforced against them.

In 460 five Buddhists arrived in China from Ceylon, *viâ* Tibet. Two of them, Yashaita, and Vudanandi, brought images.[1] In 502 a Hindu translated Mahâyâna books, called Fixed Positions and Ten Positions.[2]

During the dynasties of *Kh*î (479–502), Liang (502–557), and *Kh*in (557–589), many famous Shâmans came to China, and translated books.

The Emperor Wû of Liang (502–549) paid great honor to Buddhism. He made a large collection of the Buddhist canonical books, amounting to 5,400 volumes, in the Hwâ-lin garden. The Shâman Pao-*kh*ang compiled the catalogue in fifty-four fascicles.

In the period Yung-ping, 508–511, there was an Indian Shâman Bodhiru*k*i, who translated many books, as Kumâra*g*îva had done. Among them were the Earth-holding *s*âstra (bhûmîdhara *s*âstra?) and the Shi-ti-king-lun, the Da*s*abhûmika *s*âstra, greatly valued by the followers of the Mahâyâna.[3]

In 516, during the period Hsî-phing, the Chinese Shâman Wei-shang was sent to the West to collect Sûtras and Vinayas, and brought back a collection of 170 books. He is not, however, mentioned as a translator in the K'ai-yuen-lu.

1 Edkins, *l. c.* 2 *Ibid.*

3 Beal, *Catalogue*, p. 77; on p. 20 a translation of the Lankâvatâra is mentioned.

In 518 Sung-yun, sent by the queen of the Wei country from Lo-yang to India, returned after three years, with 175 volumes. He lived to see Bodhidharma in his coffin. This Bodhidharma, the twenty-eighth patriarch, had arrived in Canton by sea in 528, in the time of Wu-ti, the first Emperor of the Liang dynasty. Some Sanskrit MSS. that had belonged to him, and other relics, are still preserved in Japan.[1]

In the time of the Emperor Wû, of the Northern *K*âu dynasty (561–577), a Shâman, Wei-yüan-sung, accused the Buddhist priests, and the Emperor persecuted them. But in the first year of Kao-tsu, the founder of the Sui dynasty, in 589, toleration was again proclaimed. He ordered the people to pay a certain sum of money, according to the number of the members of each family, for the purpose of preparing Sûtras (the Buddhist canon) and images. And the Government caused copies of the whole Buddhist canon to be made, and placed them in certain temples or monasteries in the capital, and in several other large cities, in such provinces as Ping-*k*âu, Hsiang-*k*âu, Lo-*k*âu, etc. And the Government caused also another copy to be made and to be deposited in the Imperial Library. The Buddhist sacred books among the people were found to be several hundred times more numerous than those on the six Kings of Confucius. There were 1,950 distinct Buddhist books translated.

In the period Tâ-yeh (605–616) the Emperor ordered the Shâman *K*i-kwo to compose a catalogue of the Buddhist books at the Imperial Buddhist chapel within the gate of the palace. He then made some divisions and classifications, which were as follows:—

[1] See *Athenæum*, August 7, 1880; and *infra*, p. 370.

The Sûtras which contained what Buddha had spoken were arranged under three divisions: —

1. The Mahâyâna.
2. The Hînayâna.
3. The Mixed Sûtras.

Other books, that seemed to be the productions of later men, who falsely ascribed their works to greater names, were classed as Doubtful Books.

There were other works in which Bodhisattvas and others went deeply into the explanation of the meaning, and illustrated the principles of Buddha. These were called Disquisitions, or *S*âstras. Then there were Vinaya, or compilations of precepts, under each division as before, Mahâyâna, Hînayâna, Mixed. There were also Records, or accounts of the doings in their times of those who had been students of the system. Altogether there were eleven classes under which the books were arranged: —

1. Sûtra.	Mahâyâna .	617	in	2,076	chapters.
	Hînayâna .	487	"	852	"
	Mixed . .	380	"	716	"
	Mixed and doubtful	172	"	336	"
2. Vinaya.	Mahâyâna .	52	"	91	"
	Hînayâna .	80	"	472	"
	Mixed . .	27	"	46	"
3. *S*âstra.	Mahâyâna .	35	"	141	"
	Hînayâna .	41	"	567	"
	Mixed . .	51	"	437	"
	Records . .	20	"	464	"
		1,962		6,198	

Search for Sanskrit MSS. in China.

It was the publication of Hiouen-thsang's Travels which roused the hopes of Professor Wilson that some of the old Sanskrit MSS. which had been carried away from India might still be discovered in China.[1]

But though no pains were spared by Sir John Bowring to carry out Professor Wilson's wishes, though he had catalogues sent to him from Buddhist libraries, and from cities where Buddhist compositions might be expected to exist, the results were disappointing, at least so far as Sanskrit texts were concerned. A number of interesting Chinese books, translated from Sanskrit by Hiouen-thsang and others, works also by native Chinese Buddhists, were sent to the library of the East India House; but what Professor Wilson and all Sanskrit scholars with him most desired, Sanskrit MSS., or copies of Sanskrit MSS., were not forthcoming. Professor Wilson showed me, indeed, one copy of a Sanskrit MS. that was sent to him from China, and, so far as I remember, it was the Kâla-*K*akra,[2] which we know as one of the books translated from Sanskrit into Chinese. That MS., however, is no longer to be found in the India Office Library, though it certainly existed in the old East India House.

The disappointment at the failure of Professor Wilson's and Sir J. Bowring's united efforts was felt all the more keenly because neither Sanskrit nor Chinese schslars could surrender the conviction that, until a very short time ago, Indian MSS. had existed in China. They had been seen by Europeans, such as Dr. Gutzlaff, the hard-working missionary in China,

[1] A long list of Sanskrit texts translated into Chinese may be found in the *Journal Asiatique*, 1849, p. 353 *seq.*, *s. t.* "Concordance Sinico-Samskrite d'un nombre considérable de titres d'ouvrages Bouddhiques, recueillie dans un Catalogue Chinois de l'an 1306, par M. Stanislas Julien."

[2] Csoma Körösi, *As. Res.* vol. xx. p. 418. *Journal Asiatique*, 1849, p. 356.

who in a paper, written shortly before his death, and addressed to Colonel Sykes ("Journal R. A. S." 1856, p. 73), stated that he himself had seen Pâli MSS. preserved by Buddhist priests in China. Whether these MSS. were in Pâli or Sanskrit would matter little, supposing even that Dr. Gutzlaff could not distinguish between the two. He speaks with great contempt of the whole Buddhist literature. There was not a single priest, he says, capable of explaining the meaning of the Pâli texts, though some were interlined with Chinese. "A few works," he writes, "are found in a character originally used for writing the Pâli, and may be considered as faithful transcripts of the earliest writings of Buddhism. They are looked upon as very sacred, full of mysteries and deep significations, and therefore as the most precious relics of the founder of their creed. With the letters of this alphabet the priests perform incantations[1] to expel demons, rescue souls from hell, bring down rain on the earth, remove calamities, etc. They turn and twist them in every shape, and maintain that the very demons tremble at the recitation of them."

Another clear proof of the existence of Sanskrit MSS. in China is found in the account of a "Trip to Ning-po and T'hëen-t'hae," by Dr. Edkins. After he had arrived at Fang-kwang, he ascended the Hwa-ling hill, and at the top of the hill he describes a small temple with a priest residing in it. "Scattered over the hill," he adds, "there are various little temples where priests reside, but the one at the top is the most celebrated, as being the place where Che-k'hae spent a portion of his time, worshipping

[1] *Cf.* Beal, *Catalogue*, p. 66.

a Sanskrit manuscript of a Buddhist classic." On his return he arrived at the pagoda erected to the memory of Che-k'hae, the founder of the Thëen-t'hae system of Buddhism, in the Chin dynasty (about 580 A. D.). And a little farther on, situated in a deep dell on the left, was the monastery of Kaon-ming-sze. This is particularly celebrated for its possession of a Sanskrit MS., written on the palm leaf, once read and explained by Che-k'hae, but now unintelligible to any of the followers of Buddhism in these parts. The priests seemed to pay uncommon reverence to this MS., which is the only one of the kind to be found in the East of China, and thus of great importance in a literary point of view. It is more than 1,300 years old, but is in a state of perfect preservation, in consequence of the palm leaves, which are written on both sides, having been carefully let into slips of wood, which are fitted on the same central pin, and the whole, amounting to fifty leaves, inclosed in a rosewood box.

This may account for the unwillingness of the priests to part with their old MSS., whether Sanskrit or Pâli, but it proves at the same time that they still exist, and naturally keeps up the hope that some day or other we may still get a sight of them.

Materials on which Sanskrit MSS. were written.

Of course, it might be said that if MSS. did not last very long in India, neither would they do so in China. But even then, we might expect at least that as in India the old MSS. were copied whenever they showed signs of decay, so they would have been in China. Besides, the climate of China is not so destructive as the heat and moisture of the climate of India. In India, MSS. seldom last over a thousand years. Long before that time paper made of vegetable substances decays, palm-leaves and birch-bark become brittle, and white ants often destroy what might have escaped the ravages of the climate. It was the duty, therefore, of Indian Rajahs to keep a staff of librarians, who had to copy the old MSS. whenever they began to seem unsafe, a fact which accounts both for the modern date of most of our Sanskrit MSS. and for the large number of copies of the same text often met with in the same library.

The MSS. carried off to China were in all likelihood not written on paper, or whatever we like to call the material which Nearchus describes "as cotton well beaten together,"[1] but on the bark of the birch tree or on palm leaves. The bark of trees is mentioned as a writing material used in India by Curtius;[2] and in Buddhist Sûtras, such as the Kara*nd*a-vyûha (p. 69), we actually read of bhûr*g*a, birch, mâsi, ink, and karama (kalam), as the common requisites for writing. MSS. written on that material have long been known in Europe, chiefly as curiosities (I had to write many years ago about one of them, preserved in the Library at All Souls' College). Of late,[3] however, they have attracted more serious attention, particularly since Dr. Bühler discovered in Kashmir old MSS. containing independent rescensions of Vedic texts, written on birch bark. One of these, containing the whole text of the Rig-Veda Sa*m*hitâ[4] with accents, was sent to me, and

1 The modern paper in Nepal is said to date from 500 years ago (Hodgson, *Essays*).

2 M. M., *History of Ancient Sanskrit Literature*, p. 516.

3 Burnell, *South Indian Palæography*, 2d ed. p. 84 *seq.*

4 See *Sacred Books of the East*, vol. i., Upanishads, Introduction, p. lxxviii.

though it had suffered a good deal, particularly on the margins, it shows that there was no difficulty in producing from the bark of the birch tree thousands and thousands of pages of the largest quarto or even folio size, perfectly smooth and pure, except for the small dark lines peculiar to the bark of that tree.[1]

At the time of Hiouen-thsang, in the seventh century, palm leaves seem to have been the chief material for writing. He mentions a forest of palm-trees (*Borassus flabelliformis*) near Konka*n*apura (the

[1] Dr. Bühler (*Journal of the Royal Asiatic Society, Bombay*, 1877, p. 29) has the following interesting remarks: "The Bhûrga MSS. are written on specially-prepared thin sheets of the inner bark of the Himalayan birch (*Bœtula Bhojpatr*, Wallich), and invariably in *S*âradâ characters. The lines run always parallel to the narrow side of the leaf, and the MSS. présent, therefore, the appearance of European books, not of Indian MSS., which owe their form to an imitation of the Tâlapatras. The Himâlaya seems to contain an inexhaustible supply of birch bark, which in Ka*s*mîr and other hill countries is used both instead of paper by the shopkeepers in the bazaars, and for lining the roofs of houses in order to make them water-tight. It is also exported to India, where in many places it is likewise used for wrapping up parcels, and plays an important part in the manufacture of the flexible pipe-stems used by hukâ smokers. To give an idea of the quantities which are brought into *S*rînagar, I may mention that on one single day I counted fourteen large barges with birch bark on the river. . . . . The use of birch bark for literary purposes is attested by the earliest classical Sanskrit writers. Kâlidâsa mentions it in his dramas and epics; Su*s*tuta, Varâhamihira (*circa* 500–550 A. D.) know it likewise. As is the case with nearly all old customs, the use of birch bark for writing still survives in India, though the fact is little known. Mantras, which are worn as amulets, are written on pieces of Bhûrga with ash*t*au gandhâ*h*, a mixture of eight odoriferous substances — *e. g.* camphor, sandal, tumeric — which vary according to the deity to which the writing is dedicated. The custom prevails in Bengal as well as in Gujarât. Birch-bark MSS. occur in Orissa. The Petersburg Dictionary refers to a passage in the Kâ*th*aka, the redaction of the Yajurveda formerly current in Ka*s*mîr, where the word Bhûr*g*a occurs, though it is not clear if it is mentioned there too as material for writing on. The Ka*s*mirian Pandits assert, and apparently with good reason, that in Ka*s*mîr all books were written on bhûrgapattras from the earliest times until after the conquest of the Valley by Akbar, about 200–250 years ago. Akbar introduced the manufacture of paper, and thus created an industry for which Ka*s*mîr is now famous in India."

Western coast of the Dekhan),[1] which was much prized on account of its supplying material for writing (vol. i. p. 202, and vol. iii. p. 148). At a later time, too, in 965, we read of Buddhist priests returning to China with Sanskrit copies of Buddhist books written on palm leaves (peito).[2] If we could believe Hiouen-thsang, the palm leaf would have been used even so early as the first Buddhist Council,[3] for he says that Kâsyapa then wrote the Pi*t*akas on palm leaves (tâla), and spread them over the whole of India. In the Pâli *G*âtakas, pa*nn*a is used in the sense of letter, but originally par*n*a meant a wing, then a leaf of a tree, then a leaf for writing. Pa*tt*a, also, which is used in the sense of a sheet, was originally pattra, a wing, a leaf of a tree. Suva*nn*a-pa*tt*a, a golden leaf to write on, still shows that the original writing material had been the leaves of trees, most likely of palm-trees.[4] Potthaka, *i. e.* pustaka, book, likewise occurs in the Pâli *G*âtakas.[5]

Such MSS., written on palm leaves, if preserved carefully and almost worshipped, as they seem to have been in China, might well have survived to the present day, and they would certainly prove of immense value to the students of Buddhism, if they could still be recovered, whether in the original or even in later copies.

It is true, no doubt, that, like all other religions, Buddhism too had its periods of trial and persecution in China. We know that during such periods — as,

1 Dr. Burnell, *Indian Antiquary*, 1880, p. 234, shows that Koṅka*n*apura is Koṅka*n*ah*ll*i in the Mysore territory.

2 Beal's *Travels of Buddhist Pilgrims*, Introd. p. xlvi.

3 *Pèlerins Bouddhistes*, vol. i. p. 158.

4 Fausböll, *Dasaratha-ǵ*ataka, p. 25.

5 See, also, Albiruni, as quoted by Reinaud, *Mémoire sur l'Inde*, p. 305.

for instance, in 845, under the Emperor Wu-tsung — monasteries were destroyed, images broken, and books burnt. But these persecutions seem never to have lasted long, and when they were over, monasteries, temples, and pagodas soon sprang up again, images were restored, and books collected in greater abundance than ever. Dr. Edkins tells us that "in an account of the Ko-t'sing monastery in the History of T'ian-t'ai-shan it is said that a single work was saved from a fire there several centuries ago, which was written on the Pei-to (Pe-ta) or palm leaf of India." He also states that great pagodas were built on purpose as safe repositories of Sanskrit MSS., one being erected by the Emperor for the preservation of the newly arrived Sanskrit books at the request of Hiouen-thsang, lest they should be injured for want of care. It was 180 feet high, had five stories with grains of She-li (relics) in the centre of each, and contained monuments inscribed with the prefaces written by the Emperor or Prince Royal to Hiouen-thsang's translations.

Search for Sanskrit MSS. in Japan.

Being myself convinced of the existence of old Indian MSS. in China, I lost no opportunity, during the last five-and-twenty years, of asking any friends of mine who went to China to look out for these treasures, but — with no result!

Some years ago, however, Dr. Edkins, who had taken an active part in the search instituted by Professor Wilson and Sir J. Bowring, showed me a book which he had brought from Japan, and which contained a Chinese vocabulary with Sanskrit equivalents and a transliteration in Japanese. The Sanskrit is written in that peculiar alphabet which we find in the old MSS. of Nepâl, and which in China has been further modified, so as to give it an almost Chinese appearance.

That MS. revived my hopes. If such a book was published in Japan, I concluded that there must have been a time when such a book was useful there — that is to say, when the Buddhists in Japan studied Sanskrit. Dr. Edkins kindly left the book with me, and though the Sanskrit portion was full of blunders, yet it enabled me to become accustomed to that peculiar alphabet in which the Sanskrit words are written.

While I was looking forward to more information from Japan, good luck would have it that a young Buddhist priest, Mr. Bunyiu Nanjio, came to me from Japan, in order to learn Sanskrit and Pâli, and thus to be able in time to read the sacred writings of the Buddhists in their original language, and to compare them with the Chinese and Japanese translations now current in his country. After a time, another Buddhist priest, Mr. Kasawara, came to me for the same purpose, and both are now working very hard at learning Sanskrit. Japan is supposed to contain 34,388,504 inhabitants, all of whom, with the exception of about 1 or 200,000 followers of the Shintô religion,[1] are Buddhists, divided into ten principal sects, the sect to which Mr. Bunyiu Nanjio belongs being that of the Shinshiu. One of the first questions which I asked Mr. Bunyiu Nanjio, when he came to read Sanskrit with me, was about Sanskrit MSS. in Japan. I showed him the Chinese-Sanskrit-Japanese Vocabulary which Dr. Edkins had left with me, and he soon admitted that Sanskrit texts in the same al-

[1] See Letter to the *Times*, "On the Religions of Japan," Oct. 20, 1880.

phabet might be found in Japan, or at all events in China. He wrote home to his friends, and after waiting for some time, he brought me in December last a book which a Japanese scholar, Shuntai Ishikawa, had sent to me, and which he wished me to correct, and then to send back to him to Japan. I did not see at once the importance of the book. But when I came to read the introductory formula, Evam mayâ srutam, "Thus by me it has been heard," the typical beginning of the Buddhist Sûtras, my eyes were opened. Here, then, was what I had so long been looking forward to — a Sanskrit text, carried from India to China, from China to Japan, written in the peculiar Nepalese alphabet, with a Chinese translation, and a transliteration in Japanese. Of course, it is a copy only, not an original MS.; but copies presuppose originals at some time or other, and, such as it is, it is a first instalment, which tells us that we ought not to despair, for where one of the long-sought-for literary treasures that were taken from India to China, and afterwards from China to Japan, has been discovered, others are sure to come to light.

We do not possess yet very authentic information on the ancient history of Japan, and on the introduction of Buddhism into that island. M. Léon de Rosny[1] and the Marquis D'Hervey de Saint-Denys[2] have given us some information on the subject, and I hope that Mr. Bunyiu Nanjio will soon give us a trustworthy account of the ancient history of his country, drawn from native authorities. What is

[1] "Le Bouddhisme dans l'extrême Orient," *Revue Scientifique*, Décembre, 1879.

[2] *Journal Asiatique*, 1871, p. 386 *seq.*

told us about the conversion of Japan to Buddhism has a somewhat legendary aspect, and I shall only select a few of the more important facts, as they have been communicated to me by my Sanskrit pupil. Buddhism first reached Japan, not directly from China, but from Corea, which had been converted to Buddhism in the fourth century A. D. In the year 200 A. D. Corea had been conquered by the Japanese Empress Zingu, and the intercourse thus established between the two countries led to the importation of Buddhist doctrines from Corea to Japan. In the year 552 A. D. one of the Corean kings sent a bronze statue of Buddha and many sacred books to the Court of Japan, and after various vicissitudes, Buddhism became the established religion of the island about 600 A. D. Japanese students were sent to China to study Buddhism, and they brought back with them large numbers of Buddhist books, chiefly translations from Sanskrit. In the year 640 A. D. we hear of a translation of the Sukhavatîvyûhamahâyâna-sûtra being read in Japan. This is the title of the Sanskrit text now sent to me from Japan. The translation had been made by Kô-sô-gai (in Chinese, Khang-sang-khai), a native of Tibet, though living in India, 252 A. D., and we are told that there had been eleven other translations of the same text.[1]

Among the teachers of these Japanese students we find our old friend Hiouen-thsang, whom the Japanese call Genziô. In the year 653 a Japanese priest, Dosho by name, studied under Genziô, adopted the views of the sect founded by him, — the Hossô sect, — and brought back with him to Japan a compila-

[1] Five of these translations were introduced into Japan; the others seem to have been lost in China. The translations are spoken of as "the five in existence and the seven missing."

tion of commentaries on the thirty verses of Vasubandhu, written by Dharmapâla, and translated by Genziô. Two other priests, Chitsû and Chitatsu, likewise became his pupils, and introduced the famous Abhidharma-kosha-*s*âstra into Japan, which had been composed by Vasubandhu, and translated by Genziô. They seem to have favored the Hînayâna, or the views of the Small Vehicle (Kushashiu).

In the year 736 we hear of a translation of the Buddhâvata*m*saka-vaipulya-sûtra, by Buddhabhadra and others[1] (317–419 A. D.), being received in Japan, likewise of a translation of the Saddharma-pu*nd*arîka by Kumara*g*îva.[2]

And, what is more important still, in the ninth century we are told that Kukai (died 835), the founder of the Shingon sect in Japan, was not only a good Chinese, but a good Sanskrit scholar also. Nay, one of his disciples, Shinnyo, in order to perfect his knowledge of Buddhist literature, undertook a journey, not only to China, but to India, but died before he reached that country.

These short notices, which I owe chiefly to Mr. Bunyiu Nanjio, make it quite clear that we have every right to expect Sanskrit MSS., or, at all events, Sanskrit texts, in Japan, and the specimen which I have received encourages me to hope that some of these Sanskrit texts may be older than any which exist at present in any part of India.

The Sukhavatî-vyûha.

The text which was sent to me bears the title of Sukhâvatî-vyûha-mahâyâna-sûtra.[3]

[1] See p. 192. [2] See p. 192.
[3] The MSS. vary between Sukhavatî and Sukhâvatî.

This is a title well known to all students of Buddhist literature. Burnouf, in his "Introduction à l'Histoire du Buddhisme" (pp. 99–102),[1] gave a short account of this Sûtra, which enables us to see that the scene of the dialogue was laid at Râ*g*ag*ri*ha, and that the two speakers were Bhagavat and Ânanda.

We saw before, in the historical account of Buddhism in Japan, that no less than twelve Chinese translations of a work bearing the same title were mentioned. The Chinese tell us at least of five translations which are still in existence.[2]

Those of the Han and Wu dynasties (25–280 A. D.), we are told, were too diffuse, and those of the later periods, the T'ang and Sung dynasties, too literal. The best is said to be that by Kô-sô-gai, a priest of Tibetan descent, which was made during the early Wei dynasty, about 252 A. D. This may be the same which was read in Japan in 640 A. D.

The same Sûtra exists also in a Tibetan translation, for there can be little doubt that the Sûtra quoted by Csoma Körösi ("As. Res." vol. xx. p. 408) under the name of Amitâbha-vyûha is the same work. It occupies, as M. Léon Feer informs me, fifty-four leaves, places the scene of the dialogue at Râ*g*ag*ri*ha, on the mountain G*ri*dhra-kû*t*a, and introduces Bhagavat and Ânanda as the principal speakers.

There are Sanskrit MSS. of the Sukhavatî-vyûha in your own Library, in Paris, at Cambridge, and at Oxford.

The following is a list of the MSS. of the Sukhavatî-vyûha, hitherto known : —

1 See, also, *Lotus de la bonne Loi*, p. 267.
2 *Journal of the R. A. S.* 1856, p. 319.

1. MS. of the Royal Asiatic Society, London (Hodgson Collection), No. 20. Sukhavatîvyûha-mahâyânasûtra, sixty-five leaves. Dated Samvat 934 = A. D. 1814. It begins: Namo dasadiganantâparyantalokadhâtupratish*t*itebhya*h*, etc. Eva*m* mayâ srutam ekasmi*m* samaye Bhagavân Râ*g*ag*ri*he viharati sma. It ends: Sukhâvatîvyûha-mahâyânasûtra*m* samâpta*m*. Sa*m*vat 934, kârttikasudi 4, sa*m*pûr*n*am abhût. *S*rîsuvar*n*apa*n*ârimahânagare Maitrîpûrimahâvihâre *S*rîvâkva*g*radâsa va*g*râ*k*âryasya *G*ayânandasya *k*a sarvârthasiddhe*h*. (Nepalese alphabet.)

2. MS. of the Bibliothèque Nationale, Paris (Collection Burnouf), No. 85; sixty-four leaves. It begins, after a preamble of five lines, Eva*m* mayâ sruta*m*mekasmi samaya Bhagavân Râ*g*ag*ri*he viharati sma G*ri*dhrakû*t*e parvvate mahatâ Bhikshusanghena sârddham. Dvâtri*m*sratâ Bhikshusahasrai*h*. It ends: Bhagavato mitâbhasya gu*n*aparikîrttana*m* Bodhisattvâmavaivartyabhûmipravesa*h*. Amitâbhavyuhaparivartta*h*. Sukhâvatîvyûha*h* sampur*n*a*h*. Iti *S*rî Amitâbhasya Sukhâvatîvyuha nâma mahâyânastûra*m* samâpta*m*.[1] (Devanâgarî alphabet.)

3. MS. of the Société Asiatique at Paris (Collection Hodgson), No. 17; eighty-two leaves. (Nepalese alphabet.)[2]

4. MS. of the University Library at Cambridge, No. 1368; thirty-five leaves. It begins with some lines of prose and verse in praise of Amitâbha and Sukhavatî, and then proceeds: Eva*m* mayâ srutam ekasmi*m* samaye Bhagavân Râ*g*ag*ri*he nagare viharati sma, G*ri*dhrakû*t*aparvate mahatâ Bhikshusanghena sârddha, etc. It ends: iti srîmad amitâbhasya tathâ-

1 I owe this information to the kindness of M. Léon Feer at Paris.

2 See *Journal Asiatique*, 3d series, vol. iii. p. 316; vol. iv. p. 296–298.

gatasya Sukhâvatîvyûha-mahâyânasûtra*m* samâptam. (Nepalese alphabet, modern.)

5. MS. given by Mr. Hodgson to the Bodleian Library Oxford (Hodgson 3). It begins with: Om namo ratnatrayâya. Om nama*h* sarvabuddhabodhisattvebhya*h*, etc. Then Eva*m* mayâ *s*rutam, etc. It ends with sukhavâtîvyûhamahâyânasutra*m* samâpta*m*. (Nepalese alphabet, modern.)

But when I came to compare these Sanskrit MSS. with the text sent to me from Japan, though the title was the same, I soon perceived that their contents were different. While the text, as given in the ordinary Devanâgari or Nepalese MSS., fills about fifty to sixty leaves, the text of the Sûtra that reached me from Japan would hardly occupy more than eight or ten leaves.

I soon convinced myself that this MS. was not a text abbreviated in Japan, for this shorter text, sent to me from Japan, correspond in every respect with the Chinese Sûtra translated by Mr. Beal in his "Catena," pp. 378–383, and published in your Journal, 1866, p. 136. No doubt the Chinese translation, on which Mr. Beal's translation is based, is not only free, but displays the misapprehensions peculiar to many Chinese renderings of Sanskrit texts, due to a deficient knowledge either of Sanskrit or of Chinese on the part of the translators, perhaps also to the different genius of those two languages.

Yet, such as it is, there can be no doubt that it was meant to be a translation of the text now in my possession. Mr. Beal tells us that the translation he followed is that by Kumâra*g*îva, the contemporary of Fa-hian (400 A. D.), and that this translator omitted repetitions and superfluities in the text.[1] Mr. Edkins

[1] *J. R. A. S.* 1866 p. 136.

knows a translation, *s. t.* Wou-liang-sheu-king, made under the Han dynasty.[1] What is important is that in the Chinese translation of the shorter text the scene is laid, as in the Japanese Sanskrit text, at *S*râvastî, and the principal speakers are Bhagavat and *S*âriputra.

There is also a Tibetan translation of the short text, described by Csoma Körösi (" As. Res." vol. xx. p. 439). Here, though the name of the scene is not mentioned, the speakers are Bhagavat and *S*âriputra. The whole work occupies seven leaves only, and the names of the sixteen principal disciples agree with the Japanese text. The translators were Pra*g*nâvarman, Sûrendra, and the Tibetan Lotsava Ya-shes-sde.

M. Feer informs me that there is at the National Library a Chinese text called O-mi-to-king, *i. e.* Amitâbha-sûtra.[2] The scene is at *S*râvastî; the speakers are Bhagavat *S*âriputra.

Another text at the National Library is called Ta-o-mi-to-king, *i. e.* Mahâ Amitâbha-sûtra, and here the scene is at Râ*g*agr*i*ha.

There is, besides, a third work, called Kwan-wou-liang-sheu-king by Kiang-ling-ye-she, *i. e.* Kâlaya*s*as, a foreigner of the West, who lived in China about 424 A. D.

[1] *J. R. A. S.* 1866, p. 136.

[2] Beal, *Catalogue*, p. 23. *J. R. A. S.* 1856, p. 319. Beal, *Catalogue*, p. 77, mentions also an Amitâbha-sûtra-upade*s*a-*s*âstra, by Vasubandhu, translated by Bodhiru*k*i (Wou-liang-sheu-king-yeou-po-ti-she). There is an Amitâbha-sûtra, translated by Chi-hien of the Wu period — *i. e.* 222–280 A. D. — mentioned in Mr. Beal's *Catalogue of the Buddhist Tripitaka*, p. 6. The next Sûtra, which he calls the Sûtra of measureless years, is no doubt the Amitâyus-sûtra, Amitâyus being another name for Amitâbha (Fu-shwo-wou-liang-sheu-king, p. 6). See, also, *Catalogue*, pp. 99, 102. Dr. Edkins also, in his *Notices of Buddhism in China*, speaks of a translation of "the Sûtra of boundless age," by Fa-t'ian-pun, a native of Magadha, who was assisted in his translation by a native of China familiar with Sanskrit, about 1000 A. D.

We have, therefore, historical evidence of the existence of three Sûtras, describing Sukhavatî, or the Paradise of Amitâbha. We know two of them in Sanskrit, Chinese, and Tibetan — one long, the other short. The third is known as yet in Chinese only.

Of the two Sanskrit texts, the one from Nepal, the other from Japan, the latter seems certainly the earlier. But even the fuller text must have existed at a very early time, because it was translated by *K*i-lau-kia-*kh*ai, under the Eastern Han dynasty (25–220 A. D.) — *i. e.* at all events before 220 A. D.

The shorter text is first authenticated through the translation of Kumâra*g*îva, about 400 A. D.; but if the views generally entertained as to the relative position of the longer and shorter Sûtras be correct, we may safely claim for our short Sûtra a date within the second century of our era.

What Japan has sent us is, therefore, a Sanskrit text, of which we had no trace before, which must have left India at least before 400 A. D., but probably before 200 A. D., and which gives us the original of that description of Amitâbha's Paradise, which formerly we knew in a Chinese translation only, which was neither complete nor correct.

The book sent to me was first published in Japan in 1773, by Ziômiô, a Buddhist priest. The Sanskrit text is intelligible, but full of inaccuracies, showing clearly that the editor did not understand Sanskrit, but simply copied what he saw before him. The same words occurring in the same line are written differently, and the Japanese transliteration simply repeats the blunders of the Sanskrit transcript.

There are two other editions of the same text,

published in 1794 A. D. by another Japanese priest, named Hôgŏ. These are in the possession of Mr. Bunyiu Nanjio, and offered some help in correcting the text. One of them contains the text and three Chinese translations, one being merely a literal rendering, while the other two have more of a literary character and are ascribed to Kumâra*g*îva (400 A. D.), and Hiouen-thsang (648 A. D.).

Lastly, there is another book by the same Hôgŏ, in four volumes, in which an attempt is made to give a grammatical analysis of the text. This, however, as Mr. Bunyiu Nanjio informs me, is very imperfect.

I have to-day brought with me the Japanese Sanskrit text, critically restored, and a literal translation into English, to which I have added a few notes.

Translation.

Adoration to the Omniscient.

This is what I have heard. At one time the Blessed (Bhagavat, *i. e.* Buddha) dwelt at *S*râvastî,[1] in the *G*eta-grove, in the garden of Anâthapi*nd*aka, together with[2] a large company of Bhikshus (mendicant friars), viz. with thirteen hundred Bhikshus, all of them acquainted with the five kinds of knowledge,[3]

[1] *S*râvastî, capital of the Northern Kosalas, residence of King Prasena*g*it. It was in ruins when visited by Fa-hian (init. V. Sæc.); not far from the modern Fizabad. *Cf.* Burnouf, *Introduction*, p. 22.

[2] Sârdha, with, the Pâli saddhim. Did not the frequent mention of 1,200 and a half (*i. e.* 1,250), 1,300 and a half (*i. e.* 1,350), persons accompanying Buddha arise from a misunderstanding of sârdha, meaning originally "with a half"?

[3] Abhi*gñ*ânâbhi*gñ*âtai*h*. The Japanese text reads abhi*gñ*âtâbhâ*gñ*âtai*h* —*i. e.* abhi*gñ*âtâbhi*gñ*âtai*h*. If this were known to be the correct reading, we should translate it by "known by known people," *notus a viris notis*—*i. e.* well-known, famous. Abhi*gñ*âta in the sense of known, famous, occurs in Lalita-Vistara, p. 25, and the Chinese translators adopted that meaning here. Again, if we preferred the reading abhi*gñ*ânâbhi*gñ*â-

elders, great disciples,[1] and Arhats,[2] such as *S*âriputra, the elder, Mahâmaudgalyâyana, Mahâkâ*s*yapa, Mahâkapphi*n*a, Mahâkâtyâyana, Mahâkaush*th*ila, Revata, *S*uddhipanthaka, Nanda, Ânanda, Râhula, Gavâmpati, Bharadvâ*g*a, Kâlodayin, Vakkula, and Aniruddha.[3] He dwelt together with these and many other great disciples, and together with many noble-minded Bodhisattvas, such as Ma*ñg*u*s*rî, the prince, the Bodhisattva A*g*ita, the Bodhisattva Gandhahastin, the Bodhisattva Nityodyukta, the Bo-

tai*h*, this, too, would admit of an intelligible rendering — viz. known or distinguished by the marks or characteristics, the good qualities, that ought to belong to a Bhikshu. But the technical meaning is "possessed of a knowledge of the five abhi*gñ*âs." It would be better in that case to write abhi*gñ*âtâbhi*gñ*ânai*h*, but no MSS. seem to support that reading. The five abhi*gñ*âs or abhi*gñ*ânas which an Arhat ought to possess are the divine sight, the divine hearing, the knowledge of the thoughts of others, the remembrance of former existences, and magic power. See Burnouf, *Lotus*, Appendice, No. xiv. The larger text of the Sukhavatîvyûha has abhi*gñ*ânâbhi*gñ*ai*h*, and afterwards abhi*gñ*âtâbhi*gñ*ai*h*. The position of the participle as the uttara-pada in such compounds as abhi*gñ*ânâbhi*gñ*âtai*h* is common in Buddhist Sanskrit. Mr. Bendall has called my attention to the Pâli abhi*ññ*âta-abhi*ññ*âta (Vinaya-pi*t*aka, ed. Oldenberg, vol. i. p. 43), which favors the Chinese acceptation of the term.

1 Mahâ*s*râvaka, the great disciples; sometimes the eighty principal disciples.

2 Arhadbhi*h*. I have left the correct Sanskrit form, because the Japanese text gives the termination adbhi*h*. Hôgŏ's text has the more usual form arhantai*h*. The change of the old classical arhat into the Pâli arahan, and then back into Sanskrit arhanta, arahanta, and at last arihanta, with the meaning of "destroyer of the enemies" — *i. e.* the passions — shows very clearly the different stages through which Sanskrit words passed in the different phases of Buddhist literature. In Tibet, in Mongolia, and in China, Arhat is translated by "destroyer of the enemy." See Burnouf, *Lotus*, p. 287; *Introduction*, p. 295. Arhat is the title of the Bhikshu on reaching the fourth degree of perfection. *Cf.* Sûtra of the 42 Sections, cap. 2. Clemens of Alexandria (d. 220) speaks of the Σεμνοί who worshipped a pyramid erected over the relics of a god. Is this a translation of Arhat, as Lassen ("De nom. Ind. philosoph." in *Rhein. Museum*, vol. i. p. 187) and Burnouf (*Introduction*, p. 295) supposed, or a transliteration of Samana? Clemens also speaks of Σεμναί (*Stromat.* p. 539, Potter).

3 Names of Disciples in Sanskrit, Pâli, Chinese, Tibetan, and Japanese MSS. Beal, *J. R. A. S.* 1866, p. 140: —

dhisattva Anikshiptadhura. He dwelt together with them and many other noble-minded Bodhisattvas, and with *S*akra, the Indra or King[1] of the Devas, and with Brahman Sahâmpati. With these and many other hundred thousands of Nayutas[2] of sons of the gods, Bhagavat dwelt at *S*râvastî.

Japanese MS.	Sanskrit. (Burnouf, *Lotus*, pp. 1 and 126.)	Chinese. (Beal, *Catena*, p. 378.)	Tibetan.	Pâli
1 *S*âriputra	*S*âriputra	*S*âriputra	Sharihi-bu	Sariputta
2 Mahâmaudgalyâyana	Maudgalyâyana	Maudgalyâyana	Mougal-gyi-bu	Moggalâna
3 Mahâkâ*s*yapa	Kâ*s*yapa	Kâ*s*yapa	Hodsrungs-ch'hen-po	Kassapa
4 Mahâkapphi*n*a	Kapphi*n*a	Kapphina (?)	Kátyáhi-bu	Kappina
5 Mahâkâtyâyana	Kâtyâyana	Kâtyâyana	Kapina	Ka*kk*âyana
6 Mahâkaush*th*ila	Kaush*th*ila	Mahâko*tth*ila	Gsus-poch'he	Ko*tth*ita
7 Revata	Revata	Revata	Nam-gru	Revata
8 *S*uddhipanthaka (*S*udi, MS.)	(Mahâpanthaka?)	*S*rutavi*m*sati-ko*t*i	Lam-p'hran-bstan	Mahâpanthaka
9 Nanda	Sunanda?	Nanda	Dgah-vo	Nanda
10 Ânanda	Mahânanda	Ananda	Kundgahvo	Ânanda
11 Râhula	Râhula	Râhula	Sgra-gchan-hdsin	Râhula (Kumâra)
12 Gavâmpati	Gavâmpati	Gavâmpati (Pi*nd*oda; Pi*nd*ola?)	Balang-bdag	Gavampati (Pi*nd*olabhâradvâga)
13 Bharadvâga	Bharadvâga	Bharadvâga	Bharadhwaja	Bhâradvâga
14 Kâlodayin	Kâlodayin	Kâlâditya	Hch'har-byed-nagpo	Kâla (tthera)
15 Vakkula	Vakkula	Vakula	Vakula	Vakkali
16 Aniruddha	Aniruddha	Aniruddha	Mahgags-pa	Anuruddha (tthera)

[1] Indra, the old Vedic god, has come to mean simply lord, and in the *K*anda Paritta (*Journal Asiatique*, 1871, p. 220) we actually find Asurinda, the Indra or Lord of the Asuras.

[2] The numbers in Buddhist literature, if they once exceed a Ko*t*i or Ko*t*î — *i. e.* ten millions — become very vague, nor is their value always the same. Ayuta, *i. e.* a hundred Ko*t*is; Niyuta, *i. e.* a hundred Ayutas; and Nayuta, *i. e.* 1 with 22 zeros, are often confounded; nor does it matter much so far as any definite idea is concerned which such numerals convey to our mind.

Then Bhagavat addressed the honored *S*âriputra and said: O *S*âriputra, after you have passed from here over a hundred thousand Ko*t*is of Buddha-countries there is in the Western part of a Buddha-country, a world called Sukhavatî (the happy country). And there a Tathâgata, called Amitâyus, an Arhat, fully enlightened, dwells now, and remains, and supports himself, and teaches the Law.[1]

Now what do you think, *S*âriputra, for what reason is that world called Sukhavatî (the happy)? In that world Sukhavatî, O *S*âriputra, there is neither bodily nor mental pain for living beings. The sources of happiness are innumerable there. For that reason is that world called Sukhavatî (the happy).

And again, O *S*âriputra, that world Sukhavatî is adorned with seven terraces, with seven rows of palm-trees, and with strings of bells.[2] It is inclosed on every side,[3] beautiful, brilliant with the four

1 Tishth*a*ti dh*ri*yate yâpayati dharmam *k*a desayati. This is evidently an idiomatic phrase, for it occurs again and again in the Nepalese text of the Sukhavatîvyûha (MS. 26 *b*, l. 1. 2; 55 *a*, l. 2, etc.). It seems to mean, he stands there, holds himself, supports himself, and teaches the law. Burnouf translates the same phrase by, "ils se trouvent, vivent existent" (*Lotus*, p. 354). On yâpeti in Pâli, see Fausböll, Dasaratha-jâtaka, pp. 26, 28; and yâpana in Sanskrit.

2 Kiṅki*n*î*g*âla. The texts read kaṅka*n*a*g*alais *k*a and kaṅka*n*î*g*alais *k*a, and again later kaṅka*n*î*g*alunâm (also lû) and kaṅka*n*î*g*alânâm. Mr. Beal translates from Chinese "seven rows of exquisite curtains," and again "gemmous curtains." First of all, it seems clear that we must read *g*âla, net, web, instead of *g*ala. Secondly, kaṅka*n*a, bracelet, gives no sense, for what could be the meaning of nets or string of bracelets? I prefer to read kiṅki*n*î*g*âla, nets or strings or rows of bells. Such rows of bells served for ornamenting a garden, and it may be said of them that, if moved by the wind, they give forth certain sounds. In the commentary on Dhammapada 30, p. 191, we meet with kiṅkinika*g*âla, from which likewise the music proceeds; see Childers, *s. v. g*âla. In the MSS. of the Nepalese Sukhavatîvyûha (*R. A. S.*), p. 39 *a*, l. 4, I likewise find svar*n*a-ratnakiṅki*n*î*g*âlâni, which settles the matter, and shows how little confidence we can place in the Japanese texts.

3 Anuparikshipta, inclosed; see parikkhepo in Childers' Dict.

gems, viz. gold, silver, beryl, and crystal.[1] With such arrays of excellences peculiar to a Buddha-country is that Buddha-country adorned.

And again, O *S*âriputra, in that world Sukhavatî there are lotus lakes, adorned with the seven gems, viz. gold, silver, beryl, crystal, red pearls, diamonds,

[1] The four and seven precious things in Pâli are (according to Childers: —

1. suva*n*nam,	gold.
2. ra*g*ata*m*,	silver.
3. muttâ,	pearls.
4. ma*n*i,	gems (as sapphire, ruby).
5. ve*l*uriya*m*,	cat's eye.
6. va*g*ira*m*,	diamond.
7. pavâ*l*am,	coral.

Here Childers translates cat's eye; but *s. v.* ve*l*uriyam, he says, a precious stone, perhaps lapis lazuli.

In Sanskrit (Burnouf, *Lotus*, p. 320): —

1. suvar*n*a,	gold.
2. rûpya,	silver.
3. vai*d*ûrya,	lapis lazuli.
4. spha*t*ika,	crystal.
5. lohitamukti,	red pearls.
6. a*s*magarbha,	diamond.
7. musâragalva,	coral.

Julien (*Pèlerins Buddhistes*, vol. ii. p. 482) gives the following list: —

1. spha*t*ika,	rock crystal.
2. vaidûrya,	lapis lazuli.
3. a*s*magarbha,	cornaline.
4. musâragalva,	amber.
5. padmarâga,	ruby.

Vai*d*ûrya (or Vaidûrya) is mentioned in the Tathâgataguna*g*nâna*k*intya-vishayâvatâranirde*s*a (Wassilief, p. 161) as a precious stone which, if placed on green cloth, looks green, if placed on red cloth, red. The fact that vai*d*ûrya is often compared with the color of the eyes of a cat would seem to point to the cat's eye (see Borooah's *Engl. Sanskrit Dictionary*, vol. ii. preface, p. ix.), certainly not to lapis lazuli. Cat's eye is a kind of chalcedony. I see, however, that vai*d*ûrya has been recognized as the original of the Greek βήρυλλος, a very ingenious conjecture, either of Weber's or of Pott's, considering that lingual *d* has a sound akin to r, and ry may be changed to ly and ll (Weber, *Omina*, p. 326). The Persian billaur or ballúr, which Skeat gives as the etymon of βήρυλλος, is of Arabic origin, means crystal, and could hardly have found its way into Greek at so early a time.

and corals as the seventh. They are full of water which possesses the eight good qualities,[1] their waters rise as high as the fords and bathing-places, so that even crows [2] may drink there; they are full of golden sand, and of vast extent. And in these lotus lakes there are all around on the four sides four stairs, beautiful and brilliant with the four gems, viz. gold, silver, beryl, crystal. And on every side of these lotus lakes gem trees are growing, beautiful and brilliant with the seven gems, viz. gold, silver, beryl, crystal, red pearls, diamonds, and corals as the seventh. And in those lotus lakes lotus flowers are growing, blue, blue-colored, of blue splendor, blue to

1 The eight good qualities of water are limpidity and purity, refreshing coolness, sweetness, softness, fertilizing qualities, calmness, power of preventing famine, productiveness. See Beal, *Catena*, p. 379.

2 Kâkâpeya. One text reads Kâkapeya, the other Kâkâpeya. It is difficult to choose. The more usual word is kâkapeya, which is explained by Pâ*n*ini, ii. 1, 33. It is uncertain, however, whether kâkapeya is meant as a laudatory or as a depreciatory term. Boehtlingk takes it in the latter sense, and translates nadî kâkapeyâ, by a shallow river that could be drunk up by a crow. Târânâtha takes it in the former sense, and translates nadî kâkapeyâ, as a river so full of water that a crow can drink it without bending its neck (kâkair anatakandharai*h* pîyate; pûr*n*odakatvena prasasye kâkai*h* peye nadyâdau). In our passage kâkapeya must be a term of praise, and we therefore could only render it by "ponds so full of water that crows could drink from them." But why should so well known a word as kâkapeya have been spelt kâkâpeya, unless it was done intentionally? And if intentionally, what was it intended for? We must remember that Pâ*n*ini, ii. 1, 42 schol., teaches us how to form the word tîrthakâka, a crow at a tîrtha, which means a person in a wrong place. It would seem, therefore, that crows were considered out of place at a tîrtha or bathing-place, either because they were birds of ill omen, or because they defiled the water. From that point of view, kâkâpeya would mean a pond not visited by crows, free from crows. Professor Pischel has called my attention to Mahâparinibbâna Sutta (*J. R. A. S.* 1875, p. 67, p. 21), where kâkapeyâ clearly refers to a full river. Samatitthika, if this is the right reading, occurs in the same place as an epithet of a river, by the side of kâkapeya, and I think it most likely that it means rising to a level with the tîrthas, the fords or bathing-places. Mr. Rhys Davids informs me that the commentary explains the two words by samatittikâ ti samaharitâ, kâkapeyyâ ti yatthatattha*k*i tîre *th*itena kâkena sakkâ patum ti.

behold; yellow, yellow-colored, of yellow splendor, yellow to behold; red, red-colored, of red splendor, red to behold; white, white-colored, of white splendor, white to behold; beautiful, beautifully-colored, of beautiful splendor, beautiful to behold, and in circumference as large as the wheel of a chariot.

And again, O *S*âriputra, in that Buddha-country there are heavenly musical instruments always played on and the earth is lovely and of golden color. And in that Buddha-country a flower-rain of heavenly Mândârava blossoms pours down three times every day, and three times every night. And the beings who are born there worship before their morning meal [1] a hundred thousand Ko*t*is of Buddhas by going to other worlds; and having showered a hundred thousand of Ko*t*is of flowers upon each Tathâgata, they return to their own world in time for the afternoon rest.[2] With such arrays of excellences peculiar to a Buddha-country is that Buddha-country adorned.

And again, O *S*âriputra, there are in that Buddha-country swans, curlews,[3] and peacocks. Three times every night, and three times every day, they come together and perform a concert, each uttering his own note. And from them thus uttering proceeds a sound

[1] Purobhaktena. The text is difficult to read, but it can hardly be doubtful that purobhaktena corresponds to Pâli purebhatta*m* (*i. e.* before the morning meal), opposed to pa*kkh*âbhatta*m*, after the noonday meal (*i. e.* in the afternoon). See Childers, *s. v.* Pûrvabhaktikâ would be the first repast, as Professor Cowell informs me.

[2] Divâ vihârâya, for the noonday rest, the *siesta*. See Childers, *s. v.* vihâra.

[3] Krau*ñk*â*h*. Snipe, curlew. Is it meant for Kuravîka, or Karavîka, a fine-voiced bird (according to Kern, the Sk. karâyikâ), or for Kalaviṅka-Pâli Kalavîka? See Childers, *s. v.* opapâtiko; Burnouf, *Lotus*, p. 566. I see, however, the same birds mentioned together elsewhere, as ha*m*sakrau*ñk*amayûra*s*uka*s*âlikakokila, etc. On mayûra see Mahâv. Introd. p. xxxix.; Rv. I. 191, 14.

proclaiming the five virtues, the five powers, and the seven steps leading towards the highest knowledge.[1] When the men there hear that sound, remembrance of Buddha, remembrance of the Law, remembrance of the Assembly, rises in their mind.

Now, do you think, O *S*âriputra, that these are beings who have entered into the nature of animals (birds, etc.)? This is not to be thought of. The very name of hells is unknown in that Buddha-country, and likewise that of (descent into) animal natures and of the realm of Yama (the four apâyas).[2] No, these tribes of birds have been made on purpose

[1] Indriyabalabodhyaṅgasabda. These are technical terms, but their meaning is not quite clear. Spence Hardy, in his *Manual*, p. 498, enumerates the five indrayas, viz. (1) sardhâwa, purity (probably sraddhâ, faith), (2) wiraya, persevering exertion (vîrya), (3) sati or smirti, the ascertainment of truth (smriti), (4) samâdhi, tranquillity, (5) pragnâwa, wisdom (pragñâ).

The five balayas (bala), he adds, are the same as the five indrayas.

The seven bowdyânga (bodhyaṅga) are, according to him: (1) sihi or smirti, the ascertainment of the truth by mental application, (2) dharmmawicha, the investigation of causes, (3) wîraya, persevering exertion, (4) prîti, joy, (5) passadhi, or prasrabdhi, tranquillity, (6) samâdhi, tranquillity in a higher degree, including freedom from all that disturbs either body or mind, (7) upekshâ, equanimity.

It will be seen from this that some of these qualities or excellences occur both as indriyas and bodhyaṅgas, while balas are throughout identical with indriyas.

Burnouf, however, in his *Lotus*, gives a list of five balas (from the *Vocabulaire Pentaglotte*) which correspond with the five indriyas of Spence Hardy: viz. sraddhâ-bala, power of faith, vîrya-bala, power of vigor, smriti-bala, power of memory, samâdhi-bala, power of meditation, pragñâ-bala, power of knowledge. They precede the seven bodhyaṅgas both in the *Lotus*, the *Vocabulaire Pentaglotte*, and the Lalita-Vistara.

To these seven bodhyaṅgas Burnouf has assigned a special treatise (Appendix xii. p. 796). They occur both in Sanskrit and Pâli.

[2] Niraya, the hells, also called Naraka. Yamaloka, the realm of Yama, the judge of the dead, is explained as the four Apâyas—*i. e.* Naraka, hell, Tiryagyoni, birth as animals, Pretaloka, realm of the dead, Asuraloka, realm of evil spirits. The three terms which are here used together occur likewise in a passage translated by Burnouf, *Introduction*, p. 544.

by the Tathâgata Amitâyus, and they utter the sound of the Law. With such arrays of excellences, etc.

And again, O *S*âriputra, when those rows of palm-trees and strings of bells in that Buddha-country are moved by the wind, a sweet and enrapturing sound proceeds from them. Yes, O *S*âriputra, as from a heavenly musical instrument consisting of a hundred thousand Ko*t*is of sounds, when played by Âryas, a sweet and enrapturing sound proceeds, a sweet and enrapturing sound proceeds from those rows of palm-trees and strings of bells moved by the wind. And when the men hear that sound, reflection on Buddha arises in their body, reflection on the Law, reflection on the Assembly. With such arrays of excellences, etc.

Now what do you think, O *S*âriputra, for what reason is that Tathâgata called Amitâyus? The length of life (âyus), O *S*âriputra, of that Tathâgata and of those men there is immeasurable (amita). Therefore is that Tathâgata called Amitâyus. And ten Kalpas have passed, O *S*âriputra, since that Tathâgata awoke to perfect knowledge.

And what do you think, O *S*âriputra, for what reason is that Tathâgata called Amitâbhâs? The splendor (âbhâs), O *S*âriputra, of that Tathâgata is unimpeded over all Buddha-countries. Therefore is that Tathâgata called Amitâbhâs.

And there is, O *S*âriputra, an innumerable assembly of disciples with that Tathâgata, purified and venerable persons, whose number it is not easy to count. With such arrays of excellences, etc.

And again, O *S*âriputra, of those beings also who are born in the Buddha-country of the Tathâgata Amitâyus as purified Bodhisattvas, never to return again and bound by one birth only, of those Bodhisattvas also, O *S*âriputra, the number is not easy to count, except they are reckoned as infinite in number.[1]

Then again all beings, O *S*âriputra, ought to make fervent prayer for that Buddha-country. And why? Because they come together there with such excellent men. Beings are not born in that Buddha-country of the Tathâgata Amitâyus as a reward and result of good works performed in this present life.[2] No, whatever son or daughter of a family shall hear the name of the blessed Amitâyus, the Tathâgata, and having heard it, shall keep it in mind, and with thoughts undisturbed shall keep it in mind for one, two, three, four, five, six, or seven nights, that son or daughter of a family, when he or she comes to die, then that Amitâyus, the Tathâgata, surrounded by an assembly of disciples and followed by a host of Bodhisattvas, will stand before them at their hour of death, and they will depart this life with tranquil minds. After their death they will be born in the world Sukhavatî,

1 Iti sankhyâ*m* ga*kkh*anti, they are called; *cf.* Childers, *s. v.* sankhyâ. Asankhyeya, even more than aprameya, is the recognized term for infinity. Burnouf, *Lotus*, p. 852.

2 Avaramâtraka. This is the Pâli oramattako, "belonging merely to the present life," and the intention of the writer seems to be to inculcate the doctrine of the Mahâyâna, that salvation can be obtained by mere repetitions of the name of Amitâbha, in direct opposition to the original doctrine of Buddha, that as a man soweth, so he reapeth. Buddha would have taught that the ku*s*alamûla, the root or the stock of good works performed in this world (avaramâtraka), will bear fruit in the next, while here "vain repetitions" seems all that is enjoined. The Chinese translators take a different view of this passage, and I am not myself quite certain that I have understood it rightly. But from the end of this section, where we read kulaputre*n*a vâ kuladuhitrâ vâ tatra buddhakshetre *k*ittaprâ*n*idhâna*m* kartavyam, it seems clear that the locative (buddhakshetre) forms the object of the pra*n*idhâna, the fervent prayer or longing. The Satpurushas already in the Buddhakshetra would be the innumerable men (manushyâs) and Boddhisattvas mentioned before.

in the Buddha-country of the same Amitâyus, the Tathâgata. Therefore, then, O *S*âriputra, having perceived this cause and effect,[1] I with reverence say thus, Every son and every daughter of a family ought to make with their whole mind fervent prayer for that Buddha-country.

And now, O *S*âriputra, as I here at present glorify that world, thus in the East, O *S*âriputra, other blessed Buddhas, led by the Tathâgata Akshobhya, the Tathâgata Merudhva*g*a, the Tathâgata Mahâmeru, the Tathâgata Meruprabhâsa, and the Tathâgata Mañ*g*udhva*g*a, equal in number to the sand of the river Gangâ, comprehend their own Buddha-countries in their speech, and then reveal them.[2] Accept this repetition of the Law, called the "Favor of all Buddhas," which magnifies their inconceivable excellences.

Thus also in the South, do other blessed Buddhas, led by the Tathâgata *K*andrasûryapradîpa, the Tathâgata Yasa*h*prabha, the Tathâgata Mahâr*k*iskandha, the Tathâgata Merupradîpa, the Tathâgata Anantavîrya, equal in number to the sand of the river Gangâ, comprehend their own Buddha-countries in their speech, and then reveal them. Accept, etc.

Thus also in the West do other blessed Buddhas, led by the Tathâgata Amitâyus, the Tathâgata Ami-

[1] Arthavasa, lit. the power of the thing; *cf.* Dhammapada, p. 388, *v.* 289.

[2] I am not quite certain as to the meaning of this passage, but if we enter into the bold metaphor of the text, viz., that the Buddhas cover the Buddha-countries with the organ of their tongue and then unroll it, what is intended can hardly be anything but that they first try to find words for the excellences of those countries, and then reveal or proclaim them. Burnouf, however (*Lotus*, p. 417), takes the expression in a literal sense, though he is shocked by its grotesqueness. On these Buddhas and their countries, see Burnouf, *Lotus*, p. 113.

taskandha, the Tathâgata Amitadhva*g*a, the Tathâgata Mahâprabha, the Tathâgata Mahâratnaketu, the Tathagata *S*uddhara*s*miprabha, equal in number to the sand of the river Gangâ, comprehend, etc.

Thus also in the North do other blessed Buddhas, led by the Tathâgata Mahâr*k*iskandha, the Tathâgata Vai*s*vânaranirghosha, the Tathâgata Dundubhisvaranirghosha, the Tathâgata Dushpradharsha, the Tathâgata Âdityasambhava, the Tathâgata *G*aleniprabha (*G*valanaprabha?), the Tathâgata Prabhâkara, equal in number to the sand, etc.

Thus also in the Nadir do other blessed Buddhas, led by the Tathâgata Si*m*ha, the Tathâgata Ya*s*as, the Tathâgata Ya*s*a*h*prabhâva, the Tathâgata Dharma, the Tathâgata Dharmadhara, the Tathâgata Dharmadhva*g*a, equal in number to the sand, etc.

Thus also in the Zenith do other blessed Buddhas, led by the Tathâgata Brahmaghosha, the Tathâgata Nakshatrarâ*g*a, the Tathâgata Indraketudhva*g*arâ*g*a, the Tathâgata Gandhottama, the Tathâgata Gandhaprabhâsa, the Tathâgata Mahâr*k*iskandha, the Tathâgata Ratnakusumasampushpitagâtra, the Tathâgata Sâlendrarâ*g*a, the Tathâgata Ratnotpala*s*ri, the Tathâgata Sarvâdar*s*a, the Tathâgata Sumerukalpa, equal in number to the sand, etc.[1]

Now what do you think, O *S*âriputra, for what reason is that repetition of the Law called the Favor of all Buddhas? Every son or daughter of a family who shall hear the name of that repetition of the Law and retain in their memory the names of those blessed Buddhas, will all be favored by the Buddhas, and

[1] It should be remarked that the Tathâgatas here assigned to the ten quarters differ entirely from those assigned to them in the Lalita-vistara, book xx. Not even Amitâbha is mentioned there.

will never return again, being once in possession of the transcendent true knowledge. Therefore, then, O *S*âriputra, believe,[1] accept, and long for me and those blessed Buddhas!

Whatever sons or daughters of a family shall make mental prayer for the Buddha-country of that blessed Amitâyus, the Tathâgata, or are making it now or have made it formerly, all these will never return again, being once in possession of the transcendent true knowledge. They will be born in that Buddha-country, have been born, or are being born now. Therefore, then, O *S*âriputra, mental prayer is to be made for that Buddha-country by faithful sons and daughters of a family.

And as I at present magnify here the inconceivable excellences of those blessed Buddhas, thus, O *S*âriputra, do those blessed Buddhas magnify my own inconceivable excellences.

A very difficult work has been done by *S*âkyamuni, the sovereign of the *S*âkyas. Having obtained the transcendent true knowledge in this world Saha, he taught the Law which all the world is reluctant to accept, during this corruption of the present Kalpa, during this corruption of mankind, during this corruption of belief, during this corruption of life, during this corruption of passions.

[1] Pratîyatha. The texts give again and again pattîyatha, evidently the Pâli form, instead of pratîyata. I have left t h a, the Pâli termination of the 2 p. pl. in the imperative, instead of t a, because that form was clearly intended, while p a for p r a may be an accident. Yet I have little doubt that patîyatha was in the original text. That it is meant for the imperative, we see from *s*raddadhâdhvam, etc., farther on. Other traces of the influence of Pâli or Prakrit on the Sanskrit of our Sûtra appear in arhantai*h*, the various reading for arhadbhi*h*, which I preferred; sambahula for bahula; dh*ri*yate yâpayati; purobhaktena; anyatra; saṅkhyâm ga*kkh*anti; avaramâtraka; ve*th*ana instead of vesh*t*ana, in nirve*th*ana; dharmaparyâya (*Corp. Inscript.* plate xv.), etc.

This is even for me, O *S*âriputra, an extremely difficult work that, having obtained the transcendent true knowledge in this world Saha, I taught the Law which all the world is reluctant to accept, during this corruption of mankind, of belief, of passion, of life, and of this present Kalpa.

Thus spoke Bhagavat joyful in his mind. And the honorable *S*âriputra, and the Bhikshus and Bodhisattvas, and the whole world with the gods, men, evil spirits, and genii, applauded the speech of Bhagavat.[1]

This is the Mahâyânasûtra
called Sukhavatîvyûha.

1 The Sukhavatîvyûha, even in its shortest text, is called a Mahâyânasûtra, nor is there any reason why a Mahâyâna-sûtra should not be short. The meaning of Mahâyâna-sûtra is simply a Sûtra belonging to the Mahâyâna school, the school of the Great Boat. It was Burnouf who, in his *Introduction to the History of Buddhism*, tried very hard to establish a distinction between the Vaipulya or developed Sûtras, and what he calls the simple Sûtras. Now, the Vaipulya Sûtras may all belong to the Mahâyâna school, but that would not prove that all the Sûtras of the Mahâyâna school are Vaipulya or developed Sûtras. The name of simple Sûtra, in opposition to the Vaipulya or developed Sûtras, is not recognized by the Buddhists themselves; it is really an invention of Burnouf's. No doubt there is a great difference between a Vaipulya Sûtra, such as the Lotus of the Good Law, translated by Burnouf, and the Sûtras which Burnouf translated from the Divyâvadâna. But what Burnouf considers as the distinguishing mark of a Vaipulya Sûtra, viz. the occurrence of Bodhisattvas, as followers of the Buddha *S*âkyamuni, would no longer seem to be tenable,* unless we classed our short Sukhavatî-vyûha as a Vaipulya or developed Sûtra. For this there is no authority. Our Sûtra is called a Mahâyâna Sûtra, never a Vaipulya Sûtra, and yet among the followers of Buddha, the Bodhisattvas constitute a very considerable portion. But more than that, Amitâbha, the Buddha of Sukhavatî, another personage whom Burnouf looks upon as peculiar to the Vaipulya Sûtras, who is, in fact, one of the Dhyâni-buddhas, though not called by that name in our Sûtra, forms the chief object of its teaching, and is represented as coeval with Buddha *S*âkyamuni.† The larger text of the Sukhavatîvyûha would

* "Les présence des Bodhisattvas ou leur absence intéresse donc le fonds même des livres où on la remarque, et il est bien évident que ce seul point trace une ligne de démarcation profonde entre les Sûtras ordinaires et les Sûtras développés." Burnouf, *Introduction*, p. 112.

† "L'idée d'un ou de plusieurs Buddhas surhumains, celle de Bodhisattvas créés par eux, sont des conceptions aussi étrangères á ces livres (les Sûtras simples) que celle d'un Adibuddha ou d'un Dieu." — Burnouf, *Introduction*, p. 120.

This Sûtra sounds to us, no doubt, very different from the original teaching of Buddha. And so it is. Nevertheless it is the most popular and most widely read Sûtra in Japan, and the whole religion of the great mass of the people may be said to be founded on it. "Repeat the name of Amitâbha as often as you can, repeat it particularly in the hour of death, and you will go straight to Sukhavatî and be happy forever;" this is what Japanese Buddhists are asked to believe: this is what they are told was the teaching of Buddha. There is one passage in our Sûtra which seems even to be pointedly directed against the original teaching of Buddha. Buddha taught that as a man soweth so shall he reap, and that by a stock of good works accumulated on earth the way is opened to higher knowledge and higher bliss. Our Sûtra says No; not by good works done on earth, but by a mere repetition of the name of Amitâbha is an entrance gained into the land of bliss. This is no better than what later Brahmanism teaches, viz. "Repeat the name of Hari or of K*ri*sh*n*a, and you will be saved." It is no better than what even some Christian teachers are reported to teach. It may be that in a lower stage of civilization even such teaching has produced some kind of good.[1] But Japan is surely ripe for better things. What the worship of Amitâbha may lead to we can learn from a description given by Dr. Edkins in his "Trip to Ning-po and T'hëen-t'hae. "The next thing," he writes, "shown to us was the prison, in which about a dozen

certainly, according to Burnouf's definition, seem to fall into the category of the Vaipulya Sûtras. But it is not so called in the MSS. which I have seen, and Burnouf himself gives an analysis of that Sûtra (*Introduction*, p. 99) as a specimen of a Mahâyâna, but not of a Vaipulya Sûtra.

[1] See H. Yule, *Marco Polo*, 2d ed. vol. i. pp. 441–443.

priests had allowed themselves to be shut up for a number of months or years, during which they were to occupy themselves in repeating the name of Amida Buddha,[1] day and night, without intermission. During the day the whole number were to be thus engaged; and during the night they took it by turns, and divided themselves into watches, so as to insure the keeping up of the work till morning. We asked when they were to be let out. To which it was replied, that they might be liberated at their own request, but not before they had spent several months in seclusion. We inquired what could be the use of such an endless repetition of the name of Buddha. To which it was answered, that the constant repetition of the sacred name had a tendency to purify the heart, to deaden the affections towards the present world, and to prepare them for the state of Nirvâ*n*a. It was further asked whether Buddha was likely to be pleased with such an endless repetition of his name. To which it was answered, that in the Western world it was considered a mark of respect to repeat the name of any one whom we delighted to honor. The recluses seemed most of them young men; some of whom came out to the bars of their cage to look at the strangers, but kept on repeating the name of Buddha as they stood there. It appeared to us that nothing was more calculated to produce idiocy than such a perpetual repetition of a single name, and the stupid appearance of many of the priests whom we have seen seems to have been induced by some such process."

[1] In China, as Dr. Edkins states, the doctrine of Amitâbha is represented by the so-called Lotus school (Lian-tsung) or Pure Land (Tsing-tu). The founder of this school in China was Hwei-yuan of the Tsin dynasty (fourth century). The second patriarch (tsu) of this school was Kwang-ming (seventh century).

Is it not high time that the millions who live in Japan, and profess a faith in Buddha, should be told that this doctrine of Amitâbha and all the Mahâyâna doctrine is a secondary form of Buddhism, a corruption of the pure doctrine of the Royal Prince, and that if they really mean to be Buddhists, they should return to the words of Buddha, as they are preserved to us in the old Sûtras? Instead of depending, as they now do, on Chinese translations, not always accurate, of degraded and degrading Mahâyâna tracts, why should they not have Japanese translations of the best portions of Buddha's real doctrine, which would elevate their character, and give them a religion of which they need not be ashamed? There are Chinese translations of some of the better portions of the Sacred Writings of Buddhism. They exist in Japan too, as may be seen in that magnificent collection of the Buddhist Tripiṭaka which was sent from Japan as a present to the English Government, and of which Mr. Beal has given us a very useful Catalogue. But they are evidently far less considered in Japan than the silly and the mischievous stories of Amitâbha and his Paradise, and those which I know from translations are far from correct.

I hope that Mr. Bunyiu Nanjio and Mr. Kasawara, if they diligently continue their study of Sanskrit and Pâli, will be able to do a really great and good work, after their return to Japan. And if more young Buddhist priests are coming over, I shall always, so far as my other occupations allow it, be glad to teach them, and to help them in their unselfish work. There is a great future in store, I believe, for those Eastern Islands, which have been called prophetically "the England of the East," and to purify and reform their religion — that is, to bring it back to its original form — is a work that must be done before anything else can be attempted.

In return, I hope that they and their friends in Japan, and in Corea and China too, will do all they can to discover, if possible, some more of the ancient Sanskrit texts, and send them over to us. A beginning, at all events, has been made, and if the members of this Society who have friends in China or in Japan will help, if H. E. the Japanese Minister, Mori Arinori, who has honored us by his presence to-day, will lend us his powerful assistance, I have little doubt that the dream which passed before the mind of your late President may still become a reality, and that some of the MSS. which, beginning with the beginning of our era, were carried from India to China, Corea, and Japan, may return to us, whether in the original or in copies, like the one sent to me by Mr. Shuntai Ishikawa.

With the help of such MSS. we shall be able all the better to show to those devoted students who from the extreme East have come to the extreme West in order to learn to read their sacred writings in the original Sanskrit or Pâli, what difference there is between the simple teaching of Buddha and the later developments and corruptions of Buddhism. Buddha himself, I feel convinced, never knew even the names of Amitâbha, Avalokitesvara, or Sukhavatî. Then, how can a nation call itself Buddhist whose religion consists chiefly in a belief in a divine Amitâbha and his son Avalokitesvara, and in a hope of eternal life in the paradise of Sukhavatî ?

Postscript: *Oxford, March* 10, 1880.

The hope which I expressed in my paper on "Sanskrit Texts discovered in Japan," viz. that other Sanskrit texts might still come to light in Japan or China, has been fulfilled sooner than I expected. Mr. A Wylie wrote to me on March 3 that he had brought a number of Sanskrit-Chinese books from Japan, and he afterwards kindly sent them to me to examine. They were of the same appearance and character as the dictionary which Dr. Edkins had lent me, and the Sukhavatî-vyûha which I had received from Japan. But with the exception of a collection of invocations, called the Va*g*ra-sûtra, and the short Pra*gñâ*-h*ri*daya-sûtra, they contained no continuous texts. The books were intended to teach the Sanskrit alphabet, and every possible and impossible combination of the Devanâgarî letters, and that was all. Still, so large a number of books written to teach the Sanskrit alphabet augurs well for the existence of Sanskrit texts. There was among Mr. Wylie's books a second Chinese-Sanskrit-Japanese vocabulary, of which Mr. Kasawara has given me the following account: "This vocabulary is called 'A Thousand Sanskrit and Chinese Words,' and it is said to have been arranged by I-tsing, who left China for India in 671, about twenty-seven years after Hiouen-thsang's return to China, and who is best known as the author of a book called Nanhae-ki-kwei-*k*ou'en, on the manners and customs of the Indian Buddhists at that time.

"This vocabulary was brought from China to Japan by Zikaku, a Japanese priest, who went to China in 838 and returned in 847. It is stated at the end of the book, that in the year 884 a Japanese priest of the name of Rioyiu copied that vocabulary from a text belonging to another priest, Yûîkai. The edition brought from Japan by Mr. Wylie was published there in the year 1727 by a priest called Jakumio."

The following curious passage occurs in the preface of Jakumio's edition: "This vocabulary is generally called 'One Thousand Sanskrit and Chinese Words.' It is stated in Annen's work, that this was first brought (from China) by Zikaku. I have corrected several mistakes in this vocabulary, comparing many copies; yet the present edition is not free from blunders; I hope the readers will correct them, if they have better copies.

"In the temple Hôriuji, in Yamato, there are treasured Pra*gñ*âpâramitâh*ri*dayasûtram, and Sonshio-dhâra*n*i, written on two palm leaves, handed down from Central India; and, at the end of these, fourteen letters of the 'siddha' are written. In the present edition of the vocabulary the alphabet is in imitation of that of the palm leaves, except such forms of letters as cannot be distinguished from those prevalent among the scriveners at the present day.

"Hôriuji is one of eleven temples founded by the prince Umayado (who died A. D. 621). This temple is at a town named Tatsuta, in the province Yamato, near Kioto, the western capital."

Here, then, we have clear evidence that in the year 1727 palm leaves containing the text of Sanskrit Sûtras were still preserved in the temple of Hôriuji. If that temple is still in existence, might not some Buddhist priest of Kioto, the western capital of Japan, be induced to go there to see whether the palm leaves are still there, and, if they are, to make a copy and send it to Oxford? F. M. M.

SECOND POSTSCRIPT: *Oxford, August* 2, 1880.

At the end of my paper on "Sanskrit Texts in Japan" I mentioned in a postscript (March 10) that I had received from Mr. Wylie a copy of a vocabulary called "A Thousand Sanskrit and Chinese Words," compiled by I-tsing, about 700 A. D., and brought to Japan by Zikaku, a Japanese priest, in 847 A. D. The edition of this vocabulary which Mr. Wylie bought in Japan was published by Jakumio in 1727, and in the preface the editor says: "In the temple Hôriuji, in Yamato, there are treasured Pra*gñ*âpâramitâh*ri*daya-sûtram and Sonshio-dhâra*n*î, written on two palm leaves, handed down from Central India."

Hôriuji is one of eleven temples founded by Prince Umayado, who died in A. D. 621. This temple is in a town named Tatsuta, in the province Yamato, near Kioto, the western capital. I ended my article with the following sentence: "Here, then, we have clear evidence that in the year 1727 palm leaves containing the text of Sanskrit Sûtras were still preserved in the temple of Hôriuji. If that temple is still in existence, might not some Buddhist priest of Kioto, the western capital of Japan, be induced to go there to see whether the palm leaves are still there, and, if they are, to make a copy and send it to Oxford?"

Sooner than expected this wish of mine has been fulfilled. On April 28 Mr. Shigefuyu Kurihara, of Kioto, a friend of one of my Sanskrit pupils, Mr. Bunyiu Nanjio, who for some years had himself taken an interest in Sanskrit, went to the temple or monastery of Hôriuji to inquire whether any old Sanskrit MSS. were still preserved there. He was told that the priests of the monastery had recently surrendered their valuables to the Imperial Government, and that the ancient palm leaves had been presented to the emperor.

In a chronicle kept at the monastery of Hôriuji it is stated that these palm leaves and other valuables were brought by Ono Imoko, a retainer of the Mikado (the Empress Suiko), from China (during the Sui dynasty, 589–618) to Japan, in the thirty-seventh year of the age of Prince Umayado — *i. e.*, A. D. 609. The other valuable articles were:

1. Niô, *i. e.*, a cymbal used in Buddhist temples;
2. Midzu-game, a water vessel;
3. Shaku-jio, a staff, the top of which is armed with metal rings, as carried by Buddhist priests;
4. Kesa (Kashâya), a scarf, worn by Buddhist priests across the shoulder, which belonged to the famous Bodhidharma;
5. Ha*k*i, a bowl, given by the same Bodhidharma.

These things and the Sanskrit MSS. are said to have belonged to some Chinese priests, named Hwui-sz' (Yeshi) and Nien-shan (Nenzen), and to four others successively, who lived in a monastery on the mountain called Nan-yo (Nangak), in the province of Hăng (Kô) in China. These palm-leaf MSS. may, therefore, be supposed to date from at least the sixth century A. D., and be, in fact, *the oldest Sanskrit MSS. now in existence.*[1]

May we not hope that His Excellency Mori Arinori, who expressed so warm an interest in this mat-

[1] See page 191.

ter when he was present at the meeting of the Royal Asiatic Society, will now lend us his powerful aid, and request the Minister of the Department of the Imperial Household to allow these MSS. to be carefully copied or photographed ?

INDEX.

www.ingramcontent.com/pod-product-compliance
Lightning Source LLC
LaVergne TN
LVHW010253110826
845151LV00004B/1460
9781425522490